WILDERNESS
The Way Ahead

WILDERNESS
The Way Ahead

Edited by Vance Martin and Mary Inglis

FINDHORN PRESS
LORIAN PRESS

ISBN 0 905249 58 5 (UK).
    0 936878 10 X (USA).
Library of Congress Catalogue Card Number: 84-81614.

First published 1984.

The publishers gratefully acknowledge the financial assistance of the International Wilderness Leadership Foundation.

Book and cover design by Marcus Frey, Findhorn Foundation Design Group.
Cover photograph courtesy of Ray V. Collier, Nature Conservancy Council, UK.
Set in 11/12 point Garamond by Findhorn Publications.
Printed and bound by Butler and Tanner Ltd, UK.
Published by:
The Findhorn Press, The Park, Forres IV36 OTZ, Scotland, and Lorian Press, PO Box 147, Middleton, WI 53562, USA.

A portion of the profits from the sale of this book will go towards supporting wilderness conservation.

With the kind permission of Lady Fraser Darling and family, the 3rd World Wilderness Congress was convened in memory of the late Sir Frank Fraser Darling, and to honour his work. As a British naturalist, Fraser Darling was internationally respected and admired for his pioneering contribution to the science and philosophy of nature conservation. This book is dedicated to him and to all who value and work for the preservation of the world's wild places.

Acknowledgements

Many dedicated people have contributed towards helping the proceedings of the 3rd World Wilderness Congress be published in this book, which is not only interesting to read but is also visually appealing. It would be singularly difficult to name them all, but mention should be given to a few: Sandra Kramer for her eagle eye in proof-reading, Jane Engel and her team for hours of typesetting, Marcus Frey and the Findhorn Foundation Design group for the design, Lucia Spowers for her constant awareness and efficient handling of promotion and distribution while the rest of us had our heads down in the origination work—and of course the speakers themselves, who provided the text and often freely contributed photographs and illustrations. Thanks too to all those who so generously offered personal support and encouragement, particularly the Publications Department of the Findhorn Foundation, and Kate Martin, for being there. Special thanks go to all those at the Findhorn Foundation who provided efficient, warm and supportive services for 'Wilderness '83'—without the Congress this book would not have been possible.

Vance Martin, Mary Inglis, Editors

Photograph and Illustration Credits

Findhorn Visuals, Alexander Caminada, David Cairns, Finlay MacRae, Ray Collier, Nature Conservancy Council, J. Morton Boyd, Adam Watson, Drennan Watson, Hance Smith, Highlands and Islands Development Board, US Department of Interior (National Park Service), Custer National Forest, G. Salmon, Tony Morrison, Vance Martin, José Lutzenberger, Tasmanian Wilderness Society, Bob Burton, P. Drombouskis, Bob Blakers, Ramakrishnan Palat, Franco Zunino, US Department of Agriculture, Jim Hughes, Sally Ranney, Alaska Coalition, Zoological Society of San Diego, Walt Disney Productions, William P.H. Root, Glenn Gray, US Library of Congress, University of California (Bancroft Library), Tom Tarbet, Joan Price, Trevor Barrett, Simon Fraser, Richard Frear. Drawings of otter (p.10) and osprey (p.291) by John Busby; drawing of deer (p.315) by Simon Fraser. Photographic portrait of Sir Frank Fraser Darling by Douglas Stronach. Cover photograph courtesy of Ray V. Collier (NCC).

The logo of the World Wilderness Congress is the
Erythrina leaf, surrounded by arrows to indicate the
bringing together of peoples from around the world
who care about the wilderness and its protection.

Table of Contents

Foreword

As I write, the first dusting of snow is on the high mountain tops, and thin crimson easterly winds search the Moray coast. The voices of the 3rd World Wilderness Congress are scattered to distant lands, but the echoes linger for a while in Highland Scotland. It is time for quiet reflection.

Away back in the wild places, the roaring days are past and red deer come down to the forest, there to await the freshness and promise of spring. The wild geese speak freely from the stubble fields, their voices praising the fullness of autumn.

The wilderness delights in late autumn and winter when warm wind-song and tempest shake hands and part and meet again. The imprint of human beings is weak on the soft path in the glen, fading as they wander from the beaten way.

By grey crags, the old, blue-headed, red-stemmed Scots Pine holds the wind in its sail, long enough to bring forth song or tell the tale of great deeds, long, long ago, when it was young.

Gaelic—the gentle musical language of the Celts—takes its life from the tumbling burn, and the loch sparkles with a myriad tiny suns that toss and pass and slip away to the shadows, then surface again, far far away.

A thousand moods of the wild embrace us, gently but firmly, until we cry inwardly, saying, "I am part of you, the great whole, and I try to understand."

It was an honour and a great pleasure for all of us in the Highlands to host the 3rd World Wilderness Congress, and I would like to record my personal heartfelt thanks to all who came from distant lands to help us toward a better understanding of the good earth—HASTE YE BACK.

Finlay MacRae
Chairman, 3rd World Wilderness Congress

Introduction

Laurens van der Post

One of the things that emerged at the Third World Wilderness Congress was the feeling that perhaps we should be more political and scientific, and that perhaps we are too poetic and idyllic about wilderness. And I am reminded of something Jung said to me not long before he died. He said that the truth needs scientific expression, it needs religious expression and it needs artistic expression. It needs the poet and the musician. And even then, he said, you only express a part of it.

The truth is total, and the inspirational idea that falls into the human consciousness is total. It is the artist in us who is able to apprehend the original inspiration in its totality. But we are condemned by the nature of consciousness, according to our own particular gifts, to serve and express it only in part.

While both the political and scientific approaches are vitally necessary, it is important also to remember that they work well only if they serve a transcendent vision. Since the French Revolution we have lived in a time when people increasingly think all the answers to life are political ones. But while the political approach can carry out a vision, it cannot create one. The vision has to come from somewhere else. There can be a political vision of how to serve the wider plan of life, and the best politicians have it, but the values have got to come from somewhere else. Politics cannot create its own values.

However, the political approach is tremendously important. People who have a gift for politics perform an enormous service and one for which there is often very little gratitude, because we project all the failures on to them. A nation which does not take its politics seriously is doomed. In Asia, for instance, marvellous spiritually orientated cultures and civilisations have in a sense failed themselves because they didn't take the political approach sufficiently seriously. They never developed political systems for expressing the spiritual values. One of the great saving graces of the western world, from the time of the Greeks, is that we have taken very seriously this problem of expressing values in an organised manner. In one of the great moments in Dante's *Divine Comedy*, written in the middle ages, he is asked the question whether life would not have been better if there had been no citizens—which means cities, for citizens live in cities. And he said the answer was, without a doubt, no, it would not. Life needs citizens; it needs the political approach too. But the political aspect is only a very small part of the total picture. It does not create the original values. Political systems work well only if they serve a transcendent, apolitical vision.

The difference between politics and this great apolitical vision is like the difference between true science and applied science. Applied science doesn't necessarily serve the progression of science. Einstein said that his great concept of the universe, the theory of relativity, came to him in less time than it takes to clap your hands, but it took a lifetime to prove it. The vision which his science served was greater than the merely scientific vision.

Some of our scientists talk about 'managing wilderness', and this worries me a bit. It is like saying they want to control revelation. But the moment you try to control it, there is no revelation. Not one of those scientists could have created the vision of something like wilderness. The vision of wilderness is not very complicated. We try to give it elaborate definitions, but we all know what wilderness really is, because we have it inside ourselves. We know it is a world in which every bit of nature counts and is important to us, and we know when it isn't there. Every person in the modern world knows how deprived they are in this area.

Those of us who have spent time in wilderness are aware of the fact that there is something more to wilderness than we ourselves can express. This is rooted perhaps in the effect that wilderness has on human beings who have become estranged from nature, who live in industrialised environments and are estranged in a sense from their natural selves. Wilderness has a profound impact on them, as well as on those of us more familiar with it.

I can perhaps illustrate this best by the example of three boys of different families and different nationalities, whose parents regarded them as 'problem sons'. All three boys had very privileged backgrounds, but somehow they couldn't come to terms with their own environments and with their own futures. Their parents came to me and asked what they could do to help their sons, because schools, doctors and educationalists did not seem to help. And I found a strange aboriginal voice in me saying, "Send them to the wilderness." I persuaded their parents to send them out to Zululand where they went on a wilderness trail with Ian Player. Nothing was said to them about themselves. All they had was the mirror which nature presented to them, and through this experience, which had a profound psychological impact on them, they found something of themselves, something to do with their natural selves and the wilderness within. They returned to Europe and to their schools and universities and today all three are creative citizens distinguishing themselves in the world.

Wilderness is an instrument for enabling us to recover our lost capacity for religious experience. The religious area is far more than just the Church. If you look at the history of Europe since Christ, you will see that the Church has tended to be caught up, as it is today, in the social problems of its time, and to be less than the religion it serves. The churches and the great cathedrals are really, in the time scale of human history, just tents on the journey somewhere else.

What wilderness does is present us with a blueprint, as it were, of what creation was about in the beginning, when all the plants and trees and animals were magnetic, fresh from the hands of whatever created them. This blueprint is still there, and those of us who see it find an incredible nostalgia rising in us, an impulse to return and discover it again. It is as if we are obeying that one great voice which resounds and resounds through the *Upanishads* of India: "Oh man, remember." Through wilderness we remember, and are brought home again.

Dedication

Sir Frank Fraser Darling: Conservationist, Ecologist and Philosopher

Morton Boyd

In June 1931 a tall, dark-headed man bought a copy of *The Listener* before boarding the southbound train from Oban. A momentary thought of anguish at leaving the land that he had come to love had prompted him to seek solace in reading. Little did he know that this chance, everyday event was to change the course of his life.

His name was Frank Fraser Darling, a man of ideas and great motivation. He had already sharply changed the course of his life, firstly in leaving school and home against his mother's wishes on his 15th birthday and, secondly, by giving up a safe, respectable job as an estate factor in Buckinghamshire for the life of a postgraduate student in Edinburgh—which led to his taking charge of the newly created Imperial Bureau of Animal Genetics, a job he did not like. Another change was in the wind without his knowing quite what that change should be, but he had strong leanings towards a life close to nature in the Hebrides.

As the train sped towards Edinburgh, Frank noted an announcement in *The Listener* of the first Leverhulme Research Fellowships. He had had disappointments already when previous research schemes had fallen through—for reindeer in Labrador and elephant in Uganda; yet his mind and heart were quick with exciting ideas and the more he thought of the freedom which such a fellowship would bestow, the more inspired he became with one idea: a study of the ecology and behaviour of red deer, hopefully on the mountainous Isle of Rhum. Such a project, he thought, would provide a dual opportunity of describing through painstaking research the life of the red deer—a noble creature entwined in the fortunes of the Scottish Highlands—and of satisfying his desire for the freedom and spirit of the Isles.

His application was successful, and he left his office job in Edinburgh to head for the wilderness. As we know from his writings, the laird of Rhum refused him entry and he found his study area in the magnificent

15

country of Wester Ross, the rough bounds of which did so much to inspire him in later life and prepare him for his experiences in the High Sierra, Alaska, Bahr-el-Ghazal and the Luangwa Valley.

One clear morning in 1935 from the summit of An Teallach, Frank first saw the small island of North Rona on the northern horizon—the *ultima thule* of his island-going. This was the beginning in earnest of the island life which was to take him from the deer to the study of sea-birds on the Summer Isles and of Atlantic grey seals on the Treshnish Isles and North Rona.

In contrast to the results of his red deer studies, those with sea-birds were disappointing. His theory of social stimulation to the breeding condition of bird flocks was not supported convincingly by his data and was later discredited. However, it is still a live issue in the teaching of animal behaviour, known by students as 'The Fraser Darling Effect'. Later his seal work, planned to cover a national survey of the seals using a specially equipped 'Fifey' (fishing smack), was killed by the war, which found him reclaiming derelict land on Isle Tanera.

It was only a matter of time, however, until his great physical and intellectual energy made him break out of the confinement of the Isles and their local issues into the national and international arena. There were several key men in Frank's life. Some, like Frank Crewe, Charles Elton, Konrad Lorenz, Julian Huxley and Aldo Leopold, were responsible for shaping his ideas, while others, like Tom Johnston, Fairfield Osborn, Michael Swann and Max Nicholson, used his ideas to further a just cause. Tom Johnston, the then Secretary of State for Scotland, was Frank's pivot man of the 40s. Admiring his ideas on land-use and ecology, Johnston put Frank on the path leading to the West Highland Survey and appointed him to bodies concerned with the planning of national parks and nature reserves. Throughout his life Frank remained deeply grieved that Scotland was denying a system of national parks but he was well satisfied with the Nature Conservancy and the series of National Nature Reserves. One of the largest and most important of these is the Isle of Rhum, because, paradoxically, of the research on red deer. Frank had the great pleasure of seeing his aspirations for Rhum realised fully in his lifetime.

Frank saw himself as a pioneer in the frontier between animal behaviour and animal ecology. His thinking on wild animals was extrapolated gradually into human nature. His romanticism probably devalued his science on occasions but there emerged the maxim which, though perhaps obvious to the biologist, needed to be stated to a wider audience: namely that human beings and nature are a unity and that this special state of interdependence required acknowledgement and research. He propounded this in nearly all his major works using a wealth of illustrations from the world at large; his Reith Lectures entitled *Wilderness and Plenty* in 1969 were a final affirmation.

In the 1950s Frank was man of many parts—Director of the Red Deer Survey, Senior Lecturer in Ecology at Edinburgh University, Rockefeller Travelling Fellow in the USA and adviser to the Conservation Foundation in Washington on conservation in North America and Africa. His reputation as an ecologist and philosopher spread in America, while in Britain he was in decline. His West Highland Survey, he claimed was better known in the USA than it was in Britain; his red deer survey ran its course to an uneventful conclusion; under pressures caused by repeated absence, he gave up his job at Edinburgh University; his book *Wildlife in an African Territory* was not well received by Government. In his own country Frank sadly found himself in another type of wilderness which was made even more severe by the death from cancer of his second wife, Averil. Through it all, however, there were great compensations in a multitude of friendships and associations in many parts of the world. The 'establishment' in Britain might politely disregard his ecological prognosis of the human situation in all the places at which he looked, but the non-establishment, free-thinking, intellectually unfettered people lapped up his every word. His reports on the National Parks of the USA and of the Masai-Mara in Kenya were outstanding documents in conservation philosophy and planning.

Frank's first international assignment was as a delegate—not of UK, but of UNESCO, a distinction which he was always very particular to draw—to the United Nations Conference at Lake Success in 1949, where he made a big impression. There was a much greater awareness of 'conservation' and 'environment' in America than in Britain and he found himself in vogue. There is a sense of triumph in his words at the time: "...(by a special fellowship) The Rockefeller Foundation unlocked the door, Fairfield Osborn held it open and the American people said 'Come right in'." Between 1950 and 1952, Frank travelled the length and breadth of North America looking at national parks and reserves and reflecting upon the great historical episodes of colonisation and exploitation of the fabulously rich country. His eye for country and people and his fine prose make his American journal, *Pelican in the Wilderness*, a compelling commentary of people and environment in the grandest of settings from the Sierra Madre of Mexico to Mount McKinley in Alaska.

The tide of public awareness of conservation reached Britain in the 1960s, mainly through Prince Philip's Study Conference 'The Countryside in 1970'. Frank was by then a Vice-President of the Conservation Foundation of Washington DC and the editor of several key works of which *Future Environments of North America* (1966) is the most important. As an international celebrity he was welcomed back to Britain as a long-lost elder statesman of the conservation world. He was appointed to the Nature Conservancy, delivered the Reith Lectures, was knighted, became a member of the Royal Commission on Environmental Pollution and received honorary doctorates from the Universities of Glasgow, Heriot-Watt, Ulster and Williams College of Massachusetts, USA. He was a Commander of the Order of Golden Ark of the Netherlands, and received the John Philips Medal from IUCN, and the Mungo Park Medal of the Royal Scottish Geographical Society.

After an absence of some 30 years from Scotland, except for short business visits, Sir Frank and Lady Christina Fraser Darling retired to the Scottish Highlands, which throughout his life he regarded always as his first laboratory.

Sir Frank had a remarkable sensitivity to material things. In speaking about something—or in the case of a living creature to it—he would pass his huge hand over it to enhance one's appreciation of shape; and find words, often with a flicker of his natural stammer, which superbly expressed its qualities and roots in civilisation. He could provide a commentary on the material and design of his possessions which sounded authoritative, though it is possible that not all of it was well grounded. He was particularly proud of his collection of Chinese jades and ceramics, English and Jacobite glass, Persian rugs and bronzes, French clocks and clarets, and handled everything with great care and an affection which seemed to me to be far beyond the pleasure of possession. Each piece seemed to be a passport to another time, place and people, bringing a sense of triumph as in the case of the jades; heroism in the equestrian bronzes from Persia; pomp in the peafowl by the pond and peace in the cat curled upon his lap.

He came back to the place he loved more than any other part of the world he had known in his far-cast life. During this time I had the privilege of sitting with him to look again at the great canvas of his life recalling vignettes of An Teallach, North Rona and Tanera, of the Great Smokies, Yellowstone and Yosemite, of Tsavo, Amboseli and Serengeti. He died peacefully at Forres, Moray on 22 October 1979.

In conclusion, I fall again upon his words which describe his most favourite animal, the red deer:

See how the deer, now bright red-coated, lie at ease in the alpine grassland. Listen, if you have stalked near enough, to the sweet talking of the calves who are like happy children. Of your charity disturb them not in their Arcadia.

Ecological sanity
and social justice
are like the two faces
of the same coin—
they are inseparable.

José Lutzenberger

WILDERNESS

Science, Management and Politics

Forests and Their Role in the Future of World Civilisation

Alan Grainger

Lake Cristabel, alpine lake surrounded by dense Nothofagus forest in proposed Maruia National Park, New Zealand

Civilisation, according to my understanding, implies a certain dynamism, a sprouting forth of creative energy, matched by a structure which keeps everything in balance and harmony. Also important, perhaps, is a sense of tradition which is visible in both the landscape and in the actions of people, and which brings a sense of security and acceptance of past, present and future. One gets a feeling of civilisation when walking around the Moray Firth or the ancient streets of Oxford—and also when strolling through a forest.

Not so long ago virtually the whole world was covered by forests—a sylvan civilisation of global proportions, far exceeding the scope of the empires of Rome or of Britain. That civilisation paved the way for ours, in much the same way that modern civilisation can trace its roots back to Greece and Rome.

As Richard St. Barbe Baker, late founder of The Men of the Trees, said: "The trees worked for millions of years to make it possible for man to come on this planet."

To build our civilisation we have had to conquer that sylvan civilisation, whether we are talking about Saxon England, the Pilgrim Fathers

◀ Montane forest in the Impasse Falls area of Custer National Forest (USA)

in the early United States, or present day Amazonia. The forests had to be cleared and the life in them controlled if there were to be stable human settlements and farms.

The poet Charles Mair has written about the loss of the North American forests and the coming of human dominion:

There was a time on this fair continent
When all things throve in spacious peacefulness.
The prosperous forests unmolested stood,
For where the stalwart oak grew there it lived
Long ages, and then died among its kind.
The hoary pines—these ancients of the Earth—
Brimful of legends of the early world,
Stood thick on their mountains unsubdued.
And all things else illumined by the sun,
Inland or by the lifted wave, had rest.
And all the wildlife of this western world
Knew not the fear of Man; yet in those woods,

Lowland tropical rain forest directly on the beach of Cape Tribulation, Queensland, Australia

And by those plenteous streams and mighty lakes,
And on stupendous steppes of peerless plain,
And in the rocky gloom of canyons deep,
Screened by the stony ribs of mountains hoar
Which steeped their stony peaks in purging cloud,
And down the continent where tropic suns
Warmed to her very heart the Mother Earth,
And in the congealed north where silence self
Ashed with intensity of stubborn frost,
There lived a soul more wild than barbarous;
A tameless soul—the sunburnt savage free—
Free, and untainted by the greed of gain;
Great Nature's man content with nature's food.

The battle to subdue the sylvan civilisation is still continuing. The tropical moist forests which account for over a third of all forests are being cleared at a rate of more than 11 ha (28 acres) every minute. They contain half of all the species of plants and animals on this planet—a

vast diversity of life forms valuable for their own sake and for possible future economic exploitation. It is estimated that one species is becoming extinct every day. The tropical moist forests also contain half of all the carbon stored in vegetation on the surface of the planet, and their destruction threatens the balance of the global Carbon Cycle—contributing to the building up of carbon dioxide in the atmosphere and consequent changes in global climate ('the Greenhouse Effect').

While we can only guess at the possible repercussions of major losses in forest cover in the humid tropics, elsewhere in the world deforestation is a problem which affects large numbers of people on a daily basis and in a very direct way.

Millions of people in the Ganges Delta, for example, are in fear of their lives when the monsoon rains flood down from the Himalayas, unchecked by the forests that used to cover that massive watershed, and which have also been stripped away at a voracious rate in the last few decades. In September 1982, almost eight million people in just three states of northern and eastern India were either marooned or driven from their homes by monsoon floods. So far this year 403 people have died as a result of flooding in the state of Uttar Pradesh alone.

In many countries of the tropics, fuelwood is the primary source of energy for about 90% of the population. The average citizen in a developing country burns as much wood each year as a North American consumes in the form of paper. Worldwide, half of all wood cut is burnt as fuel. Yet, particularly in arid areas like the Sahel region of West Africa, deforestation has reached such critical proportions that there is a fuelwood famine. Women in Upper Volta may have to walk for between four and six hours, three times a week to gather fuelwood. Lack of wood does not just mean that it is cold at night. For people already short of food the inability to cook food and boil water poses an added threat to their health.

Despite the dire problems of the tropics, and the fact that forests still cover one fifth of the land surface of our planet and form the basis for an international trade amounting to some $59 billion a year, forests and forestry are still not accorded their rightful status at international level.

The tropical moist forests disappear, but we don't know with any great accuracy just how fast they are disappearing. Only about half of the total area of the tropical moist forests has been surveyed recently with modern remote-sensing techniques such as LANDSAT satellites, side-looking airborne radar and aerial photography. Of the 63 countries having some tropical moist forests, rates of deforestation have been measured by remote sensing for only six. The majority of the deforestation rates used to form the latest estimate of 11 ha (28 acres) lost every minute have been estimated by the UN Food and Agricultural Organisation (FAO).

Huge efforts are expended for the sake of feeding starving peoples and for agricultural development. Relatively little is done to help those suffering from a fuelwood famine who need a massive programme of reforestation to reclaim their devastated environments and provide them with a sustainable source of fuel.

The UK remains totally complacent about its low forest cover (only 9%) and its excessive dependence on imports: it spends some £3 billion a year importing 92% of its forest products needs. On the other hand, the Government is determined to maximise self sufficiency in food, and spends between £2 and £3 billion every year in subsidies, encouraging farmers to grub up even more hedgerows and woods and turn our once beautiful landscape into one vast prairie to grow food in such quantities that are far in excess of what people wish to eat.

The whole European Community spends £10 billion a year on the Common Agricultural Policy—just so it can be as self sufficient as possible in food. Yet, although collectively the Community is the largest importer of forest products in the world—accounting for some 40% of all imports—it has no common forestry policy to safeguard its present and future interests in this field.

This complacency has got to stop. The latest FAO estimates of future world wood supply and demand suggest that by the end of the century the world will be nearing maximum sustainable yields of industrial wood supplies. The fuelwood deficit in the arid tropics alone will be equivalent to an area of fast growing fuelwood plantations twice the size of France. In Africa south of the Sahara this will require the planting of an area of fuelwood plantations that together would form a green belt 6,000 kilometres across the Sahel from Senegal to Ethiopia and 34 kilometres deep. Also by the end of the century between a tenth and a quarter of the present area of the tropical moist forests will have disappeared. Such trends, I should point out, are independent of any major moves to substitute renewable resources like wood for non-renewable resources like oil and coal.

However troubled the world may be in other respects, however divided it is into developed and developing nations, it is united in its dependence on forests, whether for fuel, raw materials, foreign exchange, jobs, control of flooding, or an equable climate.

The developed nations cannot walk away from either their global responsibilities or their own self interest. Forestry must therefore be placed firmly and decisively on the international agenda. The following are some intitiatives which I think are worthy of immediate action.

The European Commission must put new impetus behind discussions to formulate a Common Forestry Policy. It should also follow the USA's lead and set up a task force to investigate the policies it might adopt towards deforestation and reforestation in the tropics. It should give strong support to the new International Tropical Timber Agreement currently being negotiated under the auspices of UNCTAD and which will support the development of more sustainable forest management practices in the tropics.

The USA should fund a NASA programme to use the NOAA-6 and NOAA-7 AVHRR weather satellites to estimate the overall area of the tropical moist forests. Just as importantly, it should build upon the successes of its satellite-based agricultural crop monitoring programme AGRISTARS and establish within the new NASA Global Habitability Programme an embryonic continuous monitoring system for the tropical moist forests so that we can know, for the first time, just how rapidly these forests are being cleared.

The USA and Canada together, as the two leading OECD forest nations, should place forests and forestry on the agenda for the next Western Summit.

The Commonwealth Prime Ministers, when they meet in the near future, should initiate studies that can lead to a new programme of assistance and cooperation by the Commonwealth countries on forestry matters of mutual concern.

Last but not least, the UK should reaffirm its commitment to a programme of afforestation involving both the Forestry Commission and the private sector. This programme should embrace both the deforested uplands (mainly in Scotland and Wales) and the English lowlands and be planned in the context of both economic and ecological rehabilitation.

The developed nations still have to come to terms with the role of forests in world civilisation. The image of the wild forest that must be conquered if a civilised agriculture is to be established is still very strong. It is also possible that sometimes, so as not to detract from the status of modern civilisation, we subconsciously wish to put behind us or ignore the forest habitats of those apes from which we are descended. But come to terms with the forests we must, and not just by mouthing platitudes about the future importance of renewable resources at a time when the tropical moist forests are being exploited in the manner of a non-renewable resource like oil. Forests are an important part of our lives now, and this fact should be recognised.

We are the heirs of that original sylvan civilisation and should not turn our backs on our forest heritage. Instead, we should treat the future of the world's forests as one of the major international issues of our time, and consider our ability to bequeath these forests to those who will follow us as one of the hallmarks of a civilised humanity.

From the Incas to C.I.T.E.S.

Felipe Benavides

Guano birds, the Guanay or Peruvian cormorant (*Phalacrocorax bouganvillii*), a valued resource of Peru

Garcilasco de la Vega was born in Peru in 1539, the son of an Inca Princess and a Spanish Conquistador. He was an outstanding writer. At 69, he wrote his famous *Royal Commentaries*, and from this comes much of our information on early Peru.

The capital of the Inca Empire was Cuzco. This, the most deeply revered place in the empire, was where all the kings held court. These great, elegant and proud people considered Cuzco the centre of the world. Cuzco in Quechua means 'navel'.

In the time of the Incas the Korikancha, which is today a convent, was entirely made of gold, similar to all the Royal mansions. In its gardens all sorts of plants, flowers, trees and animals were represented in both gold and silver. Tiny crawling creatures like lizards, snails and snakes, with butterflies of every size, were placed at spots that best suited the nature of what they represented. There were fields of corn with silver stalks and gold ears, on which the leaves, grains and even the corn silk were shown. Birds were set in trees, as though about to sing, and others hovered over flowers drinking in the nectar. These natural history museums, as we would call them today, as well as zoos of living animals, were to be found in most mansions where the Inca lived.

The Incas were brilliant engineers as well as warriors. As soon as a new province was conquered, engineers specialising in building irrigation canals were despatched to increase corn production in desert lands. Evidence of this can be seen today all over Peru. Their earthen terraces, sustained by stone walls, can be seen on mountain slopes, peaks and all rocky surfaces. Along the coast the only fertiliser used came from the unbelievably numerous flocks of seabirds. The islands not far from shore were covered with such quantities of their droppings that they looked liked mountains of snow. There was a penalty of death for anyone killing one of these seabirds or even approaching their islands during the laying season.

The Incas shared a common cult of the sea, which they called 'Mamacocha' or our 'Mother Sea', because the fish population was so abundant that it fed them like a mother. They worshipped certain fish, and the vast size and mysterious presence of whales stretched their imagination.

On the Nazca Pampa are the famous Nazca lines—artistic drawings covering at least 300 square miles of desert, mountains, valleys and rocky ground with straight lines. A single 'drawing' can be up to 30km across. Speculation about their origin still goes on, and we do not understand their purpose. Mathematicians such as Maria Reiche and Gerald Hawkins, author of *Stonehenge*, will possibly in time prove that the lines had a direct relation to astronomy.

In the valleys where the national marine reserve of Paracas lies today, lived the Chinchas. The fishermen of that area originated 9,000 years ago. The Chinchas, named after their general, decided to defy the Inca. "We want neither your god, nor your King," they said. "The sea is much bigger than the sun that only prostrates us with its burning rays; it is natural for you who live in the mountains to adore it, because it gives you warmth, but it is also quite natural that we should prefer the sea, which is our mother. Tell your General therefore, to return home and not to pick a quarrel with the King of the Chinchas, who is a very powerful lord. We shall come and show him how we defend our freedom, our lord and our faith." Their freedom, lord and faith was nature.

When I stand in Paracas today, after driving for hundreds of miles across the driest desert on our planet, and when I see the hump of a whale far out at sea or the flight of migrant birds from Arctic to Antarctica, I feel uplifted. I hear the whistling wind and see the moving sand covering my tracks. Only then can I describe what wilderness really means to me, and I thank God for it. It is an area where *homo sapiens* with modern conservation management has not yet interfered with nature.

The Incas were great conservationists, very wise in the use of their wild animals. Their great annual royal hunt took place shortly after the mating season, when some 20 to 30 thousand Indians assembled in the province chosen for that year. The Inca then divided them into two groups who walked in circular formation across the fields and prairies, rivers and mountains. As they advanced they herded all the animals they came upon, forcing them towards the centre with shouts and clapping of hands. As the circle of beaters closed in on the creatures, it became possible to catch them by hand. The big game animals called guanacos and vicuñas were caught in vast quantities, often as many as 30 to 40 thousand. Of the game collected, the females of an age to bear young were freed, along with the finest male specimens, while the old or ungainly animals were killed and their meat divided among the ordinary people. The guanacos and vicuña were sheared before they were set free, and a complete census of all this game was taken according to sex and species.

All the guanaco wool, which is coarse in quality, was distributed among the common people, while that of vicuña, which is the finest in the world, was sent to the Royal Stores. Only the Inca or those to whom he expressly granted his favour had the right to wear it. Any infraction of this law was punishable by death.

Nowadays we admire the canals built by the Incas, but modern technology finds it difficult to explain how they were built. Often the course of entire rivers was diverted from source by blocking the beds with stones. Unfortunately my ancestors, the Spaniards, did not understand the useful purpose of these valuable works, which are now in ruins, nor did they understand the Inca wildlife conservation laws. We brought them civilisation and taught them the use of the wheel; we forced them to believe in our God and destroyed their culture and their worship of the Sun God. We broke down their agriculture and slaughtered their valuable animals. We melted their gold idols and conquered their admirably organised empire. The destruction of wildlife was so scandalous that the King of Spain had to intervene. In 1577 he signed a royal ordinance prohibiting the hunting of vicuña, stating that they must be captured and sheared so they would not become extinct. He ordered these instructions to be proclaimed in all cities of the provinces. Unfortunately, as can happen today, it all remained on paper and the killing went on.

In 1815 the King decreed royal protection for whales. Again, while the legal intentions were admirable, the results were rather feeble.

General Simon Bolivar, who led the armies of independence, was a conservationist and a man of great vision. His close friendship with naturalist Alexander von Humboldt made him realise the importance of natural resources. In 1821, in Cuzco, he decreed that all efforts be made to increase the vicuña population, ordering strict punishment for their killing and decreeing that they should be captured and sheared

Vicuña (*Vicugna vicugna*) in the Andes

only in summer so as to protect them from cold. He also established the new coat of arms of Peru, featuring the vicuña.

He also decreed that millions of trees should be planted throughout South America, and that canals to improve the land should be built, following the Inca tradition. In Colombia, he decreed that the destruction of great forests should cease. But his laws also remained on paper, and the destruction went on.

In the late 1800s, the demand for Peru's rich timber became so great that European families moved to towns along the Amazon. The rubber boom in Peru and Brazil also created cities of utter luxury, where artists such as Melba and Caruso sang in the opera houses. A wealthy Frenchman even brought to Iquitos a whole pavilion designed by Eiffel after the Paris Exhibition. Extraction was abandoned in the early 1900s, companies closed down and families returned to Europe or moved to Lima. But the damage had been done.

Then the 'Guano Rush' began. Guano, the fertiliser made from bird droppings on Peru's coastal islands, had not been exploited during the Spanish colony. Now, slaves were imported from Africa to do the dirty work under a deadly sun, and there was no control whatsoever of the amount taken. In 1910 Peru exported 400,000 tons. The reason for this zeal was obvious: Peru's whole economy depended on the export of guano.

In 1925 ornithologist Robert Cushman Murphy described the bird population on Peru's coastal islands as 'the largest concentration of birds in the world'. On Chincha Island alone, he estimated the population of 'guanay', a white-breasted cormorant peculiar to the Humboldt current, at six million.

The main source of food for the birds is anchoveta, which is the fundamental link in the whole food chain of Peru's coastal waters. From time to time the 'Niño' current adversely affects this food source, and as a result the bird population decreases, but it builds up again in the intervening years.

In 1925 Murphy warned the Peruvian government, which then exported about 300,000 tons of guano a year, that if they ever went directly to fish the anchoveta, instead of keeping it as a food source for the 'guanay', they would lose both. Despite this warning, fishing of anchoveta began, and soon millions of tons were being extracted from the sea. There were no restrictions on amounts taken, and foreign companies established fishmeal plants. Peruvians, following the example of their foreign friends, joined the boom until my countrymen prided themselves on being the largest fishmeal-producing country in the world. Well over 14 million tons of anchoveta were gathered each year, producing 1.4 million tons of fishmeal to feed cattle and chicken for consumption by the rich nations.

In 1957 the 'Niño' current was very strong, and the temperature of the sea went from the usual 15° to 27° centigrade. This, together with the extensive fishing, decimated the anchoveta and led to the bird population dropping from 22 million to 7 million.

The demand for anchoveta continued to increase, with big prices being paid for fishmeal. In 1972 the coast of Peru suffered another 'Niño' current. Twelve million tons of anchoveta were caught that year, and millions of birds died. This was the *coup de grace* to both anchoveta and birds, for neither have ever recovered. In 1982 it was estimated that there were around five million birds but with the present

'Niño' current, the strongest on record, 60% of the population have already died and the recovery will be negligible due to the fact that anchoveta is on the brink of extinction. In February 1982, on an island off Paracas National Reserve, David Attenborough filmed a good number of boobies and few 'guanays'. Two weeks ago, I found the islands totally desolated and dead birds all over the area. It may well be the end of both 'guanay' and guano.

Since the time of the Incas, no laws or rules with reference to nature conservation have been respected in my country. There are two main reasons for this—the greed of other nations, and the immorality of government officials. The history of Peru's destruction of its most valuable wealth, its natural renewable resources, is a prime example of the fact that laws within the Third World will never be strong enough to stop contraband and illegal trade, as long as the demand of the rich nations prevails.

Consequently, I believe it is imperative that the civilised nations of the world make it their business to strengthen CITES—the Convention of International Trade in Endangered Species; and that all illegalities committed by officials should be internationally denounced and punished.

I blame the modern consumers for the disasters in Peru. They have the money to pay for whatever they fancy and have no respect for a nation's future basic food. Corruption and bribery are rife in connection with fishmeal, animal skins, whales and vicuña wool. Both buyers and sellers are guilty of the crime of contraband, but those who should receive the severest punishment are the wealthiest, the buyers.

Another difficulty in Peru is the illegal traffic in cocaine. The Incas chewed coca leaves, and our Indians living high in the mountains need it also, to keep up their strength and to stay warm. Now consumers elsewhere want the white powder for their vices or to enjoy a frivolous moment in life. This demand has created a gigantic problem in Peru. Hard up though it is, it has to try to control one of the greatest multi-million dollar rackets ever known in South America. In some countries, the illegal trade in drugs is larger than their national budget. The Mafia has modern weapons and fast planes, and through its money it corrupts authorities at all levels. Even more tragic, they work together with terrorist organisations which have already accounted for the lives of thousands of innocent people. It is not the coca leaves chewed by humble Indians that do the damage, but the people abroad who pay large sums of money for these drugs.

There is great concern these days about the destruction of the Amazonian rain forests, particularly among scientists in the industrialised world and in IUCN (International Union for the Conservation of Nature). Yet the industrialised nations themselves support some of the government projects in the rain forest areas. In 1981, a 12-man team of specialists in ecology, biology, agronomy, forestry and social anthropology spent a month in an area projected for one of these projects, and issued a report stating: "Poor soils, poor quality of the local forest, high rainfall and steep terrain render this area difficult to cultivate under normal circumstances, and from these observations this much publicised plan to settle 150,000 colonists will lead to disaster."

Nevertheless, today this project is going full speed ahead. It has the support of industrialised nations, while IUCN's Regional Counsellor for Central and South America has publicly stated that it has been managed with common sense and efficiency. This is in total contradiction to the report of the team of foreign experts.

At the CITES conference in Costa Rica in 1979, the Peruvian delegate did his utmost to move vicuña from Appendix I to Appendix II, so as to increase trade in vicuña furs and skins. Fortunately this was defeated. A later Peruvian Parliamentary Investigation Commission on the vicuña found that government officials had violated the La Paz treaty and that mismanagement and serious irregularities had occurred. It recommended that government officials connected with the project be taken to court. This is the first time a parliament has investigated a case concerning illegal request for a change in one of CITES appendices.

I realised at Costa Rica the importance of just one vote to the conservation of an endangered species. As a member of my government's Advisory Commission on vicuña conservation, I will see that our delegates in future have proper credentials.

Meanwhile, due to gross mismanagement, 6,000 vicuña (on Appendix I of CITES) have been shot by inexperienced marksmen. This tragic slaughter deserves the public trial of those who gave the order to kill, as well as of those outside my country who encouraged them. Two million dollars of Peruvian and West German tax-payers' money turned a national reserve for endangered species into a game farm, with the shady intentions of putting the wool and skins on the open market. The headquarters of what was ironically called 'The Vicuña Rationalisation Project' included a slaughter house and a deep freeze plant—in the high Andes of all places!

After 30 years of struggling to save the wild creatures of my country, I believe that CITES is the greatest weapon we have at our disposal to save endangered animals—as long as the officials running the convention give priority to the animals we are trying to save. However, the attitude of the recent meeting in Botswana towards illegal sales of vicuña cloth in Hongkong and Washington makes CITES weak.

The populations of many countries in the world are exploding. They need more land to till, more sources of income, more schools, hospitals, roads. Their governments often find themselves with their backs to the wall. If they do not provide the means for people to earn a livelihood, precarious as this may be, they are overthrown. Consequently, politicians will often agree fully on the necessity for a particular conservation step, but will then explain that it is not the right time and that the measure is not vote-catching.

Fortunately this is not always the case. For instance, Peru's position on the cessation of commercial whaling in 1985 means unemployment in the whaling station areas, which are the most depressed in Peru. In the North, where the 'Niño' current has resulted in ten months of rains and floods, thousands are homeless and hungry children roam the streets. In spite of this, I recently asked for the closure of a whaling factory which employs and feeds 200 workers and their large families. The owners, in an attempt to keep the factory open, promoted the idea that they were giving whale meat away to the hungry. However, the whales won. In a starving nation, it takes very decent rulers to take such steps. We shall save the whales, and we hope the industrialised nations will help us save the hungry children, who will not otherwise live to see a whale.

Hard-pressed countries of the Third World at times enact laws that cancel previous conservation legislation, or do not have the means to enforce their conservation laws. Many people in the industrialised world donate large sums of money to private conservation organisations which channel funds to some of the projects in Third World countries. But not all these funds are well administered after they are received, and some get into the wrong hands.

In my own country a law has recently been passed determining that areas previously proclaimed as reserves can be opened up. This has far-reaching implications which are obviously not being taken into account by the financial and policy planners of my country. Our national forests, declared as reserves, are being cut down by both Peruvians and foreign countries. Our national parks and reserves are no longer protected. Mining and oil drilling have priority. One of the largest rain forest reserves in the world is now in great danger, with plans to build a road across the park to join two watersheds. This last true wilderness in Peru's Amazonia was declared a biosphere reserve by the United Nations in 1977, but this appears to make no difference.

It is amazing to see the low profile some of our government officials take about these serious problems, never uttering a word on behalf of whales, seals, guano birds, sea turtles or vicuñas. I do not see why taxpayers should pay the salaries of officials who fail to protect our wildlife, forcing *us* then to raise funds from generous donors to repair the mischief they have done.

Industrialised countries often give large amounts of financial aid, called 'soft loans', for various Third World projects including roads, dams, buildings and even cities. Here technology and economics come into the picture. We need the technocrats and financiers of these countries to get together and to plan their projects with the far-reaching objective of conserving watersheds, natural resources and biological banks. Unless this is done, those same industrialised countries giving loans will no longer have their source of raw materials, without which they cannot subsist. It is a vicious circle.

We need also to see an end to narrow financial interests in the industrialised nations. These countries say the Third World should become more industrialised, but protectionism and lack of the latest innovations negate the markets for our industrial products, so the only things we can export are raw materials. For most of our people, agriculture is their only means of livelihood.

Urgent action is needed *now*. Those I call the 'conservation mercenaries'—ecologists, economists and bureaucrats—*must* act according to their consciences to work out clear-cut plans for the future. If they do not do this, our voices will continue to cry in the wilderness...or what will be left of it.

Brazilian Wilderness:
A Problem or a Model for the World?

José Lutzenberger

Tropical forests worldwide are a valuable resource, and Brazil contains the largest areas of this fast diminishing ecological treasure house

With eight and a half million square kilometres, and only 120 million people, Brazil should be a model of wilderness preservation. But it certainly is not, unless by this we mean a model of how to devastate nature. We have enough space to afford to leave three-quarters of our land in its wild state, and we could have the best national parks in the world. However, we have less than 1% of our land in parks, and these are so badly kept and preserved that they don't even deserve the name of parks. Even now one of our beautiful large reserves, which is not only a nature reserve but also the home of an Indian tribe, the Xavantes, is being destroyed. It is being crossed by a new road. One of the chieftains of the Xavantes, Juruma, was elected to our federal parliament last year, and in one of his speeches he referred to all our ministers, our president and our military, as bandits, thieves, liars and bad characters. This caused a tremendous scandal in government circles, and was on the front page of all our newspapers. The government reacted in an extremely violent way and wanted to have Juruma thrown out of parliament. Fortunately, practically all the other deputies voted for him, and he remains in parliament. At least we now have enough democracy to make it possible for the representative of the oppressed Indian tribes, who have constantly been subject to genocide and rape of their land, to speak out.

Today we are witnessing a biological holocaust the like of which has never been seen in the three and a half billion years of the history of life on this planet. We are witnessing the wholesale systematic demolition of all natural systems. It is not just beautiful landscapes that are being destroyed, but whole ecosystems and biomes. This is occurring in areas all over the world, including Europe, although here it is sometimes less apparent.

Let me give you some figures on the demolition of the Amazonian rain forest. In *Deforestation in the Brazilian Amazon: How Fast is it Occurring?* Fearnside, an American scientist working in the Amazon, put together data on the demolition of the rain forests. He made extrapolations showing that if present trends continue, the state of Parama, which is the largest state in Brazil, at the mouth of the Amazon, will be completely deforested by 1991. The state of Roraima will be naked by the year 2002. Maranhão will be cleared by 1990, and Goiaz by 1988, five years from now. The state of Acre will be deforested by 1995, Mato Grosso by 1998. Amazomas, the second largest state in Brazil's Amazonian basin, will be naked by 2003. If these rates continue, the whole Amazonian forest will be deforested by 1991, less than ten years from now. Of course, this is not going to happen, because things will change in time. But they will change only if we all fight for it.

What is really being destroyed? *Everything* is being destroyed! The rain forest is going, as I have said. The Atlantic forest, another type of forest along the Brazilian coast, is almost completely gone, as is the Araucaria forest, the large southern pine forest in the states of Rio Grande do Sul, Santa Catarina and Parama. I was born in Parama and when I was a young man 30 years ago that forest was still almost intact in its majesty. Today it is gone, and the few small relics that remain are now being demolished too.

In Cerrado, Cerradao and Caatinga, is another biome, a savannah type ecosystem as large in area as the Amazon. This is being destroyed at a rate close to 100,000 sq km a year—equivalent to half the size of Great Britain. Our coastal ecosystems such as the Restinga, the salt marshes and the mangroves, are all either being demolished or degraded. The same thing is happening to our swamps. We have a government agency which considers it to be its sacred duty to dry up every last swamp either by drainage, by filling it in or by making polders. The prairies in the south, the Pampas and the Panalto, are being ploughed and destroyed by erosion, and precious ecosystems such as those existing on steep mountain slopes, mountain tops, rock outcroppings or on cliffs are also being demolished.

How is all this destruction occurring? First there is clearing on an enormous scale. Cattle ranches in the Amazon are usually between 10,000 and 200,000 ha in extent. The alcohol producing programme in Brazil is on a similar scale. Forests are also subjected to clearance through a programme of the Brazilian Settlement Agency, Incra, which is called 'the largest agrarian reform in the world'. Taking settlers into the jungle is a way of not facing agrarian reform in other areas, where we do need it.

Outside these colonisation schemes, we also have wild settlers in areas that as yet have no owners. Here deforestation often takes on forms that are totally absurd. A wild settler has a chance of receiving deed to the land he claims if he can show that he improved it. Incra accepts forest clearing as improvement. Wild settlers thus have an interest in clearing as much as they can, even more than they can use. I visited a place where a Brazilian agronomist had cleared 150 ha of forest to make pasture, but he had no cattle and no money to buy them. He openly conceded he had cleared much more than he could use, but he claimed 500 ha and he got them. This gives some idea of the stupidity of the present settlement policies. Although he has no cattle, this settler burns down the tall grass every year to keep 'worth-less scrub' from coming up.

Commercial logging is another form of destruction. Until recently the type of logging in the Amazon valley was more or less compatible with the survival of the forest. It was carried out only in the flood plains, where the soils are fertile due to the annual flooding which deposits rock powder from the Andes. Here logging is done by small loggers, in a selective way. The trees are cut when the water level is low, and floated out when the water is high. They are bound into rafts and taken to the saw mill, usually a small, local enterprise. In the fertile soils of the flood plains, big trunks grow back in 20 to 30 years. Older loggers can resume logging where they started in their youth.

The export of rare plants is another form of devastation which is very little known, as it is not spectacular, but which causes irreversible destruction and affects some of the most fragile ecosystems. Those of you who like cacti, orchids, bromeliads and other exotic plants should think twice before buying a beautiful 'import'. When the exporters find a new species or variety they take all they can. But most of these plants are very limited in their habitat. Sometimes a species has a population of only a few hundred individuals, in some cases only a few dozen. Its discovery by the exporter is equivalent to its extinction.

Another factor contributing to large-scale destruction is indiscriminate mining. The Carajás Project, for instance, entails the demolition of a whole mountain range for the export of minerals. Fortunately, the world recession has put a brake on this project, and for this reason I hope the recession gets worse. We seem only to learn from adversity.

Large hydro-electric schemes such as Itaipú and Tucuruí will each flood up to 200,000 ha of forest. Two Indian tribes have been displaced, which almost amounts to exterminating them. The real reason for these mega-technological schemes is not to provide electricity—we already have too much of it—but because of the building contracts and corruption that goes with them. This also applies to nuclear energy. We don't need it. We could get all the electricity we need from small, decentralised, locally-owned plants.

The worst factor for destruction in our country is perhaps the way in which agriculture is practised today. It is rape of the land. The few peasant cultures we had are disappearing. Throughout the history of Brazil, the big landlords have done all they could to prevent healthy peasant cultures from developing. The landlords want all the good land for themselves, and they need a poor population to provide cheap labour. This is particularly evident in the amount of misery and starvation in the north east of Brazil, where there is certainly no lack of land or water. All the good land which can be farmed and irrigated is in the hands of the landlords who are less interested in producing food than in making money. They create monocultures of sugar, cocoa and other crops that under given conditions offer the most profit. The peasants are actually prevented from growing food. That is why we see millions of *nordestinos* in the slums of Rio, São Paulo, Belo Horizonte and other towns further south.

It is often said, by those who have an interest in continuing the devastation, that the population explosion is responsible for the wholesale destruction of the last wilderness areas. This is a lie. The rain forest is being destroyed by forces that lie outside it. If we left the rain forest to its inhabitants, to the Indians, the caboclos, the rubber tappers or the small urban population, the forest would be safe for at least another 500 years. We would have plenty of time to learn to handle it intelligently and in a sustainable way. The destruction that the inhabitants of the forest cause is on a scale that hardly matters. Large-scale devastation originates in outside interests, in technocratic and political interests in other regions of Brazil and overseas.

Large areas of tropical forest are burned daily

What happens in the Amazon region is an example of classical imperialism. Whether the imperialist power is overseas or within the borders of the same political union makes no difference. The local people are being robbed of their resources, marginalised and driven off their land. They either end up as poor day-labourers, chronically unemployed, or they go to the slums of the big cities.

The Jarí Project of the American multi-billionaire, Daniel Ludwig, is an example of one that caused much controversy. He somehow managed

to acquire six and a half million ha of land, and cleared close to 200,000 ha. The clearing work is done either by spraying a tree-killer—'agent orange' of Vietnam fame—and then burning off the forest; or by 'coorentão', where two super-heavy tractors pull a thick chain between them and tear everything down. There may also be armies of men wielding chainsaws. The timber is then all burned, and wasted. In the ashes, Ludwig planted a monoculture of a fast-growing tree—first Gmelina and then, when that failed, Caribbean pine. From

Japan, he brought a floating cellulose factory. He also planted some 30,000 ha of rice monocultures in the 'varzea', the flood plain. Fortunately the project failed, and Ludwig had to sell. But the new owners, Brazilian industrialists from the south, will probably be more devastating. They can certainly count on more government help.

This kind of project does not improve the lives of the people who live in the forest. All they may get are seasonal, badly paid jobs with no security. In fact, when Ludwig decelerated the project, thousands of people brought from far away were left stranded.

Today there are hundreds of large-scale projects in the Amazon region. Some are those of European and American companies such as Volkswagen, Nixdorf Computer, Nestlé, Liquigas, Kennkot Copper, Borden and others, or of Brazilian enterprises from the south—even a farmers' cooperative, Cotrijui, which is mostly setting up cattle ranches. It is a fundamental dogma in our modern industrial society that all capital must grow. An 'empty' jungle is seen as a good place to make money grow. But this happens at the expense of the people who have lived in harmony with the forest for millennia, like the Indians, or centuries, like the caboclo, and who have an interest in its preservation.

Rubber tappers in Amazonia live a much better and more abundant life than metal workers in São Paulo, actually making more money. But they hardly need it. They get all their food from the forest—fruit, game, fish and a few crops such as maniok, sweet potatoes and maize. They hunt only for their own subsistence and do not exterminate game. Today they are no longer the slaves they once were. Their transistor radios tell them the price of rubber in São Paulo or Chicago, so they cannot be exploited the way they used to be. They get half their income from rubber, half from Brazil nuts. But, because the rubber tappers, like the Indians, have only a sense of territory rather than land ownership, they can suddenly be confronted by a 'jagunco', a hired pistol man who tells them they are squatters and must go. The 'owner' is usually someone powerful who secured a deed for an enormous tract of land, marked out on a map, without reference to the people living there. The *seringueiro* has no choice—he either goes or becomes a day-labourer on the holding of the big guy.

I must emphasise that the destruction of our last wilderness areas has nothing to do with the population explosion. In fact, the big cattle ranches actually contribute to starvation. In a film I made recently with ITV, there is a scene in which we show a felled Brazil nut tree rotting in a field. The trunk was some 40 metres long. When that tree lived, it must have produced several hundred kilos per year of a very precious food, and there were several such trees per hectare. The cattle ranches produce ridiculously low yields of meat, less than 50kg per hectare per year during the first year, with yields going down rapidly in the following years. Compare this to yields in northern Europe—about 600kg per hectare per year, plus some 6,000 to 7,000 litres of milk on the same hectare. No milk is produced on the Amazonian cattle ranches. That is why the caboclo wisely says, "Where cattle come, there comes starvation, and we go." The irony of it all is that the little meat produced is meant for export. The owners of these projects rely on subsidies, and low yields are compensated for by the enormous areas.

In the case of the big dams, for example Tucuruí, the advantages also go to the powerful people who live outside the region. The reason for producing eight gigawatts of electricity in the middle of the jungle, where there is no demand for energy, is to produce aluminium for export to Japan. The next time you take beer in aluminium cans, think of it! It cannot be stressed enough—the destruction of the rain forest is done in the interests of outside capital. Most of the time that capital doesn't even need multiplying. What makes a man like Ludwig, 80 years old and with no heirs, who owns a fortune close to ten billion dollars, set up that kind of project in the jungle, thereby destroying the lives of the people living there? This is one of the great indecencies of our modern way of life.

Earlier I mentioned the small settlers. It may seem that they are also responsible for the destruction of the rain forest, and in fact they are. But they are there because they have been driven off the land elsewhere. Down south, where I live, the only relatively healthy peasant culture that developed in Brazil is being destroyed. There we have relatively fertile soils that, if well treated, can produce high yields on a sustainable basis. But the agrarian order of the Common Market which led to a situation where now more than ten billion dollars are spent annually to destroy food, has also promoted soybean monoculture on those good soils. The small guy cannot compete with the big mechanised and chemicalised farms, and government policies promote only cash crop monoculture for export. There is very little left today of the once beautiful and locally adapted peasant culture that German and Italian immigrants created there.

The Brazilian central government has set aside the state of Rondonia and other regions in the Amazon basin to serve as escape valves for farmers displaced elsewhere, in south and central Brazil, and for the masses of people from the north east who were never allowed to develop a peasant lifestyle. However, while the soils in the regions where they come from are fertile and able to support sustainable agriculture, the soils in the regions of the tropical rain forest are the poorest in the world. The settlers will soon be uprooted again. When the last tract of forest is cut down, there will be no more place for them to go.

Ecological devastation and social injustice always go together—or, in other words, ecological sanity and social justice are one and the same thing, two faces of the same coin. We ofter hear the phrase, "we have to find ways to make development compatible with the preservation of ecosystems and of wilderness." I believe that what we call development today is fundamentally incompatible with survival and social justice. It is development itself that is a disaster, because it means using and consuming nature, not living in harmony with it. We must question the fundamental tenets of this fanatical religion by which all live, the religion of 'progress' and technocracy.

Technocracy wants us to believe that both science and technology have nothing to do with ethics, politics or morals. They deliberately confuse science with technology, making the two terms almost synonymous. But, in fact, every technology is political. Every machine, technique or patent is an instrument of somebody's power. We need a political critique of technology. Whenever a new technology is introduced in the name of 'progress' and 'higher efficiency', we must ask: higher efficiency for whom and at the expense of whom? Is it good for the people or only for the powerful? Who profits by planned obsolescence, by one-way containers, by wasteful management of raw materials and by pollution? Is it the consumer, the people or the powerful? These techniques, philosophies and devices are invented by the powerful for the powerful.

It is not enough merely to change our own individual lifestyles, because those in power are changing the world in such a way that we have no choice. We cannot avoid buying poorly-made or non-ecological products. Nor, because our cities are organised in the way they are, can we avoid continually driving long distances.

The fundamental point is that if we want to change these things, then we must change the whole philosophy of development and all our economic thinking. For this to become politically feasible we must get the ear of the common people. I have noticed that in Europe and the USA these people still think of the environmental movement as an elitist one. We will only get their attention if we can show how social justice and ecological sanity are one and the same. In Brazil, in our movement, we have from the start attempted to do just that. This is why, even though we are very small in terms of organisation and finance, we have achieved a certain amount of political power. Politicians are beginning to listen, and we have won some very important victories. For instance, in the last 13 years we have achieved a very significant victory in terms of fighting pesticides. Today Brazil consumes less poison in agriculture than it did in 1973, while the chemical industry expected to be selling ten times as much by now.

What we need is to find ways to make science and wisdom come together again. Today, unfortunately, science, more often than not, is the whore of technocracy.

The Franklin Saga

Barry Cohen

Rock Island Bend, Franklin River

On July 1, 1983, at 10.30am, the High Court of Australia delivered its judgement on the future of a World Heritage area, the South West Tasmanian Wilderness Region. By a majority of four votes to three, the Court ruled that the Federal Government had the power to prevent the Tasmanian State Government from building the Gordon-below-Franklin Dam, which would have severely damaged one of the largest areas of temperate wilderness in Australia and one of the last such areas remaining in the world.

Thus ended the most important and controversial conservation issue in Australia's history—the battle to 'Save the Franklin', one of the last wild rivers in the world. To say it was a bitter struggle is to put it mildly. It raged for over three years and in the process ended the careers of two State Premiers, a State Government and many Parliamentarians, both State and Federal. It aroused large public demonstrations, not seen in Australia since the anti-conscription days of the war in Vietnam. It ended lifelong friendships, divided families and turned politics on its head in the serene and beautiful island of Tasmania, in a manner unprecedented in its near two hundred years of recorded history.

In my capacity as Minister for the Environment, I am responsible for the World Heritage (Properties Conservation) Act, specifically enacted

47

by the Labour Government to avert the threat to the wilderness area, and thus I was deeply involved in that battle. I now have a crucial role to play in ensuring that the South West Heritage Area is looked after in a responsible and careful manner for the benefit of future generations, as it is one of the few unspoiled natural wonders of the world.

The State of Tasmania comprises the major island and several smaller ones off the south-east corner of the Australian mainland, and is one of the six States forming the Commonwealth of Australia. It is the smallest State, with an area of about 68,000 sq. km., approximately 1% of the total area of Australia, and has a population of less than half a million.

Tasmania's industries have always been disadvantaged because of very high freight costs. As the island contains many short and fast flowing rivers, successive Tasmanian Governments, in an effort to reduce this disadvantage, have developed cheap sources of hydro-electric power to attract energy-intensive industries to the State. These include forest-based industries such as timber-milling, newsprint, woodchipping and mining. The metal smelting works resulted in the hills around Queenstown being turned into a moonscape. Tourism is a new industry currently being vigorously developed, and many Tasmanians now realise that the stripping of forests and the destruction of rivers is damaging the State's major economic asset, its rural beauty of great scenic charm.

It would be easy to assume that Tasmanians are careless of their environment because of the nature of their logging and mining industries, but in fact the value of the South West Tasmanian Wilderness Area has long been recognised. As far back as 1927 the Cradle Mountain-Lake St. Clair National Park was set aside, followed by the Gordon River State Reserve in 1939 and Frenchman's Cap National Park in 1941.

The South West Conservation Area—approximately one fifth of Tasmania—was declared a Conservation Reserve by the Tasmanian Labour Government in July, 1980, and was entered in the Register of the National Estate on the same date. The Register is an inventory of those parts of the cultural and natural environment of Australia, which have aesthetic, historic, scientific or social significance. Listing on the Register does not ensure preservation, but does impose obligations on Federal Government Authorities not to act in a way that adversely affects the area.

In 1982, at the request of the State Government of Tasmania, the Federal Government nominated for inclusion in the World Heritage list three parks within this South West area—the South West National Park, the Franklin Lower Gordon Wild Rivers National Park, and the Cradle Mountain-Lake St. Clair National Park. The World Heritage Committee accepted the nomination in December 1982, but expressed grave concern about the adverse effects to the area which would result

Keyhole Cavern, a limestone arch through which the intact and pristine Weld River passes. Mining and forestry interests pose potential conflicts to this river.

from the construction of a dam, and even went so far as to say: "The Australian authorities should ask the Committee to place the property on the list of 'World Heritage in Danger' until the question of dam's construction is resolved."

Why did the Tasmanians want to build a dam?

The Hydro-Electric Commission (HEC) has often been described by mainland Australians as the State religion of Tasmania. The Hydro, as it is known locally, is a statutory corporation operating under the Hydro-Electric Commission Act of 1944. It is not only dedicated to the generation of hydro-electricity, but is also a major employer of labour in the State. Its altars are the dams, as the Hydro is also its own construction company. Unless the Hydro keeps building dams, it cannot produce electricity and it ceases to grow.

The Hydro is no stranger to bitter litigation. From 1967 to 1973 the South West of the State was the site of a major conflict between conservationists—contemptuously referred to as 'Greenies'—and the Hydro over the construction of Lake Pedder dam. The Greenies lost and Lake Pedder was flooded. However, battle lines had been drawn and in regrouping, the Greenies became even more determined to stop any further 'development' of the South West area.

In October 1979, the Hydro recommended to the Tasmanian Government that a Gordon-below-Franklin dam be built. The fight to 'Save the Franklin' had begun.

The Tasmanian Parliament is bicameral. The Lower House, where the Labour Government had the majority, rejected the Hydro's proposal of the Gordon-below-Franklin on environmental grounds, favouring instead the Gordon-above-Olga dam. The Upper House, under control of the opposition parties, favoured the Hydro proposal on economic grounds and repeatedly blocked the Lower House's recommendations for the less environmentally damaging Gordon-above-Olga dam. It was in order to block the Upper House's scheme for a dam that the Tasmanian Government in the Lower House declared the Franklin-Lower Gordon Wild Rivers National Park in July 1980.

But the fight was far from over. By mid-1981, the dams issue dominated Tasmanian political life and had become increasingly important to the rest of Australia. In September, the Federal Government set up a Senate Select Committee on South West Tasmania which concluded, in its report tabled a year later, that the Franklin River must not be flooded both for environmental reasons and because of caves of major archaeological significance located along its banks. Also, there was no need for at least three years to decide on schemes for the additional power needs of the State. Finally, a number of alternative power options were in any case available.

Meanwhile, the issue was boiling up in Tasmania to the point where the Government decided to hold a referendum. Despite widespread public demand, the referendum did *not* canvass the 'no dams' option, merely putting to the people the choice between two dam sites, the Gordon-below-Franklin favoured by the Hydro and the Upper House, or the Gordon-above-Olga favoured by the Lower House.

In response to the call by the conservationists, 38% of the voters wrote 'no dams' on their ballot papers, thus rendering them invalid. The initial count of the referendum, which was later challenged legally, showed that 53% of voters favoured the Gordon-below-Franklin, with only 9% supporting the less environmentally damaging Gordon-above-Olga scheme. The pro-dammers claimed a victory, the Greenies claimed a victory, the Government licked its wounds and recessed Parliament for 15 weeks.

Scenes reminiscent of the pre-Civil War South followed. In May 1982, elections were held in Tasmania and for only the second time in forty years the voters elected a non-Labour Government. The new Premier, Robin Gray, claimed that the referendum result and the election victory gave him a clear mandate to go ahead with the building of the dam and had passed the *Gordon River Hydro Electric Power Development Act* which authorised construction of the dam. There is no question that the majority of Tasmanians, possibly around 60% of the adult population, favoured the building of a dam.

The Tasmanian Wilderness Society and other conservation groups sought a High Court injunction to restrain the Prime Minister and Treasurer from taking action in the Federal Loan Council which would have to consider the application by the Government for funds to build the dam. The request for the injunction was refused.

Throughout 1982, the Federal Government comprised the Liberal/National Party coalition led by Malcolm Fraser, who announced that under the terms of the Australian Constitution the Federal Government had no role to play in the dam issue as it was solely a State matter. The Australian Labour Party was actively opposed to the building of the dam and spoke vigorously against it in the Federal Parliament.

Public opinion was strongly and very vocally opposed to the dam. Pressure reached such proportions that in January 1983, Prime Minister Fraser offered State Premier Gray a $500 million economic aid package in return for a commitment to preserve the South West Region. Gray immediately refused.

The following month, a Federal election was called and the dam issue was one of the principal issues before the voters, though the major one was that of the nation's pressing need of economic recovery. The Labour Party Government which was elected on 5 March came in with clear policies to stop the construction of the dam.

Under the Australian Constitution, Federal Parliament is not given plenary power to legislate in respect of all matters for the whole of Australia. The powers are divided between the Government of the Commonwealth and the States. Because the Founding Fathers made no mention of the environment nor of conservation when they drafted the constitution, the division of power in these areas is subject ultimately to judicial interpretation. However the Commonwealth Parliament can draw on various powers to give effect to environmental policies on a national scale.

The issue was not clear cut in the case of the dam, so the Federal Government had to draw on the following powers: first the Foreign Corporations and Trading or Financial Corporations formed within the limits of the Commonwealth (Section 51(XX) of the Constitution); secondly, the rights of people of any race for whom it is deemed necessary to make special laws (Section 51(XXVI) of the Constitution); thirdly, the External Affairs (Section 51(XXXIX) of the Constitution).

The Federal Parliament approved the regulations which I made entitled *World Heritage Western Tasmania Wilderness Regulations,* which specifically prohibited the construction of any dam in an area of about 14,000 hectares in the South West. This was the first legal shot in the battle, as the regulations were based only on existing legislation and on the foreign affairs power.

The Act itself prohibits any clearing, excavation and building taking place in any 'identified property' which is defined as property forming part of the cultural or natural heritage included in the World Heritage List, or so declared by the Regulations of the Act.

The Tasmanian Government challenged the Federal Government's claim to have the constitutional power to stop the building of the dam, so on 31 May 1983, the matter was taken to the High Court of Australia, which rules on Constitutional matters. Tasmania argued that though Australia had signed the relevant UNESCO Convention, this did not impose an obligation on the Federal Government to conserve the heritage of a State of the Commonwealth. The Tasmanians further argued that the Federal legislation was tantamount to acquisition of property without compensation on just terms and therefore invalid under the Constitution. Furthermore the Corporations and Trading powers did not apply as the Hydro was not a trading corporation.

The High Court upheld the critical sections of the *World Heritage Properties Conservation Act of 1983* and all work on the dam was stopped.

Lake Selina—this place will be adversely affected by the construction of the hydro scheme which replaced the Gordon-below-Franklin power development

The Tasmanian Government claimed that the decision had tolled the death knell of the rights of individual States under the Constitution. This is nonsense. The decision merely recognised the need for the Federal and State Governments to consult on the question of accession to treaties and their application. The Tasmanian Government had refused consultation with both past and present Federal Governments, preferring to persist in its unilateral course of vandalism to an area protected under the terms of the World Heritage List.

Since the High Court decision the Federal Government has had three main aims: to assist the Government of Tasmania to find alternative employment for those working on the Gordon-below-Franklin project; to develop long-term programmes for Tasmania's economic advancement—tourism is an obvious choice; and to provide, with the cooperation of the Tasmanian Government, for the conservation and management of the World Heritage Wilderness Area.

Premier Gray claimed compensation of $3,500 million from the Federal Government for Tasmania's loss, the claim being based on the long-term value of all resources in the area. This clearly verges on the fanciful, as it would amount to a sum in excess of $7,500 for every man, woman and child in the State.

Federal Government disbursements to Tasmania are based on an individual project approach. The Prime Minister, Mr. Bob Hawke, and Premier Gray met on 31 August when they discussed an interim financial agreement which would provide $25.8 million in 1983-84 for job-generating projects, mainly in Western Tasmania. They agreed on a number of projects including roadworks, a rail deviation, tourist improvements, a sewage treatment plant at Queenstown, and the upgrading of the airport in the State's capital, Hobart. The total assistance committed this year is for projects totalling up to $30 million. I have been involved in the continuing process of consultation, especially as much of the work will be done in the World Heritage area to upgrade facilities to attract tourists.

We recognise that the management of the World Heritage area is a national responsibility, and we have provided funds for the restoration of damaged areas. I have found my State counterpart, Geoff Pearsall, most willing to cooperate and to let the past bury itself. Funds are being made available for immediate management needs. Shortly, for example, the number of park rangers will be substantially increased to cope with the coming summer and with the large number of visitors expected in the area.

Details of the formal management structure for the Western Tasmania Wilderness National Parks is still to be decided, but it will be a cooperative effort, as the Wilderness belongs neither to the State, nor to the Commonwealth. The wilderness soothes our longing for desolate, remote places where the spirit can rejoice in the beauties of nature. The wilderness belongs equally to us all.

The Silent Valley Story

Ramakrishnan Palat

Silent Valley contains the last substantial piece of tropical evergreen forest in all India

Silent Valley is a unique tract of tropical rain forest in South India, one of the few such areas in the world that remains relatively undisturbed by human beings. Tropical rain forests are the richest expressions of life that have evolved on this planet, with a continuous history of several million years of evolution. Silent Valley is estimated to have a record of 50 million years of evolution. It is unique in many ways, and is important for the survival of certain endangered species. Its flora is so diverse that plant breeders would find it an invaluable gene pool, and much of its fauna is very rare.

Situated in the Palghat district of Kerala State, about 45km north of Mannarghat, the Silent Valley Reserve covers 8,952 ha and contains many hills and valleys. The entire forest is on a plateau. Silent Valley contains India's last substantial stretch of tropical evergreen forest and is perhaps the only vestige of a near virgin forest in the whole of South India. Because of its impenetrable nature and the lack of means of communication, the area has long remained in a near virgin state. But more recently it has been subjected to disturbances by various anthropogenic activities such as plantations, agriculture, tribal settlements, poaching and fire. However, the heart of the Valley proper has remained comparatively undisturbed.

For the last five years I have been conducting research on the bird community of this undisturbed area. For a detailed ecological study of the bird community, a fairly good knowledge of the habitat is essential. I adopted the multiple stage sampling method for vegetation studies. Ten major plots, each 100m by 100m, were selected in the forest. The plants were classified into three categories based on their size. All plants exceeding 5cm DBH (diameter at breast height) were classified as class I. Plants with less than 5cm DBH and more than 50cm height were grouped as class II and plants with less than 5cm DBH and less than 50cm height were class III. In my study plots there were 111 species of class I, 83 of class II and 32 of class III plants. In the major plot the average number of class I, class II and class III plants were 521, 572 and 711 respectively, thus showing that the forest is very dense.

Both the height and the crown position of plants in these study plots were recorded. Trees were classified into five categories based on the crown possibilities. Trees receiving direct sunlight from above and from the sides were classified CP I; those receiving direct sunlight from above and partially from the sides, CP II, and those receiving direct sunlight only from above, CP III. Trees receiving no direct sunlight from the sides and only partially from above were classified CP IV, and those with no direct sun from either above or the sides, CP V. In my study plots 12% of plants were CP I, 30% CP II, 27% CP III, 21% CP IV and 10% CP V. This shows that the forest is well striated.

Each bird species has preferences for specific crown positions. When the diversity of crown position increases in a habitat, such as in evergreen forests with numerous plant species, the niche availability for bird species also increases. If the forest is homogenous or consists of one or only a few species, the crown position diversity will be low. This affects the niche availability, and only a few bird species can exist in such habitats.

The phenology and morphological condition of plants were classified into nine categories: those with 1) leaf bud, 2) mature leaves, 3) leaf shedding, 4) flower bud, 5) flower, 6) flower shedding, 7) fruit bud, 8) fruit and 9) fruit shedding. Because of the numerous plant species in Silent Valley, all the phenological conditions were present in certain percentages throughout the year. This helped those bird species with very specific food and other niche requirements to live there all year round. This may be why most of the birds of Silent Valley are residents. A forest homogenous in plant species has only flowers during certain months and only fruits during others. This means that birds which feed, for instance, only on fruits have to leave when there is no fruit in the forest. Because of the high plant species diversity, this is not the case in Silent Valley.

Foliage density on different vertical zones is another important factor which influences birds. The foliage height, density and diversity were also high in Silent Valley. This helped different bird species with different niche requirements to co-exist.

Bird censusing was also carried out using line transect and point transect methods. I recorded 112 bird species in this forest, with high abundance and diversity.

In 1977 the State government of Kerala started the preliminary work on the Silent Valley hydro-electric project, which resulted in the destruction of some forest area. The first thing to affect the birds was the blasting of rocks, which took place continuously from February to October 1977. When I took a census in December 1977, I recorded only 73 species. Five months later, in May 1978, I recorded 103 species, but nine species never returned to the area. The sound of blasting might have disturbed them but, since it did not affect the food potential, many returned when the blasting was over. However, some bird species were so sensitive that they never came back.

About 5% of the vegetation in my study area was destroyed for roads and temporary sheds, with a consequent 1.89% decrease in bird species and a 3.65% decrease in bird species abundance.

A temporary bund built in a free-flowing river resulted in the submergence of the natural shoreline which provided habitat for many birds. Certain amounts of biomes, represented by the original vegetation, disappeared, and the impounding shoreline did not have the same vegetation as the natural shoreline. The shoreline also offered nesting sites for various bird species. In particular, the boulders on the shoreline are very important and essential for the nesting of most birds of prey. When the boulders were submerged these birds had to migrate to other parts and this resulted in a population explosion of rodents which feed on the eggs and nestlings of birds. The sudden increase in the rodent population thus affected the population of many birds, some of which are responsible for the dispersal of seeds and for the natural propagation of vegetation. Their elimination will therefore affect the vegetation, which in turn will affect the herbivores and then the carni-

Indian conservationists succeeded in saving Silent Valley by taking the conservation message directly to the villagers. Drama, poetry and art played an important part in the campaign.

vores. The submergence of the river shore may not affect the entire bird community but it certainly affects the species which are completely dependent on riparian habitat.

Of the many wild animal species in Silent Valley, three are endangered—the tiger (*Panthera Tigris*), the Nilgiri tahr (*Hermitragus Hylocrius*) and the lion-tailed monkey (*Macaca Silenus*). The lion-tailed monkey is the only true arboreal monkey species and is considered extremely important in understanding the biological and social evolution of humankind. About half of their known world population of 500 live in Silent Valley, which is one of their two remaining viable habitats. Each troupe of these monkeys requires a minimum of 5 sq km of continuous evergreen forest, while a viable breeding population requires about 130 sq km of unbroken forest with a minimum of 33 troupes. Any destruction of their habitat in Silent Valley would be disastrous to these monkeys, which are obligate rain forest dwellers which cannot adapt to a new environment. They have been functioning in this particular ecological niche and are adapted to that particular ecosystem. The popular belief that once an animal habitat is destroyed the species will move into another one is not correct. The lion-tailed monkeys have a specific trophic status in the food web, and if forced to leave their natural habitat a chain of reactions would begin which would ultimately lead to their extinction.

The uniqueness of Silent Valley as the only vestige of a virgin forest in the Western Ghats of India has led many ecologists and conservationists to raise their voices against the construction of a hydro-electric project in this area. Both national and international organisations interested in nature conservation have drawn attention to the need to preserve it for the benefit of posterity. But it has been the efforts of the local people to save this forest that have been the most important.

Most of the people living in villages near Silent Valley are very poor and uneducated. They were led to believe that a hydro-electric project in the forest would solve most of their problems, providing job opportunities, more irrigation facilities and so forth. So they favoured the project. For them, it was more important to get food for their children than to preserve the forest for monkeys.

When the preliminary work on the dam was started, we who were concerned with nature conservation protested. But the government decided to continue the work. Then we sought help from other bodies outside Kerala and outside India. Conservationists came to Silent Valley and addressed the local people in many meetings. Unfortunately they could not feel the pulse of our poor village people. Some of them from the first world explained that forests are important as picnic spots, and in a meeting with school children one explained that only from forests can we get material to make ice-cream cups! Others emphasised the importance of the gene pool. All this went over the heads of our villagers. They did not want to go on picnics. They did not want to conserve forests just for ice-cream cups—they had never tasted ice-cream in their lives. This type of conservation effort did more harm than good, and our villagers began to think that conservation of forests was only for the recreation of rich people.

We realised that without the help of the local population nothing could be done, and that therefore our first task should be to help them realise the importance of nature conservation. We formed the 'Save Silent Valley Society' which included people from all walks of life—doctors, engineers, professors, labourers and students. We went to our villages in small squads, met our people and tried our best to understand their problems. We explained the ill effects of deforestation, and selected examples from their daily life to illustrate this. We made short dramas, songs, dances and puppet shows with a conservation theme, and staged these not in established theatres but in busy market places, at roadsides and street corners. Slowly more and more people began to attend our meetings and many of them joined us. We helped the people realise that the preservation of Silent Valley had implications far beyond the requirements for preserving the monkeys. That was our real success. By the end of 1981 the entire population of the Palghat villages had rallied under the 'Save Silent Valley' banner. With the emergence of this popular mass movement, the government had to change its decision. Finally our Prime Minister, Indira Gandhi, took a personal interest in the issue and stopped work on the dam. A powerful committee was appointed whose recommendations are yet to be published. For the time being Silent Valley is free from the noise of developers and bulldozers. This is the first time in India that a movement of the common people has successfully fought for conservation and won.

Let Silent Valley be silent forever. Let not the bulldozers and cranes destroy the tranquillity of this cradle of evolution.

A Wilderness Concept for Europe

Franco Zunino

Brown bear of Abruzzo National Park; a symbol of the last wild nature in Europe

I had planned to speak about the wilderness I have experienced in the Gran Paradiso National Park and in alpine loneliness among peaks, glaciers and wide, silent valleys in which waters thunder and marmot screams echo. I had planned to speak about the ancient beech forests in Abruzzo National Park in the heart of Italy, and of their wonderful fauna; and in particular about the brown bear, wild symbol of a world that is being engulfed by machines, civilisation and mass tourism. The brown bear is now being expelled from the protected boundaries of the National Park to be exterminated by poachers. I had planned to speak of the message I understood one day when I first met this animal face-to-face. Wilderness was all around me then, in a little lonely valley at the edge of the wood, when a brown bear mother and her cubs appeared in a meadow yellow with flowering dandelions. In that place my mind enlarged because they were there, alive, with only silence surrounding us.

However, I will speak instead about philosophy, laws, problems, roads and buildings. I will speak about how human beings move against wilderness and about how and why we should stop this. I do this so that others in the future will be able to see and feel in their hearts all that I have no time to express here.

Wilderness is not only a geographical feature or an environmental situation. It is also a state of mind, a psychological feeling of space that can differ from one individual to another; but it is always related to territories which foster an experience of human solitude and of intimacy with nature. Often it is not the actual extent of a space that gives us the feeling of wilderness. There are special morphological and environmental features that enlarge our horizons, allowing us a unique experience which tells us we are in touch with the wild. In Europe this is particularly important, because it allows us to find wilderness even in our over-developed and over-crowded countries. Even though much of the land bears the marks of thousands of years of human habitation, there are still certain coastlines, river gorges, valleys, mountain peaks and marshes that have the primaeval qualifications of wilderness. The impulse which compels us to seek and enter these areas is similar to that which compels American people to preserve and experience their wilderness, to discover their past in it, and to save critical habitats for the most threatened fauna.

In Europe we have lost much of the land from which the spirit of wilderness springs, and what is left is increasingly threatened. Past generations have tamed, forested, harrowed and urbanised the European lands, and have done so at the expense of those who today feel a spiritual need for the wild. They have also done so at the expense of the animals which need these lands for their very lives. Brown bear, wolf, lynx, ibex and big birds of prey now live only in the remnants of the European wilderness, and it is their last refuge. To compel these animals to live in mountains, woods or marshes broken by roads, houses and human developments which simply satisfy our desire for technological growth is to make slaves of them. For us that means losing forever the awareness of freedom and balance which these animals give us.

The 'Wilderness Concept' is a philosophy which sees human life in balance with the natural world around it. This balance is still psychologically within us, although it has almost no way to manifest itself today, like a seed which cannot grow without the proper ground. It is a philosophy of balanced use of natural resources based on the idea of creating an environmental heritage for posterity, and it entails imposing limits on human developments in order to preserve an everlasting space for nature and its wild creatures. If we in Europe wish to leave such a heritage for those who come after us, we must allow the spirit which moved in the USA and which resulted in the Wilderness Act to spread in us also.

Today only a few European countries, apart from those in the far north, can boast of having large areas of land which fit the Wilderness Concept. Most of these areas are generally not protected, but the very nature of their physical defences has until now kept their morphology uninjured and their unique solitude intact. However, if they are not protected, only a few will remain in years to come. Every year more roads, mountain shelters, electric lines, dams and ski-lifts are planned and built. Increasing tourism in natural areas is another pressing danger.

Even National Parks, Nature Reserves and other protected areas are injured every day. Frequently management agencies condone rash use of the environment through so-called 'active conservation', which alters the primary purpose of protected areas and often allows more economic considerations to prevail on conservation needs. In many of these areas, irrevocable options are open to whoever is managing them at the time. These managers may be influenced by local and transitory economic pressure coming from tourism, forestry or sheep-raising developments.

Even in the last ten years the natural environment in the European National Parks has decreased significantly. Laws misinterpreting the purpose of the Parks, incorrect management policy, lack of interest and management mistakes have all contributed to this. Viewpoints based purely on economic and tourism considerations often cause authorities to increase public use of the environment in a way that alters and degrades it, instead of limiting human use to a carrying capacity which allows for the preservation of the land and the continuity of our psychological ties with nature.

Many of the tenets of nature conservation, particularly in Europe, are based on economic, scientific and cultural needs of the present generation. But the Wilderness Concept calls upon us to look further than this, to our spiritual needs, which are durable and immutable. The need for peace and solitude in wild and free spaces is as old as civilisation itself.

Unless special measures are adopted, in a few years it will be impossible to speak of wilderness in Europe. The most dramatic ecological disaster in Europe today arises not from forest fires or pollution—which can be contained, although with considerable economic effort—but from the loss of the last areas that contain wilderness values. With their loss we will not only lose a priceless environmental heritage, but also cut the final umbilical cord with our past. Elsewhere in the world, conservationists still have some time to stop the encroachment of civilisation into the wilderness areas. In Europe, however, it is our generation which must act, and act now, on behalf of wilderness. If we do not, those succeeding us will have only a few faint memories of what Europe once was.

The recovery and restoration of European wilderness is imperative. A first step in this direction would be for the Council of Europe to promote an international Convention based on a specific definition of wilderness areas and including rules for their management and protection. This Convention, patterned on the US Wilderness Act, could induce European governments to promulgate laws to safeguard both protected and unprotected wild areas. Areas with unique wilderness features should form part of a European Wilderness Preservation System under sponsorship and moral control of the Council of Europe.

I would like to put forward proposals both for the definition of European Wilderness Areas and for rules to safeguard them.

Proposal for the Definition of a European Wilderness Area

To be classed as 'Wilderness', a natural environment area should have the following qualifications:

1. It must be uninhabited, with a wild and natural look. Generally speaking, its landscape and morphology should be uninjured. However, areas degraded by human interference could also be included provided they can restore themselves in the future.

2. It should not have any lasting or unalterable modern human structures; neither should it be crossed by roads unless these are unpaved and closed to car traffic, or due to be dismantled.

3. It must be large enough to give visitors a feeling of solitude, but its extent may change according to its morphology and environment.

4. It must generally conceal from the sight and hearing of visitors every sign and sound of human activities.

5. While previous conservation measures related to the area would be helpful, these would not be strictly necessary for its classification and protection as a Wilderness area.

Proposal for Rules to Safeguard European Wilderness Areas

1. No intervention upon woods, fauna and flora should be allowed in any designated Wilderness areas. Exploitation of fauna and other natural resources in non-designated wild areas should be rational and respectful of these rules.

2. No human works should be allowed, except for the restoration of old buildings for cultural or recreational purposes (or, in non-designated wild areas, for the building of temporary shelters and for forestry and sheep-raising purposes).

3. There should be no displacement of earth or deviation of waters, except for the restoration of previous landscapes or for the preservation of ancient unique environmental features (or, in non-designated wild areas, for forestry or sheep-raising activities).

4. No roads, trails or pathways should be opened, even on a temporary basis, to motorised vehicles, including engines employed in management of the area. Vehicles should also be forbidden off-road, even on water or snow.

5. Fly-over should be forbidden below a height of 1,000 metres, and landing by helicopters and aircraft should be forbidden.

6. The area should be kept in its most natural state, and managed in such a way that does not conflict with its environmental features and with the Wilderness Concept.

7. The number of visitors and the kinds of recreational use should be limited to a level that is in balance with the environment, and that guarantees people's enjoyment of the peace and solitude that are the main features of wilderness.

8. Any deviation from these rules should be approved by the authority responsible for the designation of the Wilderness area, after hearing the opinions of the Council of Europe and of the main conservation organisations, both public and private, in the involved State.

Wilderness in the European Community

Anthony Fairclough

Coastlines could play a major part in new conservation legislation in EEC countries

The relationship of the European Community to wilderness is a difficult subject when, by definition, the Community is a common market dedicated to the removal of barriers to trade and movement and to the establishment of common policies in a few very practical fields—agriculture, transport, trade and so on. However, the questions raised in my mind are much the same as those being faced throughout the world.

What is wilderness? Is there any true wilderness left when, for example, PCBs can be traced in the body tissues of every penguin in the Antarctic? Is wilderness a positive or negative quality? Are we thinking of the beauty and harmony of vast tracts of land untouched by human beings or of the harsh and bitter places which rapidly destroy life and hope? Is wilderness only wilderness when people are not there or, if they have a place, what is it? And what sorts of people—only those who live in (and in harmony with) the wilderness areas, or is there room also for visitors to come and share the experience of wilderness on a temporary basis?

In reading the objectives, theme and purpose of this Congress, my mind was cast back—as far as the UK is concerned—to the Dower and Hobhouse Reports which laid the groundwork for the National Parks. Dower defined a National Park as "an extensive area of beautiful and relatively wild country in which (a) the characteristic landscape is strictly preserved, (b) access and facilities for public open-air enjoyment are amply provided, (c) wildlife and buildings and places of architectural and historical interest are suitably protected, while (d) established farming use is effectively maintained." Hobhouse recognised that "here are no vast expanses of virgin land...which can be set aside for public enjoyment or conservation of wild life...almost every acre of land is used in some degree for the economic needs of man and has its place in a complex design of agriculture, industrial or residential use." Even more important was his recognition that "since it is not possible to sterilise great tracts of land...it is all the more urgent to ensure that some at least of the extensive areas of beautiful and wild country in England and Wales are specially protected as part of the national heritage...."

These definitions already clearly saw the need to reconcile potentially competing uses of land. But they left unanswered the questions of how to achieve that reconciliation, what the priorities should be, and how to balance the various interests. And herein lies the problem.

The National Park Policies Review Committee (the Sandford Committee) tackled the question of reconciling conflicts. The designation of areas as National Parks was intended, *inter alia*, to exclude incompatible development; whilst as to conflicts between the two objectives of National Parks—the preservation and enhancement of natural beauty and the promotion of public enjoyment—the Committee had "no doubt that where the conflict between the two purposes, which has always been inherent, becomes acute, the first one must prevail in order that the beauty and ecological qualities of the national parks may be maintained."

More recently the Countryside Review Committee discussed what it called 'the conservation ethic' which, whilst acknowledging the necessity of accepting change, also seeks to minimise its adverse effects because of "a recognition that resources are limited and that we can no longer afford a careless, still less a profligate, approach to their use and enjoyment." Conservation must thus "be regarded as a key element in national thinking...no longer the icing on the cake...(but rather) something to be taken into account from the outset."

CRC went on to propose a two-tier system of designation of protected areas. This was not pursued, but it is interesting to note that, for the top tier, they were thinking of 'small areas of outstanding quality' where the purpose of designation would be the conservation of the environment and quiet enjoyment by the general public to the extent

Coastal sand dune systems have significant wilderness qualities: Findhorn dunes on the Moray coast, Scotland

compatible with this, and where there would be 'the strongest possible presumption against any development or other activity' in those areas likely to conflict with conservation.

This is all UK history, and I have spoken of it in some detail because similar conflicts have arisen in all the relatively densely populated and industrialised countries of the European Community, and a comparable evolution of thought has taken place. Everywhere, there has been a growing recognition that it is folly to neglect conservation and that, quite apart from the ethical arguments for the protection of wild life and wild places, people themselves have a need that they should not be destroyed.

The European Community's most recent Environmental Action Programme, adopted in February 1983, puts it this way: "The resources of the environment are the basis of but also constitute the limits to further economic and social development and the improvement of living conditions." For this reason it must be recognised that "environment policy is a structural policy which must be carried out without regard to the short-term fluctuations in cyclical conditions, in order to prevent natural resources from being seriously despoiled and to ensure that future development potential is not sacrificed." Thus, to "implement a preventive environmental protection policy in a full and effective manner, the Community should seek to integrate concern for the environment into the planning and development of certain economic activities as much as possible" thus leading to "a greater awareness of the environmental dimension, notably in the fields of

68

agriculture (including forestry and fisheries), energy, industry, transport and tourism."

What is involved here is the acceptance at Community level of the significance of the world-wide evolution of thought which has led to the recognition (highlighted by the World Conservation Strategy) that environmental needs and industrial, agricultural and other developments cannot be regarded as incompatible, and that a way must be found of reconciling them. The central point in the WCS is the clear acknowledgement that development and conservation are interdependent, and that to neglect conservation in fostering development is to live on capital rather than income, thereby diminishing the capacity of the environment to support future development. It also needs to be recognised that this is as true for the developed countries of the Community as it is for developing countries, which *must* be developed if the people are to escape from the margins of survival.

Let me say something about what action the Community has taken on the environment in fields of concern to this Congress. The Treaty of Rome said nothing about the environment: it was essentially aimed at the creation of a Common Market and at ensuring the free movement of goods and the avoidance of distortions of competition. But it also spoke of improving living standards and the quality of life, and so in 1972, when the Community's action programme on the environment was launched, it was based on both these strands.

As the guardian of the Treaty, the Commission's duty is to make proposals to harmonise action in individual Member States when it considers them necessary in order to achieve both these objectives. A good deal of action has followed the adoption in 1973 of the First Environmental Action Programme—most of it by way of the adoption of legislation, and mostly concerned with pollution control.

In addition, numerous studies are being undertaken, information exchanged and disseminated, and cataloguing carried out. In the field of land management and nature protection, this type of activity—rather than legislation—has, to date, predominated. One reason for this is the view that harmonisation at Community level should be proposed only when necessary, and that in many fields—land management amongst them—the national or even local levels are more appropriate for action than the Community level.

Even though priority was initially given to pollution control (essentially to protect human health), the Community environmental legislative measures that have been adopted—some 70 in all since 1973—have almost all had indirect effects that benefit wildlife and the natural environment generally.

Increasingly a preventive approach has come to be seen as crucial in appropriate environmental action. To this end—to quote the latest Action Programme—"environment impact assessment is the prime instrument for ensuring that environmental data is taken into account in the decision-making process. It should be gradually introduced into the planning and preparation of all forms of human activity likely to have a significant effect on the environment."

To achieve this, there are two basic requirements. The first is a change of attitude on the part of decision-makers at all levels, both in the Community as such and in Member States, and a recognition that 'cutting environmental corners' for short-term gains is a false economy which will lead not only to unacceptable environmental damage but also in the medium and longer term to greatly increased costs; and, associated with this recognition, the development of appropriate environmental awareness at all levels of management.

The second is the establishment of regular procedures for the advance assessment of the environmental impact of proposed developments so as to ensure, before decisions are taken, that developments are acceptable environmentally. This also implies a readiness to change proposals to ensure compatibility with the environment and an acceptance of the fact that the costs of necessary environmental protective measures (or even of associated positive measures to promote conservation or environmental improvement) should be accepted as an appropriate part of the costs of the developments themselves.

A draft Directive concerning prior environmental impact assessment of major projects likely to have an impact has been under discussion by the Community's Council of Ministers for some time. Such a Directive would require Member States to adopt certain procedures. There is also a need for the Community's own policies and actions to respect environmental requirements including, in appropriate cases, the use of prior impact assessments. I think in particular of the Common Agricultural Policy and the Less Favoured Areas Directive, about which there has been concern in Britain. The Commission as a whole is committed by the preventive approach adopted in the Third Environmental Action Programme, and by the commitment to integrate environmental requirements into policy in other fields. When the Commission's proposals on agricultural structures are published, I hope it will be felt that environmental needs have satisfactorily been built in.

So far I have addressed the question of preventing damage occurring. But there are also much more positive aspects to the Community's work to date in the environmental and conservation fields.

For instance, the Birds Directive prohibited the killing and capturing of wild birds, the taking of their eggs and their deliberate disturbance, etc. It also, with a view to the protection of habitat, required Member States to classify the most suitable sites 'as special protection areas for the conservation' of the species concerned, and asked them to notify the Commission of the special protection areas designated, as well as of areas which they had designated (or intended to designate) as internationally important wetlands. Since then a major study has been prepared for the Commission, and published, on important bird areas in the Community.

Important studies have also been undertaken of coastal zones and mountainous areas. The object of these studies has been to examine the nature of the pressures facing these areas, and to define principles which would permit necessary development whilst maintaining environmental quality.

The Commission has also undertaken the classification of protected areas. This study, which was completed a few years ago, attempted to define a common language to assist in distinguishing between different types of protected zones on a compatible basis in the different Member States, despite wide differences in terminology and definitions. Such a common language could be of considerable practical importance in a number of fields—not least in relation to possible Community financial support.

The designation of protected zones started in most countries with the protection of those which were rare or considered to be of scientific interest. But the differences from country to country (and often from region to region) in population density, economic activity, land use and natural conditions, as well as in the social attitudes towards nature, have resulted in a mosaic of types of protected zones differing (sometimes greatly) from one member country to another. Our study on 'Protected Areas in the European Community' therefore looked first at the different types of protected zones existing in the EEC Member States. This inventory made it clear that zones with the same name can cover very different realities, and that zones fulfilling the same function can have different names.

These differences in typology and definition have obvious disadvantages for international cooperation in the field of wildlife. For example, if different countries agree to protect biotopes of migratory species—say birds—it is not enough to know that the biotopes will be classified as 'Reserves'. It is necessary to be sure that these biotopes will receive the same degree of protection in reality. Many attempts have therefore been made to establish widely accepted definitions and criteria, especially by the Council of Europe and the International Union for the Conservation of Nature and Natural Resources (IUCN).

Our study has reviewed the results obtained at international level. On this basis, in cooperation with the IUCN and Council of Europe, we have developed a classification system fully compatible with existing systems but which better meets the specific situation of the European Community. The system distinguishes eight types of zones: Strict Nature Reserve; Nature Reserve; National Park; Protected Natural or Semi-Natural Landscape; Protected Cultivated Landscape; Protected Cultural Monument and Natural Features; Specific Protected Areas; and Green Belt. For each of these categories the system describes the type of area and the reasons for protection, the form of protection and management, and the use of the area.

Another activity undertaken by the Commission is the 'Ecological Mapping' project. This had its origins in suggestions made by the Italian government and was launched by the Council of Ministers in 1974. Its aim was to develop a method, based on cartography, of mapping together environmentally related data and values, economic and social demands, and basic physical characteristics. The idea is to provide another 'common language', and to lead to the development of methodologies for establishing a European information system on the state of the environment related to other relevant characteristics.

In the course of the project's development, initial ideas have been modified and the system will now aim, in general, at bringing together information either already existing or readily derived from existing data about the environment. This could be particularly important in assisting the Community by providing good information on the environmental characteristics of zones where Community actions (eg under the Regional Development Fund) were contemplated. We hope to make proposals to the Council very shortly for the next steps in the development of this important information system.

Given that the Community is an economic one, another area of important action is that which has been taken in relation to trade in threatened species. Perhaps the most important is the implementation, by way of a Regulation, of the Washington Convention on Trade in Endangered Species. The Regulation will enter into force in January 1984, and will provide for much stricter protection of the species covered by the Convention than by the provisions of the Convention itself. The Regulation will also cover all Member States not yet parties to the Convention, ie, Belgium, Greece, Ireland, Luxembourg and The Netherlands. In this field, I should also mention the 1982 ban on whale products (which will be absorbed by the application of the CITES Regulation) and the Directive adopted in 1983 requiring Member States to take steps to prevent the import of baby seal skins and products. The Community has also become a party to the Berne Convention on the conservation of European wildlife and natural habitats, and will shortly become a party to the Bonn Convention on migratory species. It has also signed the protocol of the Convention of Barcelona relating to specially protected areas of the Mediterranean Sea.

The Community has done a good deal to contribute to conservation and the protection of wilderness, but more is certainly needed. One hopeful note is that in 1982 the European Parliament for the first time voted money in its budget for actions of an environmental nature. The scale of financial provision is small, and no decisions have yet been taken on a Community Regulation to control the future use of such funds. But by 1982 there were already a number of descriptive analyses defining projects to be carried out. Also, to illustrate what can be achieved, there has been action to restore a salt water lagoon destroyed by the building of a dike (Denmark); the restoration of a wetland threatened by the indirect effects of surrounding drainage (Germany); development contracts with local authorities in France resulting in the commitment of these authorities to maintain publicly owned land as extensive grazing areas; and the monitoring of the environmental effects of an integrated development programme (Great Britain, Western Isles).

The future is unknown. But the Community's commitment to conservation, to the wise and sensitive management of all natural resources, and to the progressive integration of environmental needs into the decision-taking processes in all fields, is clear. That is perhaps the best long-term guarantee that, within the framework of the Treaty of Rome and of the Environmental Action Programme, the European Community will continue to make its contribution to conservation and to the protection of wilderness.

Evolution of the Wilderness Concept in the US

John Block

A trail maintenance crew *en route* with pack animals: Glacier Peak Wilderness, Washington State, USA

To discuss wilderness in the realities of our present-day age it is necessary first to gain an appreciation of its historical significance. Wilderness is the arena in which the civilisations of humankind have slowly been shaped. For thousands of years, we challenged the forces of nature, seeing them as the enemy. But as we began to understand them and to work with and around nature, they became less of an enemy.

The benevolent idea of wilderness first came to life in the minds of poets and philosophers centuries ago, eventually taking on the aura of heritage. In 1905, this heritage concept began to develop as national policy in the United States. Forest reserves, which had earlier been set aside by Congress, became national forests, and the US Forest Service was established in the Department of Agriculture. The National Park Service and the US Fish and Wildlife Refuge System were set up as part of the Department of the Interior in 1916 and in the 1930s respectively. These three agencies were all later to play prominent roles in designating and managing wilderness areas.

The idea for a special designation of 'wilderness' came when two Forest Service employees suggested that certain areas be set aside away from the threat of roads and vehicles and any forms of developed recreation. In the next couple of decades, other areas were added to the wilderness list.

In the 1950s, a citizen organisation called the Wilderness Society, along with other support from inside and outside government, concluded that areas designated as wilderness by administrative action could be un-designated in the same way. They urged statutory designation of the areas. With the nation standing on the threshold of a great period of industrial growth after World War II, this idea of 'locking up' vast natural resources was not universally embraced. It took eight years of discussion, debate and hearings before the Wilderness Act of 1964 was passed. The purpose of this landmark legislation was "to assure that increasing population, accompanied by expanding settlement and growing mechanisation, does not occupy and modify all areas within the US."

Considering the conflict in which the new law was forged, some compromises had to be made in developing the legislation. Grazing, mineral exploitation, oil and gas leasing, and some previously established uses were allowed to continue, at least for a time.

The nucleus of the new wilderness system was already in place in the National Forests. Some 9.1 million acres (over 3.5 million ha) of this land were instantly proclaimed part of the system. Directions were also given for study of other National Forest areas, plus areas under the National Park Service and the Fish and Wildlife Service, with a view toward recommending these areas for possible addition to the wilderness system.

Since 1964, Congress has designated many additions to the system. The current 264 designated wildernesses encompass 80 million acres (over 32 million ha) of Federal land, almost 3½% of the surface area of the US. Some 56 million acres (22.4 million ha), roughly 70% of the system, are in Alaska. Under a 1976 law, the Department of the Interior's Bureau of Land Management is studying the land it administers for the purpose of recommending to Congress some additions to the wilderness system.

Growth of the wilderness system continues—and so does the debate. There is strong controversy about proposals to make further additions to wilderness from the National Forests. The land base designated as wilderness in the US is larger than many countries of the world, and some consider the designation of so much wilderness as prodigal, stemming from an embarrassment of riches.

However, there is more validity and importance to the action than that. We are learning lessons that will be of value not only to us, but to the international community.

Wilderness is relatively independent of human influences, generally uncultivated and uninhabited, and shaped only by the interactions of air on water, water on soil, soil on plant and animal. All are dependent on each other in a mix of constant natural change. We use wilderness for scientific, educational and recreational purposes, but do not modify it. Therefore, it has a special value as a scientific yardstick and possibly as a gene pool. It is useful to be able to compare modified environments with those perpetuated in near-natural condition. Quantities of data, valuable to the scientist and no longer available elsewhere, are likely to be contained in these wildland resources. Wilderness areas can serve as benchmarks against which we can model and predict favourable and adverse impacts of developmental works on non-wilderness land elsewhere.

A second and more subtle value of wilderness is sociological. In wilderness, people can, if they wish, isolate themselves from human activity. For most people, wilderness is probably simply a magnificent natural arena for rest and recreation away from the pressures of society.

Wilderness is not a concept which is universally embraced. Many people perceive it in the same context as art and music—nice, but not absolutely necessary. Others are indifferent to it.

Many who acknowledge and appreciate the wilderness concept still question how much is needed or can be afforded, especially in view of the obvious uses to which land can be put. For instance, the US today is not self-sufficient in oil, nor is it richly endowed with certain rare minerals critical to implementing modern technology applicable particularly to national defence. Deposits of oil or of critically rare minerals may exist in already designated wilderness areas. But so long as these areas are closed to exploration, we will never know. And although the Wilderness Act authorises mineral surveys by the US Geological Survey, an agency in the Department of the Interior, adequate funding to conduct such exploration is most unlikely.

These concerns have been expressed in the decades of debate over the issue, and will be questioned even more sharply as other countries consider establishing wilderness systems. Many nations are struggling desperately to provide the basic needs of food, fuel, clothing and shelter. These are all products of the land, and must be served first. However, a key consideration in acceptance of wilderness is that the wilderness resource is enduring. If situations change—if needs for food, fibre, minerals and fuel become so overwhelming they cannot be met by the land available—wilderness will still be there as a last resort. Meanwhile, we will be prompted to do a better job of managing other land resources, so as to avoid having to invade the wilderness.

The continuing debate over wilderness in the US is now focused on two matters: how much wilderness is enough, and what management practices should be followed in retaining the qualities of the designated wilderness areas? The issue of designating more wilderness arises because of the continued existence of rather large roadless areas. There are also numerous proposals to designate wilderness in areas which have returned to a natural state after initial disturbances for logging, ranching or even farming.

As far as already designated wilderness areas are concerned, experience has shown that these need management, even though the term 'wilderness' and 'management' may appear to be contradictory. One management problem is that of protecting wilderness areas from the very people for whom they were set aside. With the growing popularity of wilderness for recreation, some places have been so heavily used they are in danger of being loved to death, particularly in areas near large population centres. As a result, Federal land managers in some areas have had to institute permit systems and other controls, such as limitations on group sizes, length of stays and use of certain overworked camping sites. Such measures are instituted only as necessary, and land managers are finding they can minimise this necessity through public education, encouraging wilderness visitors to leave few traces of their presence.

Another management challenge, and also cause for national debate, is the role of fire. For thousands of years fire has been part of wilderness, and is not always a destructive force. Complete control of wildfire in wilderness has in fact caused some unnatural conditions, such as buildup of downed trees and other forest debris. This could be the source of extensive destruction if uncontrollable fires or insect and disease epidemics break out. Researchers and managers are consequently studying areas where fire has been a significant natural influence, with the objective of determining the effects of planned or naturally-caused fires burning under controlled conditions.

We in the US are proud of our wilderness system, and thankful to have a legacy of our nation's natural heritage. This legacy is one that can be enjoyed and used today, and then passed on to future generations. With balance and planning, the system is working. Its creation was not easy, but its success may provide an example to other countries in devising similar systems suited to their own resources, needs and desires. We now have a body of experience and knowledge that can help other nations in their efforts.

There is nothing finer to pass on to future millions than the rich heritage of well-managed natural resources. It is a worldwide legacy of resource use which includes food, fibre, wildlife, quality water—and wilderness. It will be tangible proof that we cared for them too.

Working to Conserve Wild America: The Wilderness Movement in the US

Sally Ranney

Wildlands in Alaska have been the focus for tremendous achievements in the effort to conserve North American wilderness

There is an enduring conceptual eloquence about wilderness. It speaks to us in a panoply of paradigms. It consistently demands definition of the subtle differences between intellect and intuition, awe and fear, reality, real intangibles and the intangible. It ignites a very gut-level, primaeval passion in our hearts and stirs longings and fantasies that are beyond, as some would say, the King's English.

Yet, as author Roderick Nash stated in *The Future of Wilderness: Need for a Philosophy*, we stand "quite plainly on the edge of decision about wildness as a factor of significance in human culture and natural process....The 15,000 year effort of man to modify and control nature is amazingly complete....As 500 years of continued technological transformation of the planet concludes, the debate is on...joined by scholars, policy makers and the public about the long-term future of wild in an ever-increasing synthetic environment." And, thank God, that debate is now joined by theologians.

Within contemporary political, cultural, social and economic contexts, wilderness increasingly represents critical choice. This choice is not only confined to the question of whether or not to protect wild country, but also, and more importantly, it involves the question of our very survival, for it deals with the essentials to existence itself.

The challenge of choice, of alternatives that wilderness represents, is a challenge to our individual and collective wisdom, to our imagination, intelligence, foresight and sense of history. It is a challenge to recognise our inescapable linkage in the fragile fabric of ecosystem diversity; a challenge to consciously acknowledge the value of wilderness.

Environmentalism is an enigma on the list of social consciousnesses and political actions. Previous significant social movements—for example, suffrage, civil rights, labour, women's liberation and even political independence—all dealt with the human condition apart and separate from the genuine meaning of a quality existence, even the true sense of survival. All derived from and evolved around concerns for human interactions with other humans. While their achievements have been significant, they have not addressed the primary relationship of human beings with their natural environment, their very source. All else is really of secondary importance. As Aldo Leopold, one of the fathers of the land ethic and American conservation, put it: "The shallow-minded modern who has lost his rootage in the land assumes that he has already discovered what is important."

Wilderness advocates and environmentalists in America have been accused of being anti-growth, anti-construction, anti-water development, anti-progress, anti-high rise, anti-low rise, anti-pollution, anti-pesticides and, of course, anti-American—but pro-bug, pro-tepee, pro-wooden wheeled bicycle, pro-cave. We have been labelled as the men with ear-rings and the women with hair under their arms who are always looking cross-eyed at developers and industry.

As we became more sophisticated, more politically savvy, articulate and effective, we were then characterised as the 'hired guns'—those hired to cause trouble, raise money, squash or start rumours (depending on what was appropriate at the time) and to whip both pro and con constituencies of an issue into shape.

It is difficult to separate the wilderness component from what is now a many-faceted environmental movement. To distill its origins is even more elusive, yet nevertheless important.

The early and noteworthy American conservationists and authors, Henry Thoreau, John Muir and Aldo Leopold, were responsible for the conceptual architecture of the American conservation effort. But awareness of the natural environment and the permanent value of its integrity did not begin with them. Its roots are deeper and less definable.

It really began with the shamans, the medicine men who were the spiritual forebears of today's environmental consciousness. They knew where humankind's life came from, its substance and how it was sustained. They knew the heart of being in one relationship and in harmony with the Earth, and had a sense of their place and purpose in the universe.

This knowledge came from a life in and of the wilderness. Values were shaped by ancestral bonds to the land and caring for that source. This approach, however, was rudely riddled by white settlers pressing ever deeper into the wild part of the country, toting with them a distorted sense of the 'American Dream' of riches, land, homes and highways paved with gold. They were unaware of the cultural heritage in the wilderness. Americans became independent, self-reliant, ingenious and tough because of their contact with wilderness, but they saw it as something to be conquered, to be lived separate from. It was there to be hoed, burned, cut, built on, settled, roaded, used, stripped, tamed and subdued. America's wild country began to diminish at an alarming rate, and the qualities of the land that had developed the American character increasingly disappeared.

However, it was this American character which built our particular brand of democracy and which established the United States as the most successful goods-producing country in the world. The new entrepreneural breed flourished over the last 200 years, but, in keeping with the law of balance, a critical counterpoint developed in the hallmark works of Thoreau, Muir, Arthur Carhart and others. They eloquently shared the essence of what the shamans knew, blending their observations and feelings about the natural world, so that the modern intellect could grasp and understand what was being lost: the ethics of land stewardship.

The initial impact of this philosophy led to the establishment of New York City's Central Park in 1857. But what had more significant national impact was the setting aside of Yellowstone as a National Park in 1872. The idea of government withdrawing land from settlement, and of protecting a resource of this magnitude for the value of its wildness, scenic wonder and ecological significance, was revolutionary.

In 1880, two more parks were established, Yosemite and Sequoia, and this began the National Park System which now comprises over 60 million acres.

In the early years of this century, President Roosevelt, along with Gifford Pincho, developed the idea of forest preserves which later became our National Forest System of over 190 million acres. In 1924 the first wilderness area was established in the still bandit-ridden country of New Mexico and named in memory of Aldo Leopold. Efforts to protect forests were accelerating.

In the mid-1920s a remarkable man, Robert Marshall, then a Forester with the US Forest Service, was hiking and mapping hundreds of thousands of acres of what was then called 'the country beyond the roads'. Stationed in Montana, he worked his way into most of the wild country of the West and Alaska. Marshall felt it imperative to inventory what was wild for the purpose of protecting it for future generations. In his short life of 38 years, he saw more wildlands and walked more miles than an average person would in ten lifetimes. He quickly became the most powerful voice for wilderness in public and political arenas. More than any other single person in American history, he influenced the future of 'wild' in our culture because he directly or indirectly impacted wilderness decisions both of his day and of the future on administrative, management and political levels. As a consequence of his efforts, the Forest Service formally reported in 1926 that it had some 79 roadless areas, each of 230,000 acres or more, and comprising a total of 55 million acres. The largest single tract was seven million acres in the state of Idaho in the Rocky Mountains.

Four years before his death, Marshall and a handful of like-minded individuals founded what is now known as the Wilderness Society, whose sole purpose was to work for the preservation of wilderness. Other organisations were also developing, including the Sierra Club, now one of the largest and strongest conservation groups in the States.

However, America was still suffering from what Nash calls 'frontier hangover'. We were still rolling back the edges of untouched country under pavement and polyester. Rumblings of the 'All American Dream' became a roar. As we emerged from World War II, our economy was booming. We embarked upon three decades of a 'buy it, sell it, trade it, release it, drill it, dig it, pawn it, strip it, flood it, manipulate it and dam(n) it' philosophy which put the 'classic' American Dream into a twilight zone, hazy with uncertainties about the future of our natural resources and consequently our economy.

To the horror of many, and the delight of others, the dream of owning one's own home, two cars, a vacation cottage, a boat and a large quantity of unnecessary paraphernalia to make life supposedly easier, along with the 'get rich quick' theme of the first half of the century, began to go through a transformation. The basis upon which the dream was predicated—accessibility and availability of unlimited natural resources—was invalid, and it could no longer be sustained.

This transformation of the 'classic' American dream into what I believe is a more lucid one has been fostered, promoted and nourished by a wave of awareness and caring that began with a small number of visionaries with their hearts and heritage in wildness. It has been carried forward by contemporary wilderness advocates like Sigurd Olson, Olaus and Mardy Murie, Howard Zahniser, Joseph Krutch, David Brower and others. Their vision and commitment has infiltrated and nudged the American public as well as the whole of the environmental movement.

Once the seeds of alarm about our destructive course had been planted, it did not take long for individuals here and there to come in

contact with others with the same concerns. As these seeds grew, 'roots' developed and networks formed. As the 'roots' spread, the concerns expanded from wild country protection to air, water, toxic substances and threatened species. The 'roots' became stronger, more resolute, thicker-skinned and decidely more articulate.

This networking of people all over the country who were ready to stand up for the protection of their one and only habitat was named 'grassroots'. As committed people came in touch with each other, they organised their efforts and discovered their power to effect change in an elective, pluralistic system.

There is a very large degree of public support for environmentalism and wilderness conservation. But the real test comes when decisions are to be made at the political level—in the town council, the county commission, state government or Congress. The *immediate* translation is in the action of our elected officials. The *ultimate* translation is not, however, in politics, but in the lives of individuals…in concrete, on-the-ground changes which reflect evolved awareness. Consciousness or awareness that survives comes about through education, actual restructuring and re-thinkng, not through propaganda or crisis management. 'I hear, I forget; I see, I remember; I do, I understand' seems to be the most effective rule to remember when creating change.

In the late 60s and early 70s the environmentalist movement began a change in *modus operandi,* promoting a return to self-restraint, less waste and more regard for the Earth's finite resources. We buckled down, read *Rules for Radicals* and tooled up with the facts. The movement baffled politicians because it was based on common sense—and a humility which recognises the value and interrelationship of all things. The American public began to recognise that perhaps it was time to live a new dream, one that acknowledged both sides of the equation: action = consequence.

In 1964 the Wilderness Act was passed, establishing our National Wilderness Preservation System and legislating enduring security for wildness in America. For the first time, legislation mandated public involvement and solicited public participation in a land allocation decision. Uses incompatible with wilderness values were prohibited or restricted, such as the cutting of timber, building roads, use of vehicles and, within a given time frame, mineral exploration. Hunting continued to be allowed.

Before passage, a series of public hearings were held throughout the country. Dr. Ed Zahniser, then Executive Director of the Wilderness Society, said the wilderness legislation in itself indicated "that an increasing population accompanied by expanding settlement and growing mechanisation, was destined to occupy all areas within the United States and its possession except those areas that are designated for the preservation and protection of their natural condition."

◄ The Grand Canyon, with Colorado River flowing at the bottom, presents one of the most complete exposed geological records on Earth

This was quickly becoming the case. When the Forest Service reviewed its roadless lands in 1961, there were only 19 areas of 230,000 acres or more, compared with 79 in 1926. The total area had dropped from 55 million to 17 million acres, and the largest tract had shrivelled from 7 million to 2.5 million acres. With larger areas becoming more scarce, the rule of measure was changed to 100,000 acres or more.

Americans were staggered by the loss. It was apparent that a national policy for wilderness preservation was needed. The Wilderness Act of 1964 established 9.1 million acres in 54 areas as protected areas. Today, the National Wilderness Preservation System includes 79 million acres in over 260 areas.

Passage of this historic legislation gave an infusion of energy and resolve to environmentalism. However, many wilderness proponents were looking primarily at preserving areas within National Parks, National Wildlife Refuges or designated Forest Service Primitive Areas. Few recognised that millions of acres of *de facto* wilderness, primarily in the West, were the real opportunity.

Two more roadless area reviews within the past twelve years have made that opportunity very clear. After refined analysis and individual legislative measures in various states, there still remain some 40 million acres of Forest Service lands that will either be preserved or 'released' to uses which will destroy the wilderness values. The pressure is on to have the debate resolved. There is also another possible approximate 50 million acres of Bureau of Land Management lands which could be added to the System. These decisions will be made in the political theatre in the next two to seven years.

With the challenge so dramatically magnified, it became imperative to stimulate organised local wilderness committees to affect local politicians and Congressional representatives. In the years following the passage of the Wilderness Act, American environmentalism came of age. The Environmental Protection Agency estimates there are now some 12,000 environmental groups in the United States with a combined membership, not including overlap, of six to ten million. Concerns of these organisations range from solar energy, toxic wastes, mass transit, wilderness, wildlife, parks, clean air, energy conservation, consumer rights, agricultural preservation, less consumption, alternative lifestyle systems and nuclear disarmament.

Collectively we celebrated sterling victories like the National Environmental Policy Act which established our environmental impact review process, the Wilderness Act, the Wild and Scenic Rivers Act, getting solar tax credits in place, the Resource Conservation Recovery Act, Land and Water Conservation Fund Act, arrival of the photovoltaic cell (although still not economically competitive) and cancellation of several nuclear reactors.

We were sickened by the devastating blows of such losses as Glen Canyon, the upper reaches of the Grand Canyon which were flooded by a dam that still has questionable benefits; the slaughter of whales; the Three Mile Island nuclear reactor accident; oil spills; the great 'terrain' robbery—destruction of thousands of acres of wetlands, farmlands and prime wildlands and forests; the quickening pace of the loss of species and the insidious effects of herbicides and pesticides.

We pushed hard, and succeeded in getting legislation in place to protect endangered species and to control water pollution and, to some degree, toxic substances. The pinnacle of our increasingly professional approach came with the passage of the Alaska Lands Conservation Act, which not only established approximately 100 million acres of wilderness, wildlife refuges, national parks and wild and scenic rivers, but also designated areas by topographic and hydrographic boundaries rather than arbitrary section lines. Watersheds and ecosystems were protected in their entirety.

However, there have been dark passages too, such as certain administrations and tough economic times. But because we have been 'number two', we try harder. We have become very adept at coalition building, one of the keys to our success. Agency and government receptiveness to environmental concerns has been a direct result of this kind of organised, informed public pressure. Persistent and informed citizen activity succeeded in getting wilderness acknowledged as a multiple vs a single use concept, and in getting the areas we have in the System today in place. But every inch, every acre, watershed, stream, lake, mountain, desert, forest and canyon has been hard fought for.

Why will we not compromise? It is because only 300 years ago, 100% of the country was wilderness. Today only 3½% is legally protected in the Wilderness System, with only another 10½% estimated to remain in a wilderness condition. That means approximately 87% has been either altered or destroyed. If we were bankers managing a client's principal financial resources and allowed such losses, we would be charged with criminal misconduct.

Our current challenges are many. The Wilderness System has been under attack by the current administration and a contingent of members of Congress who propose to 'release' millions of acres of potential wilderness lands from any further consideration for protection within the Wilderness System. This would condemn qualified areas to other uses that most probably will significantly alter or destroy those values needing protection. Environmental policies and regulations that were carefully constructed to ensure environmental protection are in danger of being dismantled or weakened and a constant vigilance on the part of the citizen organisations is essential.

Wilderness management is receiving more attention from both conservationists and government agencies, who are working to develop management schemes integrated with current research and that address recreational and non-recreational use as related to both the biophysical and social uses of wilderness.

Another opportunity available to conservationists is Wild and Scenic Rivers. Our Wild and Scenic Rivers Act created a National Wild and Scenic Rivers System. Recent nationwide inventories reveal that of some 300,000 miles of river, approximately 65,000 miles are still free-flowing and could qualify under the requirements of the System.

I have been professionally involved in conservation for 15 years, and in that time I have seen the movement evolve and become more sophisticated. On some levels it has been bureaucratic, and on others extremely innovative and creative. I have seen people of commitment carry the cause forward when morale and financial resources were down. Our objective has become to imbue the nation and the world with an environmental ethic.

"Wilderness needs no defence, only more defenders," my friend, author Edward Addey said. America's wilderness conservationists are committed to using every sensibility, every internal and external resource, every talent available to preserve what remains of Wild America. We recognise that turning the other cheek on this one, or losing heart at this stage, would be like a stamp of approval for letting it all go and being too apathetic to care. We are part of a bloodless, backyard revolution—and we had best never forget it, nor let down our guard for a moment.

Conservation and Management of American Wilderness Areas

Ray Arnett

Wild horses, while beautiful and free, pose a serious threat to many fragile ecosystems

"We need the tonic of Wilderness," Henry David Thoreau wrote in *Walden* in 1854. One hundred years later the United States Congress agreed with the spirit of Thoreau's sentiment and passed the Wilderness Act of 1964. Thus began a brave new era in the history of American natural resource conservation, an era now entering one of its most interesting and challenging phases.

This landmark legislation assigned the land managing agencies of the Federal Government the difficult task of identifying and protecting unique and essentially unspoiled wilderness areas. These are what could be called 'capital W' Wilderness areas, places "where the earth and its community of life are untrammelled by man, where man himself is a visitor who does not remain." They were to offer latter-day Thoreaus what the Act termed "outstanding opportunities for solitude or a primitive unconfined type of recreation."

The Wilderness Act codified a gradual, but ultimately massive, reversal of American opinion about the value of wilderness. Prior to the mid-19th century, wilderness was seen by most as hostile territory, something to be subdued and settled before it could be of benefit to civilised human beings. The passing of the American frontier, however, kindled a new, more benign attitude wherein wilderness came increasingly to be valued for its own intrinsic merits of beauty, naturalness and wildness.

Wilderness untamed became a subject for poets and philosophers. Conservation of wildlife and wild places became government policy with establishment of parks, refuges and national forests around the turn of the century. A wilderness movement was spawned and has become international in scope. Its penultimate expression in the United States may have been the Wilderness Act.

The Act presented Federal land managers with two stiff challenges: first, to identify and recommend to Congress *bona fide* wilderness areas from those lands already managed by the Federal Government; and second, to manage these areas for their perpetual preservation in as pristine a condition as when they were designated.

The task was and is enormous. The US government is the nation's largest landlord, owning 750 million acres or one-third of the country's land mass. Within this domain, managers were to seek out lands in excess of 5,000 acres that possessed three broadly defined wilderness characteristics: naturalness; the opportunity for solitude and primitive recreation; and special features such as ecological, geological, scenic or historic uniqueness.

In the 19 years since passage of the Act, the wilderness study process has entailed hundreds of thousands of working hours, countless public meetings and hearings, and millions of pages of reports. The result of this enormous labour is a Wilderness Preservation System totalling 80 million acres. In addition, over 20 million acres remain in study status but must be managed as 'capital W' Wilderness until Congress decides their fate.

The Wilderness study process has been far from painless and, although slowed, is far from complete. But increasingly the focus of land managers has shifted to the question of how best to manage the designated areas in a manner that satisfies the mandates of the law and, at the same time, honours the 'visitation' rights of wilderness-hungry citizens in a highly mobile society.

This is a question we are grappling with at the Department of the Interior, where I serve as Assistant Secretary for Fish and Wildlife and Parks. It is also a question of importance to those responsible for managing wilderness-type preserves elsewhere on this shrinking planet.

The 334 National Park Service units and 417 US Fish and Wildlife Service units for which I am responsible encompass 167 million acres of land set aside for conservation, recreation and wildlife purposes. Of this total, over 54 million acres, or nearly one-third, is now being managed as wilderness. An additional 25 million acres has been designated wilderness in Forest Service areas.

Wilderness areas are places where people must leave behind no sign of their passing. This means, primarily, no roads, no water systems, no toilet facilities, no mining, no drilling, no timber harvesting and no use of motorised equipment. Trees that fall on trails cannot be removed with chainsaws as in other areas.

These proscriptions seemingly have done little to diminish people's appetite for wilderness experiences. Mount McKinley in Alaska, our highest peak, is one example. Ten years ago only about 25,000 visits were recorded in a good year. Today, transportation into the area has improved to the point that an apartment dweller in New York City can leave home tonight and reach the slopes of McKinley tomorrow. In 1980, the park recorded nearly 300,000 visits, a ten-fold increase in a decade. The same story is recorded in steadily increasing annual park and refuge visitor counts around the nation. It is as if all of America has decided to put on hiking boots, hoist rucksacks to their backs and head for the mountains.

Little wonder so many observers worry we are in danger of loving our wilderness to death. Compounding the problem is the conflict over recreation rights that often attends wilderness designation. Everybody seemingly has their own idea of what wilderness is and how it should be used. One purist hiker in the Pecos Wilderness in New Mexico, for example, became so enraged when he encountered another individual walking a dog on the same trail that he slit the poor dog's throat.

In the Boundary Water Canoe Area, located along Minnesota's border with Canada, local residents still object vociferously to the large-scale ban on use of motorised boats to reach distant fishing areas in this lake-dotted area. Similarly, efforts by the Park Service to phase out motorised rafting down the Colorado River in the Grand Canyon resulted in an uproar that led to the plan being scuttled by Congress.

Even more disturbing for wilderness managers are the growing numbers of marauding pot hunters who pilfer artifacts from remote cultural sites, pot growers who cultivate their illegal but lucrative crops in the wilderness, and even 'survivalists' who occasionally use these lands to practise military tactics as they prepare for Armageddon.

Managing this near tidal wave of human activity on and about our conservation and wilderness areas is testing the expertise of our resource managers in ways not even dreamed of 20 years ago. Slowly we are coming to realise these areas must be the subject of active and even aggressive management strategies and continual resource monitoring if their resources are to be protected as the law intended.

There is no doubt that the notion of 'managing' a wilderness would seem wholly contradictory to some of the Act's original partisans nearly 20 years ago. Even today, several groups in the United States would publicly decry such a concept.

However, I believe we have arrived at an era in resource management wherein most of the principal advocates and administrators of wilderness agree that effective human management is absolutely essential if our designated wilderness areas are to retain the attraction and the intrinsic worth that has made them so popular. The challenge to both the manager and the wilderness enthusiast alike is this: how do we reconcile the altruism of the 1964 Act's language with the current demand for legitimate wilderness uses?

Some examples of how US land managers are responding are:

● Wilderness areas within Cumberland Island National Seashore, a National Park Service unit in Georgia, are being damaged by a deer herd that, under protection, has outgrown the carrying capacity of its habitat. To solve this problem, the Park Service has proposed a controlled hunt this year. More often than not, hunts of this kind are opposed vigorously by anti-hunting organisations and leave-nature-alone advocates. Yet the Park Service, following a careful programme to involve the public in this decision, reports virtually no opposition.

● In Mesa Verde National Monument, Arizona, park officials have had to severely restrict use of the 8,000-acre wilderness area within the monument because of the extensive damage being done to the park's cultural and archaeological sites by vandals and artifact hunters. Regular users of the park reportedly understand and support the reasons for instigating these restrictions.

● In 1977, fully 90% of Bandelier National Monument, New Mexico, was officially designated wilderness. It was like putting up a neon sign. In a recent news article, the monument's resource manager was quoted as saying: "Nothing really changed, but to some people wilderness is a drawing card. It is a word that denotes purity, cleanliness and no people—to a lot of people." Bandelier back country use jumped 30% after wilderness designation. Almost immediately, the park instituted a wilderness permit system. One of the reasons was to find out what kind of people went where in the park. The data revealed that most of the 5,000 backpackers using the park went to approximately the same places at the same time of the year. As a result, many campsites were showing distinct signs of wear, including beaten paths and browse lines amongst trees around firesites, caused by campers seeking firewood. In some places, stones from ancient ruins were being used to form fire-rings. Another, more smelly, problem generated by the park's popularity is unburied human waste.

All of this information is being used by park managers to protect the resources in their charge. Open campfires, for instance, will probably be banned in many of the more fragile parts of the park. I don't know what they intend to do about the human waste problem, but in some parks we are helping the plastic bag industry by requiring people to pack it out. After all, they packed it in.

Bandelier's problems are not atypical of those being encountered in other wilderness areas. The studies under way there and elsewhere provide evidence of the increasingly scientific approaches resource managers need in order to develop data bases for sound decision making. We will be seeing much more systematic review and monitoring of ecological, social, psychological and physical factors affecting wilderness and other fragile areas in the future.

It would be wrong, however, to dwell just upon examples of potentially destructive human uses. There are many wilderness areas that 'function' quite well—thanks to a fortunate balance between public wants and management goals.

The Okeefenokee wilderness in south Georgia provides an excellent example. Congress took a special interest in public use within this wilderness area, and the establishing legislation provided for 120 miles of canoe trails, the use of mechanical equipment to maintain the trail, and the use of power boats in certain areas with motors of less than 10 horsepower. About 4,000 people a year use the wilderness canoe trail for two- to six-day trips. Almost half of this use takes place during March, April and May. Another 4,000 people are day users.

To enhance the wilderness experience no more than 20 campers are allowed on the overnight trail at a time. Covered, elevated campsites with flush toilets are provided every eight to twelve miles along the 120 mile canoe trail. These sites are not only safe, but they also prevent degradation of the habitat by trampling and pollution from human waste. Trail users have demonstrated a strong wilderness/environmental ethic. Litter is a very minor problem. Most wilderness users police the areas they use and frequently pick up litter left by the few careless users. A motorised mechanical vegetation cutter is used to maintain about 50 to 60 miles of trail per year.

A few purists might object to the efforts at Okeefenokee; but most wilderness users there overwhelmingly agree that the measures initiated have been an excellent compromise that hasn't jeopardised the essential wilderness character of the area.

The more we move into this brave new frontier of wilderness management, the more we realise we are just beginning to understand what these unique preserves have to offer the future. We must guard our wilderness zealously. But we must also realise the close linkage between these resources and the people in whose trust they are held. We cannot shut the people out. To do so would be to risk losing the public support that has made protection of these areas possible in the first place. Instead, we must continue to find ways of both preserving these wilderness wonders and sharing them with those who wish to taste Thoreau's 'tonic of Wilderness'.

Attitudes Towards Wilderness and Environmental Protection in the US

John Hendee

A Forest Service ranger gives information to two of the many—and ever-increasing—users of American wilderness areas

Positive attitudes toward wilderness and environmental protection in the United States are reflected in public opinion surveys, in the growth of membership in environmental organisations, and in the addition of areas to the National Wilderness Preservation System. The concept of wilderness—land areas preserved as they are—has come to symbolise environmental quality, and support for wilderness has grown with the environmental movement. The Wilderness Act of 1964 created a National Wilderness Preservation System (NWPS), set aside 54 areas totalling 9.1 million acres and identified another 34 areas to review for suitability for classification. Today the NWPS has grown to about 80 million acres, and 25 additional Bills classifying more acreage as Wilderness have been introduced in the US Congress.

During the 60s several national opinion polls documented rising concern for environmental issues. This concern peaked after Earth Day in 1970, and has now stabilised into broad and deep support for environmental protection. In 1980, among topics of public concern, the environment drew 48% support. Although this was down from more than 60% in 1973, nevertheless only crime (69%), drugs (59%), defence (56%), health (55%) and education (53%) exceeded the environment as topics perceived as having inadequate expenditures in 1980 (Council on Environmental Quality 1980).

A more recent survey asked people to rate 'three national problems you would like to see the government devote more of its attention to in the next year or two.' Reducing pollution of air and water (24%) ranked sixth among ten categories behind only crime, unemployment, killer diseases, improving education, and helping the poor (Bloomgarden 1983).

A 1980 poll found 'sympathy with the environmental movement' among 55% of the public, with 'active participation' in the movement reported by 7%, down from 13% in 1978 (Council on Environmental Quality 1980). No more than 6% in any category was 'unsympathetic' to the environmental movement, but 'sympathy' and 'active participation' were highest among the young, those with at least some college education, and those with incomes over $12,000. The same survey found 12% of the public 'had occasion to write a letter or contact a public official directly about an environmental matter' in the previous two years, and that nine out of ten of their letters favoured *more* environmental protection.

These findings were confirmed by an April 1983 poll (ABC News-Washington Post) that found 61% of the public sympathised with the environmental movement, 7% said they were environmental activists and only 4% were unsympathetic toward the environmental movement. The remaining public were either neutral (29%) or had no opinion (6%).

All these findings indicate solid environmental support but less concern than in the 1970 Earth Day era—possibly a reflection of environmental protection accomplishments as well as a stabilising public opinion. One pollster, Louis Harris, testified before Congress about the broad and deep consensus of the public to fight pollution as "...one of the most overwhelming and clearest we have ever recorded in our 25 years of surveying public opinion."

Polls of the American public also indicate positive support for preservation of wilderness and wildlife. A 1980 survey found that 73% agreed that 'an endangered species must be protected, even at the expense of commercial activity' (Council on Environmental Quality 1980). A more recent survey (Bloomgarden 1983) reported that 79% believe 'we must prevent any type of animal from becoming extinct, even if it means sacrificing some things for ourselves.' The same survey found that 65% favoured 'leaving parts of our country in their natural state, untouched by man.'

In a 1977 survey by Opinion Research Corporation for the American Forest Institute, people were offered a choice to ' ... increase the yield and sales of timber from our national forests or ... preserve those trees in their natural state.' Sixty-two percent chose 'preserving trees', 28% were for 'increasing timber sales' and 10% expressed no opinion. In the same survey 'the present amount of wilderness' was 'about right' for 46% of the public, and 'too little' for 32%. Those saying 'too little' indicated concern that wilderness and wildlife habitat were being lost to development and population pressures. In a more recent survey (Yankelovich, Skelly and White 1982) the public were asked to select from a list those resources they thought would be in short

National Forest workers install a 'hikers only' sign on a wilderness trail, protecting a particularly sensitive area from damage caused by horses and pack stock

Mount McKinley, at 20,320 feet the highest peak in North America

supply in the future. Their priorities were farmland (55%), wilderness (52%), water (51%), lumber (44%), food (43%), recreation areas (32%) and paper (27%).

Finally, a poll of citizens in Montana (Utter 1983) found that 85% favoured designation of wilderness areas in general, 52% 'strongly favoured wilderness', 33% 'somewhat favoured' and only 11% were 'opposed to wilderness areas'. Deeper probing in this survey indicated, as have others, that some people were unclear about exactly what wilderness was, even though they supported it. Such views may reflect general environmental support, for which wilderness is a symbol.

Support for the environmental movement is also reflected in expanded membership in environmental organisations. The largest group, the National Wildlife Federation, has 4.3 million members and has grown 2.7-fold since 1970. The Sierra Club, with almost 350,000 members, has grown more than four-fold since 1970. The National Audubon Society, with over 400,000 members, has more than tripled since 1970. The Wilderness Society, with 85,000 members, and Friends of the Earth, one of the youngest and smallest of the environmental groups with 32,000 members, have similarly grown.

One recent survey compared the views of environmental group members with small business and corporate executives (Bloomgarden 1983). Environmentalists tended to support more philosophical aims for society such as 'protecting nature' (92%), and tended to describe themselves as liberals, while executives described themselves as political conservatives. But about half of the executives said they and their families 'benefit from the government's and environmental groups' efforts'.

The US National Wilderness Preservation System is supported not only by public opinion and environmental group membership but by other social trends as well. For example, research has shown strong associations between level of education and pro-environmental values, wilderness appreciation and wilderness use. In the 1970s the surging increase in wilderness appreciation and use was often attributed to educational gains during the 50s and 60s. But there were even greater educational gains between 1970 and 1980. The United States Bureau of Census reports: (1) a nearly 25% increase in the proportion of Americans aged 25 and over who have high school diplomas (up from 55% to 68% during the 70s); (2) a nearly 50% increase in the proportion who have at least one year of college (up from 21% to 31%); (3) a nearly 50% increase in the proportion graduating from college (up from 11% to 16%), with even bigger gains among women (up from 13% to 21%). Furthermore, large and small colleges and universities in the US offer courses that teach various aspects of wilderness values, benefits, use skills and management. College graduates who have taken such courses and become opinion leaders are likely to reinforce positive views of wilderness.

Other trends also nurture support for wilderness. Social forecaster John Naisbitt, in his book *Megatrends*, identifies a major trend in the US away from representative democracy where elected officials dominate the important decisions, toward participatory democracy where people affected by decisions insist on having a direct voice in them. Increasingly, citizens are expressing this voice through ballot initiatives, referenda, recalls and demand for consumer and workers' rights and participation. The growth of environmental organisations already described reflects this trend, as does increasing public involvement in natural resource decisions. For example, the US Forest Service's Roadless Area Review and Evaluation in the late 1970s (RARE II) to identify lands potentially suitable for wilderness, drew several times as many public comments (360,000) as did a similar review (RARE I) in the early 1970s.

All these factors—public opinion favourable to environmental protection, wildlife and wilderness; growth of membership in environmental organisations; rising educational levels; and increasing public involvement in wilderness allocation decisions—have contributed to expansion of the size and use of the National Wilderness Preservation System. They have also increased the challenge of wilderness management.

In the United States, Wilderness Areas are set aside under the Wilderness Act to protect their naturalness and to provide outstanding opportunities for solitude and primitive forms of outdoor recreation. To meet these goals, wilderness management is required. The guiding principles of such management are to do only what is necessary to meet the wilderness objectives set forth in area management plans, and, when management actions are necessary, to use the approach that will least impact the area and its visitors.

Wilderness management must address many issues. At popular locations, crowding by hikers and backpackers can destroy fragile wilderness vegetation and the quality of experience for users. In a few locations recreational activity must be regulated to prevent impacts. In many areas visitors are contacted by wilderness rangers to educate them about the need to behave in ways that will protect the environment and the experience of other visitors. Trails must be maintained and patrolled, and occasionally new ones built. Campsites need to be evaluated and closed for rehabilitation if they become too heavily impacted. Because of rising costs, many of these wilderness management activities are increasingly being carried out by volunteers with supervision by managers.

Natural wildlife is a special attraction in wilderness, and regulation of hunting and fishing, fish stocking, and protection of wilderness-dependent wildlife are special management problems. Wilderness conditions must be monitored to assess their naturalness and the limits of acceptable change. Increasingly, exclusion of fire is causing unnatural change in some areas. Wilderness fire management plans are therefore being developed to reintroduce fire to natural levels by letting some wildfires burn under safe conditions. Planned ignition of prescribed fire to restore naturalness may some day be considered. Perhaps most important is the preparation of wilderness management plans for each area, to address all these problems with full public involvement before any actions are implemented.

Within a decade or two, all the wilderness allocation decisions will have been made in the US. Thereafter, the enhancement of wilderness values will depend entirely on wilderness management. Even closer cooperation among environmentalists, wilderness visitors, volunteer workers and wilderness resource managers will be required. The future of the National Wilderness Preservation System depends on these partnerships.

Marine Wilderness Areas and Multiple Sea Use Management

Hance Smith

The sea is perhaps the greatest wilderness of all: the Stonga Banks, Shetland Islands (UK)

The world ocean covers 71% of the globe. Despite publicity from time to time on the feasibility of human settlement in this vast area, in reality it belongs, in the words of David Attenborough, to the fish. The sea is arguably the greatest wilderness of all, yet its emptiness is deceptive. For the past century or so, parts of it have been under great pressure from certain industries in the developed countries, notably whaling, the pelagic fisheries and bottom trawling. Since World War II there has been a great intensification in fisheries generally and in navigation, especially of ships carrying hazardous cargoes. There has also been a vast expansion in uses of little importance before the 1940s, including oil and gas exploitation, waste disposal, the use of coastal areas for recreation, and a heightened importance of the sea for science and for defence.

These developments have proceeded in association with an unprecedented effort in global law-making, beginning with the Geneva Convention of 1958 and culminating in the new Law of the Sea Convention of 1982, now awaiting ratification. These legal developments give a formal aspect to a process of enclosure of the sea by coastal states which will encompass over 40% of the 71%, including most of the shelf seas which are rich in resources.

All these events bring the potential wilderness value of the sea into sharp focus, and highlight the fact that the maintenance and development of marine conservation approaches will take place largely in relation to and at times in competition with other sea uses.

The wide range of sea uses may be classified into eight groups representing fundamental purposes which, from a management standpoint, may be further reduced into five groups. The first and earliest, apart from fishing, is the use of the sea for navigation and communication, including navigation and related activities for the other uses. Until the advent of motor ships and the carrying of hazardous cargoes (of which by far the most important is crude oil), this use had limited environmental impact, apart from numerous wrecks and the modification of port approaches for navigation purposes.

The second three groups involve varying degrees of manipulation of the marine environment through extraction or addition of materials. These are respectively mineral and energy resource exploitation, most of which requires the establishment of large fixed installations in the marine environment; fisheries and fish farming; and waste disposal. The fifth group consists of those uses in which the marine environment as a whole is the object of use, including strategy and defence, research, recreation and conservation.

The inclusion of conservation as a specific use may appear as something of a departure: most marine conservation activity has been aimed at aspects of other uses such as the control of marine pollution from shipborne sources. Depletion of oil and gas resources is largely a function of national and international political and economic circumstances, the rate of exploitation being a major determinant of environmental impact. The large effort directed at fisheries conservation is greatly complicated by the objective of allocation of resources, which is really the primary political problem, as in the recurring controversy over the Common Fisheries Policy of the European Economic Community. The elimination of pollution through waste disposal is more obviously a conservation issue in that maintenance of the integrity of

Marine pollution is one of the greatest dangers to coastal birdlife. Puffin (*Fratercula arctica*)

the environment is clearly a key objective, although straightforward hazards to human life are often the driving force. In the field of environmental management *per se*, reasons for conservation put forward include maintaining environmental quality for scientific and aesthetic purposes—research and recreation. Even the defence interest is often the first to promote wideranging environmental studies, as has happened recently in the North Sea.

There are two reasons for considering conservation as a primary use group cutting across the other activities. First is the obvious effort to preserve endangered species, together with the beginnings of control of specific areas at a number of scales, ranging from localised habitats to extensive regions with complex objectives in which conservation *per se* is of primary importance. The second is that conservation, at whatever scale, involves the designation of specific areas of sea, and the establishment of priorities among uses.

The impetus for marine conservation thus comes from two sources. The first, and currently most important, is the conservation activities of other use groups, notably fisheries and waste disposal which are extensively institutionalised at local, regional, national and international levels. The second, and fast developing, source is the designation of conservation uses through the activities of conservation organisations. Out of these groups arise a diversity of management regions, with specific ordering of objectives, ranging from fishery conservation regions such as that instituted in the USA to a series of designated conservation areas such as the Great Barrier Reef.

Although marine wilderness areas have been recognised in many places, notably tropical and polar regions, much of the initiative has come from international bodies such as IUCN and UNEP in research and the establishment of regional seas programmes. At national level the response is less obvious, a significant point in relation to the enclosure of the sea and considering the paramount importance of states in maritime administration. Perhaps the most notable initiative is the planning of the Great Barrier Reef. In the UK, statements relating to marine conservation are appearing in response to the World Conservation Strategy. The Nature Conservancy Council are about to designate a number of relatively small coastal areas, while a significant number of coastal sites are covered by national park and related legislation. These include heritage coasts and sites possessed by private trusts.

The designation of marine conservation areas, which includes those of both natural and human interest, may be classified into four scales. The first are individual sites, such as prominent natural features or historic wrecks. Second are the reserves, restricted areas often of special scientific interest, perhaps as habitats for endangered species. Third are the marine parks, which include a wide variety of conditions of national or international significance, such as coral reef coasts. Fourth are the very large regional sea areas required for the control of pollution, such as the UNEP Regional Seas, and those areas necessary for the protection of marine mammals, which may be of oceanic scale as in the case of whale conservation in the Indian Ocean.

Broadly speaking, the range of objectives and tightness of control decrease with increasing scale. The conditions for individual sites and reserves can be strict, as in the designated areas within the Great Barrier Reef Marine Park. At small scales, natural wilderness attributes may be maintained and even human aspects conserved, such as very early maritime artefacts connected with early voyages. Most of the human interest aspects are necessarily conserved in maritime museums, which are perhaps the most significant development in the marine conservation field overall. At the marine park scale, zoning approaches are generally necessary to accommodate other uses within a proper geographical and legal framework. At the regional seas level, use objectives are relatively few, and the main problem, as in the North Sea case, is the establishment of a sufficient degree of political, legal and administrative cooperation to make even limited objectives workable.

An increasingly important aspect in the context of the 1982 Law of the Sea Convention is the institutional framework of conservation activity, particularly as regards designated areas of explicitly conservationist bodies. In an area such as the North Sea, political and administrative authority resides at four levels: regional, national, supranational (the EEC) and international. Local laws may also be relevant. Sites may be located partly on the coast (land and sea), in internal waters, the territorial sea, continental shelf, exclusive economic zone or high seas, or combinations of these. Only in the first two is the state's authority perhaps great enough, or the influence of voluntary bodies strong enough, to promote effective conservation. As it happens, many of the most important sites are located on or close to coasts, at least in the North East Atlantic, but jurisdiction to seaward may be just as important, especially as it affects marine ecosystems and environmental quality. The number of jurisdictional zones is great and therefore legal complexities are many.

For a review of sea uses and the development of marine conservation approaches in the waters around Scotland, see p. 269, The Seas Around Scotland.

Energy and Environment: Preserving a Delicate Balance

William Moffett

Production platform off the US coast, in the Gulf of Mexico

One Scotsman did a lot to teach Americans to appreciate their own wilderness areas—John Muir, born in Dunbar, Scotland in 1838. It was Muir who took the first long walk along the misty ridges of America's Appalachian mountains, who called Alaska 'God's crystal temple' and who reminded us that 'the clearest way into the universe is through a forest wilderness'.

I am both a nature lover and an oil man. While it may be surprising to some to find an oil man so enthusiastic about wilderness, I find no inherent contradiction in those two roles. After all, energy development and wilderness preservation are not mutually exclusive. As human beings we need both: energy to heat our homes and run our cars and factories, and wilderness to cherish and enjoy. There is no real reason for industry and society to disagree about environmental responsibility. Business and the public live in the same environment. People in corporations breathe the same air, drink the same water and enjoy the same scenery as everyone else, and when the physical environment deteriorates, business declines.

The relationship between energy and wilderness has been a long and intimate one. Oil, coal and other natural resources are most often found in remote wilderness areas, and in developing these resources, energy companies have necessarily been deeply involved with nature.

The relationship has not been without problems. As in any long marriage, it has had its ups and downs. We have had some rocky points, especially in the early years, but, as in any *good* marriage, we have learned from our experiences and now find it natural and necessary to work in harmony with the environment.

In my view, energy companies and environmentalists have a shared goal: to seek a balance between economic growth and environmental protection. We need to think less about conflict and more about finding reasonable ways to balance human activities, so both business and the environment can prosper; and it has been encouraging to see the relationship between energy companies and environmentalists evolve from one of mutual suspicion and hostility to one of communication. Hopefully this will soon move to cooperation.

For energy companies, the main issue is that of land access. In the US, the Federal Government owns or manages nearly one-third—720 million acres—of all land. Except for National Parks, monuments and historic sites, most of this land is in principle open to oil and gas activity. In practice, however, vast areas are closed to all commercial activity, without any serious thought about their resource potential.

However, if we are to develop any form of energy—oil, coal or natural gas—we must have access to some of this land to determine its energy and mineral potential. We do not want to trample through designated wilderness areas or to destroy our nation's wilderness heritage, but we do want to explore lands which have not yet been designated as protected wilderness areas. We have had problems with this because government laws and regulations keep even wilderness candidate areas off limits, even for exploration purposes. These are areas which are merely being considered for protected wilderness status.

We suggest that lands not designated as protected wilderness areas should be opened up for multiple use, that energy companies should be permitted to conduct seismic surveys and use other research methods to discover the energy and mineral potential of the land, and determine whether it would be economically feasible to produce the reserves, if they exist. But the land should also be preserved for recreation.

In those areas where the natural environment is unique and irreplaceable, as well as those areas where technology does not exist to probe the land without disturbing its natural balance, neither industrial or recreational development should be permitted. However, on most public lands, controlled and regulated multiple use would maximise the benefits for as many people as possible. It is not necessary to waste energy resources to preserve environmental riches.

It is important to remember that energy and mineral use of land or water is temporary. Although energy exploration and production might cause some disruptions in the short-term, in the long-term the land can be restored to its original state. Nowadays, energy companies take great care to ensure that the most modern and environmentally sound technology is used. For example, the Alaska pipeline was built below ground in some places, and quite high above it in others, depending upon which method would have the least impact on the surrounding environment. In the same way, seismic surveys today generally avoid the old method of drilling a hole of about 200 feet and then exploding a charge of dynamite in it. Now we use subtler and less environmentally disruptive methods of seismic survey.

Further, once energy extraction is completed—which generally takes a few years—we now have both the technology and the commitment to restore the land to its original state. Our own corporate policy in Gulf Oil is not to extract minerals from land unless we can restore it to its original productive state. We replace topsoil and return disturbed land to approximate original contours. We also control surface water runoff to prevent downstream sedimentation and potential acid-mine drainage.

The reason energy companies are worried about land access when there is an apparent glut of oil in the world is that we don't believe this so-called glut is a permanent condition. Once the world recession is over, demand for oil, coal and other forms of energy will pick up again. We can't be short-sighted about this. There may be enough oil for ten years, but what about 20 or 30 years from now? If Middle East instability flares again into overt war, it could quickly lead to another shortage, and I doubt whether we want to repeat that experience.

Energy companies need lead time to explore for energy *before* energy demand picks up again. If we wait for another shortage before we begin exploring in frontier areas it will be too late, because fields that we begin to explore then might not yield a commercial find for years. Hence our concern for access to land now.

While Gulf Oil is committed to energy development, we are equally concerned about protecting the environment. We want to reduce acid rain, limit air and water pollution, and minimise toxic waste. We want to secure a clean environment and preserve areas of natural wilderness both for our own benefit and for that of future generations, and to translate this philosophy of environmental protection into practical action. We have hundreds of employees whose full-time job is to monitor the environmental impact of Gulf operations on the community. We take them and their jobs seriously, listening to their evaluations and acting upon their advice.

An example of the way Gulf's coal mining company handles land reclamation can be seen in Kansas, where we operated a surface coal mine covering 8,000 acres. When mining was completed in 1974, Gulf spent over $1 million in reclaiming and restoring the land. We then donated the restored land to the Kansas State Fish and Game Commission which now manages the land for many uses. Most of it is used as a recreation area for fishing, swimming and hiking. Some serves as forage and pasture land for nearby farmers, and some is used as a research facility by scientists from the Pittsburgh State University who try to determine what kinds of fish would best survive in water habitats in the area.

On a national level, Gulf has been the sole sponsor of the award-winning National Geographic TV series for the last eight years, and we also support a yearly programme honouring outstanding conservationists in the US for their achievements. In 1983 we were proud to receive the Outdoor Writers Association of America's Mountain of Jade Award for Environmental Work, especially because Gulf is the first corporation to be so honoured.

We also support conservation and environmental projects in the UK, and have sponsored books on wildlife, conservation and country walks, among others. A grant from Gulf enabled the Royal Society for the Protection of Birds to make *Osprey*, a 40-minute award-winning film which traces the return of the osprey to the Scottish Highlands after many years' absence.

We have certainly not solved all the problems connected with energy development and wilderness preservation. Acid rain and toxic waste disposal are not issues that will disappear overnight, and there is still a lot of serious work to be done. Essentially, however, the energy companies have recognised the problem and are making an honest effort to arrive at solutions which will preserve the delicate balance between social, economic and environmental needs.

Nature is both beautiful and bountiful. In developing her bounty, it is possible to destroy her beauty. We in Gulf are interested in developing energy—but we are only interested in that kind of energy development which is compatible with wilderness preservation. For, as human beings, we need more than just material comforts. Our spiritual need for an untarnished and natural wilderness must also be satisfied.

Restocking the Wilderness with Captive-Bred Animals: The California Condor Story

Sheldon Campbell

The California condor story could develop into a successful model for captive breeding programmes

A stated purpose of most efforts to breed vulnerable or endangered wild animals in captivity is to provide cadres that can augment dwindling populations or completely restock a former habitat. Captive breeding is no substitute for keeping a species alive and well in its own habitat—it is either a hedge or a last recourse, resorted to when adverse trends in animal populations become apparent. Serious breeders realise also that some of their charges will no longer be acceptable in areas from whence their ancestors came. One does not conceive of breeding Sumatran tigers or Scottish wolves with the idea that the people occupying their former space will welcome them back. Some captive breeding, then, is an end unto itself—done to preserve a perceived value like beauty, strength, legendary status or admired behaviour, or to assist nature in maintaining genetic variety.

The record in breeding animals for return to wilderness is dismal, but not beyond redemption. Zoos, the principal breeders, got a late start after missing the boat completely with some animals that were once kept but are now extinct—the quagga, the passenger pigeon, the

108

Carolina parakeet and the Thylacine, to name a few, were all once in zoological collections in numbers and sexes (since both are necessary) sufficient to start captive breeding.

Against the failures, captive breeders can also place a few successes. Pere David's deer has been extinct in the wild for 3,000 years, but now exists in impressive numbers, with some 1,900 distributed in a number of zoological gardens. The European bison or wisent was captive-bred up from a population of 17 to the point where it has been returned, if not to true wilderness, at least to reserves in Poland. The New York Zoo was largely responsible for breeding American bison from the low point they had reached at the end of our Indian wars (c.1890) to the point where large new herds now populate our bison range in Montana, and bison can be found in virtually all major zoos. The Arabian oryx, one of the current success stories, has been bred up from the pitiful few that remained alive in the group captured by Ian Grimwood and his associates and a few more kept in private zoos by Arab nobles and sheiks. To date we have produced over 100 new oryx in our two collections at the San Diego Zoo and San Diego Wild Animal Park. We have also bred over 50 southern white rhinoceroses from the 20 we originally obtained from Ian Player and the Natal Parks Board in 1971 to help keep that subspecies from the endangered list on which its northern relative now finds itself. In addition, there is now talk about returning a herd or two of Mongolian wild horses to their original habitat—an objective made difficult for us, however, by the fact that the United States has no diplomatic relations with Mongolia.

All the species mentioned so far are hooved animals. For the most part, these are not as difficult to breed as are many other mammals such as primates and carnivores, some birds and several reptiles.

Captive breeders have also had some success with birds, over and above the thousands of game birds commonly bred and released for hunters around the world. The Patuxent Research Center of US Fish and Wildlife has bred, trained and released thousands of the endangered Arizona masked bobwhite, while the work done by Tom Cade and his associates at Cornell University in breeding and later releasing peregrine falcons is a good example of combining research, effective husbandry, determination and lots of money to help turn around the decline of that noble bird. A model for breeding exotic birds with a view toward saving them from extinction was set by Sir Peter Scott and the managers of Slimbridge, which probably saved our nene, or Hawaiian geese, from passing entirely into the great beyond, and eventually restored them to the volcanic slopes of their former home. Several European zoos, particularly in Germany, regularly breed the European owl for release to the wild.

When we consider that one to two million of the five or ten million plant and animal species now living are slated to be extinct by the year

2000 (according to the report of the US Presidential Commission), we can grasp how insignificant our efforts have been and are likely to be in any effort to stem the tide. We are in a retreat which will continue until either universal revelation, universal reason or catastrophe finally prevail. The efforts of captive breeders are directed at prolonging that retreat, hoping eventually for the equivalent in conservation of a Waterloo, Moscow or Stalingrad. Then we can have more remaining than we would have had we not fought.

In the meantime we can breed some species and return them to wilderness, a process which can help us accomplish a two-fold objective: first, to save the species, and second, to help save the wilderness. Ironically, in several wilderness areas all wildlife inhabitants depend for their continued existence on the perpetuation of a key species—a species for which land was originally left wild or undeveloped, and without which there would be less excuse for preventing the omnipresent earth movers from grinding through on caterpillar tracks.

The California condor (*Gymnogyps californianus*) is one such species, and one that provides a model for all that is involved in successful captive breeding. Ultimate success, of course, is guaranteed only if enough of the species' original habitat has been saved or if attitudes which have contributed to the species' demise have been altered. The steps involved in captive breeding are: identifying the need; agreeing to its desirability; developing a breeding plan; acquiring the animals; researching husbandry and reproduction; breeding; developing a release plan; and releasing the animals. All this sounds rather easy when delineated here, but in practice becomes complicated and often extremely difficult.

From evidence accumulated in the La Brea tar pits near Los Angeles, the prime days of the California condor occurred during the Pleistocene era, when there was an abundance of large animals to provide, eventually, condor fodder. Between that golden age for condors and the present day, the species has suffered a shrinkage of its former range, a shrinkage which accelerated rapidly as American pioneers moved westward and settled in California, and in particular as the megalopolis called Los Angeles burgeoned into an acre-eating monster which exhaled poisonous smoke. The condor population dwindled year by year, until their last fortress was in the rugged mountains of the Los Padres National Forest behind the cities of Ventura and Santa Barbara. Here the remaining birds nested and from here they soared forth to seek carrion along the mountain slopes on the west side of the immense San Joaquin Valley.

The need to take action to arrest the decline of the California condor was identified two to three decades ago, but at first captive breeding was not considered because those who counted the birds and found fewer each year still lived in hope that somehow the declining trend would arrest itself. Vain hope! Finally, in 1980, all but the most sentimental conservationists agreed that captive breeding would have to be tried. The question was—and still is—has captive breeding started too late? Behind the decision to start it were US Fish and Wildlife, and the National Audubon Society, the latter of which had only a few years before stood adamantly against such an undertaking with a slogan that could have been stated as 'better dead than bred'. An early decision in the process was to use the San Diego Wild Animal Park as a breeding centre, and shortly thereafter the Los Angeles Zoo, which for 14 years had kept the sole captive condor, a male called Topa Topa, was also included. Now the programme involves five institutions, the four already mentioned and the State of California Fish and Game Department, which in law has final jurisdiction over the birds.

At first, it was thought that the captive breeding would proceed with the capture of birds that could be put to nesting, starting with a female to become a mate for Topa Topa. But just after the programme got under way, a wild fledgling, one of the only two produced that year, died in the hands of a Fish and Wildlife biologist who was examining it. The publicity surrounding this nearly sank the condor ark before it got under way. The California Fish and Game Commission was reluctant to issue any capture permits, and for a period the breeding effort floundered.

While we worried about the setback at the time, it may, in retrospect, have pushed forward the development of a new plan, that of taking the first eggs laid by each of the four adult pairs—the birds mate for life—and hatching them in captivity. Behind this plan lay the success we have had in 'double clutching' the egg-laying of Andean condors.

Under normal circumstances a pair of California condors will lay one egg every two years. Thus, if the birds are allowed to raise their own first hatched, progress in restoring a viable population would be excruciatingly slow. At present, only 20-25 California condors exist. By taking first-laid eggs, however, the birds are encouraged to lay a second (the double clutch). Over the past year, we have also found that if two eggs are taken, some pairs will lay a third, making a triple clutch. If the eggs taken are successfully hatched—and we hatched four in the spring of 1983—and if any remaining fledglings are captured, the producing pairs will be encouraged to lay again the following year. Consequently, the production of new condors will more than double 'natural' production, and with fewer losses of fledglings.

When we use egg- or fledgling-napping, we will have to wait longer to breed birds in captivity, for they do not become capable of producing fertile eggs until they are seven years old. On the other hand, we will probably be able to start the release programme by 1985. To maintain a population as distantly related genetically as possible—considering

Newly hatched chick being fed with condor puppet, to assist in correct imprinting

that the founding stock is eight birds—we will not mate siblings. In 1983, we hatched one male, Sisquoc, the first ever hatched in captivity, and three females, Tecuya, Sespe and Almiyi. (These names, by the way, are all original local American Indian place names in Los Padres.) Sespe is Sisquoc's sister, so obviously they will not be mated. We shall see what 1984 brings. It appears that permission will be granted by California Fish and Game to take the first six eggs laid. However, only after the first egg is taken from four pairs can a second be taken from any pair. We see this provision as illogical, but attuned to political realities. Our view is to get as many birds into the breeding programme as possible. With existing facilities, which cost over $400,000, our San Diego Wild Animal Park and the Los Angeles Zoo can house 12 breeding pairs in 3,200 square feet apartments (we call them condor-miniums) which are 22 feet high to allow for flight.

If 1984's batch of eggs has some that don't fit for genetically sound breeding, we can release them as youngsters in a year or so. We are doing our best to avoid human imprinting on the fledglings. From the very beginning they are groomed and fed by hand puppets, each of which is a realistic replica of an adult condor's head and neck manipulated by a keeper who remains out of sight behind a curtain. If the young birds see humans, they see them in the distance. Currently the role models they can catch are Andean condors, but shortly one of two adult males at the Los Angeles Zoo may become a role model, either there or at our San Diego Wild Animal Park.

To date it appears the plan is working well. Sisquoc and Tecuya, the first two hatched, are already flying short distances quite successfully.

When these birds finally learn to soar, they are graceful and lovely, but at first they are terribly clumsy, sometimes landing in heaps of crumpled feathers as they tumble end over end in what any aeroplane pilot would term a crash landing.

Now a release plan is being formulated, one that will state the 'who, what, when, where, why and how' of releasing birds as they become available. This plan will take into account all the problems involved in any release of captive bred animals: the training, if any, they must have (like flying, eating carrion, and avoiding people); the diseases, if any, they may vector (for in releasing captive bred animals one may also release diseases exotic to the remaining wild stock, with results that might approximate the introduction of smallpox in Tahiti); and possibly, the sex education they may need in courting, nest-building, copulating and rearing young, although one hopes that behaviour in this respect is more genetically programmed than learned.

The release programme will probably follow a strategy that worked well with Andean condors, whereby birds bred by US Fish and Wildlife, the New York Zoo and our zoo were released three at a time. Of eleven birds released since 1981, seven are still alive and flying. We can hope for as good a result.

Is all this worthwhile? It is certainly expensive: the total programme will cost $25 million or more. In 1983 alone, we are spending $250,000 for labour, facilities and food (including about $50,000 for mice alone at 50c each).

But consider what we are saving: the largest of all birds in North America; a unique set of genes; a species in a world which loses a species a day; a symbol of wilderness and wildness; a wilderness itself, set aside with the justification that it was for the condor; and a symbol of immortality in the lore of some California Indians, who believed that the condor performs the role we assign to angels of transporting the souls of the dead to heaven. Even if it is not worthwhile to save the species for its own sake, for the sake of nature's future, or for any other of the reasons normally given for conserving wild animals, let us at least consider that the Indians may be right—and hedge our bets by saving this majestic bird for the sake of our immortal souls.

I would like to end with a short poem written by first grade students in a California school. It was among the thousands of congratulatory messages we received after the first condor hatching:

Dear San Diego Zookeeper:
>We're happy that your condor hatched
>We hope some day it will be free
>We know it's nature's garbage man
>And the Earth needs more than three.

Management Objectives and Goals for Wilderness Areas: Wilderness Areas as a Conservation Category

Bill Bainbridge

The Drakensberg Mountains, Natal

A great deal of emphasis has been given in the past decade to the shrinking of the world's wild places, and the need for each country to protect these. The International Union for the Conservation of Nature (IUCN) has played a leading role in coordinating a global policy for nature conservation and in providing the necessary impetus for individual nations to participate in the international conservation programme. Amongst the important contributions have been the publication of the World Conservation Strategy (IUCN, 1980) and a classification system for natural areas (IUCN, 1978).

Each nation has individual environmental, social and cultural attributes and therefore individual requirements for a spectrum of natural areas which can achieve its national objectives for nature conservation. Many countries have developed their own categories, subdividing the continuum ranging from wilderness areas through to developed natural areas. These categories are distinguished by their management objectives.

The international system was developed by IUCN to enable the conservation areas of each country to be classified according to the objectives for which it is being managed; to enable each nation to establish natural areas to fulfil conservational functions appropriate to its own circumstances, yet to receive recognition for its contribution to world conservation; and to allow an international data bank to be established for the storage of biological and other data, for assessment of the world system. The scientific community would have access to this data bank, which would also provide information about many research and environmental educational facilities.

The first classification proposed for the establishment of a global network of national parks and protected areas was completed in 1973. Subsequently a revised system was proposed in 1978. Wilderness was included as a category in the first system, but omitted in the second.

The purpose of this paper is to suggest that wilderness area should receive international recognition as a conservation category. Inclusion in the IUCN list would generate international recognition for wilderness areas already established, and stimulate the declaration of new areas.

The revised system of categories for natural areas proposed by IUCN in 1978 complemented the concept of national parks with other 'distinct categories, which when taken together, can provide land managers and decision makers with a broad set of legal and managerial options for conservation land management'. This recognised the necessity for establishing a spectrum of natural areas which should be managed in perpetuity to maintain representative samples of major ecosystems in unmodified state, for the conservation of natural communities and their component species, protection of scenery and landscapes, and the provision of recreation and tourism.

In the preamble to the revised system, IUCN specifically noted the urgent need to assess the status of nature conservation in the face of rapidly increasing physical modification of the remaining wild places of the Earth and to prescribe action to ensure adequate protection for areas not yet subject to agriculture or development. It also recognised the need for versatility in the system so that the conservation areas established by different nations could be recognised and categorised according to their management objectives.

A primary objective for the classification system was to encourage the development of a series of conservation categories and to define primary conservation objectives for each. All ten categories proposed (see Table 1) involve, to varying degrees, the protection of natural ecosystems. Of these, five principal categories have major commitments towards the permanent conservation of large ecosystems, biological diversity and genetic resources, while minimising human impact through recreation and tourism. Within these areas, sacrosanct core areas of undisturbed country should be maintained.

Other categories provide for many environmental and human needs, extending the total area of land maintained in both natural and semi-

Nomenclature for Designated Areas Proposed by the International Union for the Conservation of Nature (1978)

I	Scientific Reserves/Strict Nature Reserves
II	National Parks/Provincial Parks
III	National Monuments/Natural Landmarks
IV	Nature Conservation Reserves/Managed Nature Reserves/ Wildlife Sanctuaries
V	Protected Landscapes
VI	Resource Reserves
VII	Anthropological Reserves/Natural Biotic Areas
VIII	Multiple-Use Management Areas/Managed Resource Areas
IX	Biosphere Reserves
X	World Heritage Sites (natural)

Table 1

natural states. These categories incorporate the principles of 'ecodevelopment', in which nature conservation can be interwoven into development. Natural resources can be managed in a variety of ways both to support the quality of life and also to provide for other human needs on a sustainable basis.

Conservation categories are artificial classes which a variety of people have attempted to define in order to sub-divide the continuum of conservation areas. The original concept of a national park was that of a natural area with 'supreme' status, but opinions differ about what its management objectives should be. In particular, the provision of recreational facilities for the public in national parks has varied greatly from country to country. In the long period between the creation of the first national parks and the attempts to define an internationally accepted definition of their functions and objectives, research has brought to light the potential conflicts that arise between conservational and recreational objectives.

It seems reasonable that the *de facto* use and objectives of important categories such as national park and wilderness area will vary from country to country, according to the ecological and cultural situations of each. International definitions will need to incorporate the full range of concepts.

In relation to wilderness, the USA initiated the concept of preserving wild country in legally dedicated wilderness areas with the Wilderness Act of 1964. It has since established the most extensive wilderness system in the world. Other countries such as Australia and South Africa have also established a system of wilderness areas as part of their national natural areas. In these countries, the category wilderness is at least equivalent to the national park system in regard to conservational importance and legal security.

There have been few attempts to reconcile the different concepts held by nations which have already declared wilderness areas. In 1983 Stankey provided a comparison of these, stating that the essential characteristics of a wilderness area differ little from those generally accepted by most countries for national parks. He lists these as: a relatively large area; substantially intact ecosystems; physical and biological features possessing scientific, educational and recreational interest; reserved through the country's highest competent legal authority; and visitors allowed to enter, under special conditions, for inspirational, educational and recreative purposes.

The description of a national park given by IUCN in 1978 is as follows:

The area should perpetuate in a natural state representative samples of physiographic regions, biotic communities and genetic resources, and species in danger of extinction to provide ecological stability and diversity.

National Parks are relatively large land or water areas which contain representative samples of major natural regions, features or scenery of national or international significance where plant and animal species, geomorphological sites, and habitats are of considerable scientific, educational and recreational interest. They contain one or several entire ecosystems that are not materially altered by human exploitation and occupation. The highest competent authority of the country has taken steps to prevent or eliminate as soon as possible exploitation or occupation in the area and to enforce effectively the respect of ecological, geomorphological, or aesthetic features which have led to its establishment.

There is, however, little unanimity on the functions of a national park or on the manner in which each individual nation manages its parks. In many countries, the national parks provide an important source of revenue, and sometimes also of international currency. Concern has arisen about the impact of large numbers of people on the parks and the conflicts that may arise between the conservation management objectives and the requirement to provide recreational and tourist facilities.

In 1975 Bannikov and Krinitskii noted that the main objective for many national parks at the time of their establishment was the provision of recreational facilities with the greatest possible protection of landscapes. In contrast, the primary management objective for nature reserves was the conservation of natural communities, rare species and landscapes of exceptional beauty. Even IUCN's present description of the category national park lists the provision of recreation and tourism services as 'a primary objective for management of area resources'.

There are many differing concepts of the functions and uses of the categories national park and wilderness area. In most countries, both categories have a number of common conservation management objectives. The essential differences appear to be that in national parks particular emphasis is given to the provision of outdoor recreation, often incorporating public accommodation, and educational opportunities. In wilderness areas, great emphasis is placed on the conservation of major ecosystems and landscapes with a minimum of disturbance by human beings, and the provision of high quality recreational experience to a relatively small number of people at a time. Both areas may be used for scientific study and environmental monitoring. Wilderness areas in particular offer outstanding opportunities for scientific study of unmodified ecosystems, for comparative purposes.

At present there are various existing definitions of wilderness. The US Wilderness Act of 1964 defines a wilderness area as:

An area of undeveloped...land retaining its primeval character and influence, without permanent improvements or human habitation, which is protected and managed so as to preserve its natural conditions which,
1) generally appear to have been affected primarily by the forces of nature, with the imprint of man's work substantially unnoticeable;
2) has outstanding opportunities for solitude or a primitive and unconfined type of recreation;
3) has at least five thousand acres of land or is of sufficient size as to make practicable its preservation and use in an unimpaired condition; and
4) may also contain ecological, geological or other features of scientific, educational, scenic or historical value.

IUCN (1973) defines the primary purpose of a wilderness area as the protection of nature, '...with the area maintained in a state in which its wilderness or primitive appearance is not impaired by any form of development, and in which the continued existence of indigenous animal and plant species is assured'. The area is also used for the provision of outdoor recreation, '...for those capable of enduring the vicissitudes of wilderness travel by primitive means (without motorised transport, roads, improved trails and developed campgrounds, etc.)'.

In 1972, Raymond Dasmann wrote:

Wilderness stands as a unit of measurement against which we estimate progress or loss in our deformation of natural areas in managed areas. It stands as a reservoir and refuge for those wild plants and animals difficult to fit into the managed landscape. It stands as a sanctuary for people seeking to keep contact with primitive values. We require great tracts of wilderness land of all biotic types, from desert and high mountain to lands that are now, or will be, occupied by farm, managed forests, or managed range. Although in percentage these wilderness areas need never amount to more than a small part of the total land area, their value in the future will far exceed their extent. The present system of wilderness areas and national parks is a strong beginning but not adequate for future needs.

From these and other definitions, it is clear that the particular attributes of wilderness, and the conservation objectives for major ecosystems and natural communities in their primitive state are: that they should be of large size; that they should be maintained by active management with an absolute minimum of disturbance or development; and that the number of visitors permitted to enter at any one time should be restricted to relatively low numbers if the quality and character of their experience is to be preserved. The natural communities conserved within a wilderness area will thus have optimal survival chances, comparable at least to the level of protection offered by any other conservation category.

Wilderness areas are of major importance for the achievement of international and national nature conservation programmes. The nature conservation objectives listed by IUCN in 1978 for the principal conservation categories should be incorporated in the list of management objectives for all wilderness areas and receive high priority ranking. These management objectives have already been adapted for use in the Drakensberg State Forests of South Africa, a high proportion of which have been declared wilderness area.

There is no doubt, at least in the African context, that a management policy of benign neglect is not suitable for wilderness areas. This is partly due, as Stankey points out, to the fact that external influences from adjacent land use and global environmental pollution make a certain degree of management essential. In addition, in some places, Southern Africa for example, natural fire is a key environmental factor which no longer occurs in the prehistoric pattern which pertained before humans created boundaries and brought in modern land use machinery. It is essential for the maintenance of a number of natural fire climax vegetation communities that a prescribed system of burns be regularly applied, in a simulated natural pattern.

The manner in which wilderness areas are managed must also take into account the primary management objectives for the area. Management must not in itself become a factor responsible for the deterioration of wilderness character.

Stankey also emphasises that the provision of adequate and appropriate interpretive services and the promotion of wilderness-associated experiences are essential roles of management.

Many eloquent pleas have been made about the need to conserve areas of wilderness for the particular types of outdoor recreation and spiritual renewal that may only be obtained in extensive, undeveloped tracts of land. Historically, these relate to so-called 'primitive' types of experience where mechanised recreation forms are not permitted, but where users enter on foot, relying on their own self-sufficiency to commune with nature and to enjoy solitude and the opportunity to re-create. Modern wilderness areas can provide important spiritual and

African animals, small or large, equally depend on our attempts to conserve and maintain their wilderness homes

recreational experiences, which can have important therapeutic properties for those normally subjected to the pressures of modern life. Finson states, "In wilderness it is possible to be free, at least for a while, from the limitations that man places upon himself, and to rediscover the richness of one's whole being." It is difficult to obtain this experience in any other type of natural area.

It has frequently been asked whether land can be spared for the creation of wilderness areas in today's world of exploding human populations and ever-shrinking resources. There has been criticism of the exclusive nature of wilderness experience and the fact that relatively large areas are required for the benefit of the few people who may be admitted at any one time. Charges have been levelled that the aesthetic and social values of wilderness are currently limited in extent and are of value to a few privileged citizens with better than average education and work opportunities, who seek an exclusive social experience in pleasant outdoor surrounds.

The experience gained in wilderness is individual to the user, varying according to background, upbringing and personal perception. Some people are able to gain a personal wilderness-type experience even in semi-developed environments. Not all people who enter wilderness areas will obtain as profound and impressive a level of experience as may a person with great empathy for wilderness, just as not everyone who enters a church will have a profound religious experience. It is inevitable that wilderness users will obtain a great variety of experiences.

What is important is that wilderness managers provide adequate interpretive services to users, so that the quality of their experience may be heightened and intensified. Great emphasis must be given to encouraging youth to prepare themselves for wilderness use, initially by using parks and quasi-wilderness areas, and then by taking the greatest possible advantage of the character-building qualities and the opportunities for spiritual renewal available in wilderness. It is also important that the multiple-use aspects of wilderness areas are adequately projected through these interpretive services. Wilderness areas ought not, at least in many countries such as Africa which are critically short of land, to be created primarily for the provision of outdoor recreation and wilderness experience.

At least four countries have already established extensive wilderness areas which have legal status equivalent to national parks in several. It is desirable that these areas receive international recognition. It is also desirable that other countries, who still have sufficient wild areas, be provided with the opportunity to declare new wilderness areas in a conservation category that will receive recognition from the international community. This could be achieved by simple adaptation of the system proposed by IUCN and the inclusion of an additional category equivalent to that of a national park. This would provide versatility for each nation to design a system of natural areas for its own specific requirements.

Much attention has been given to the rapid rate at which development is destroying the last of the wilderness in virtually every country of the world. With the pressures of escalating human populations and modern development, there can be no secure sanctuary for wild areas outside dedicated natural areas which have secure legal ensconcement. If the last of the wilderness is to be conserved for posterity, it can only be done in one of the accepted conservation categories which do not cater for wilderness. There is obvious need for a specific wilderness category for this purpose.

Wilderness area is also an appropriate category for the conservation of fragile or environmentally sensitive landscapes such as high mountain ecosystems and watershed areas. The implied low recreational levels appropriate for the provision of wilderness experience makes the category particularly suitable for the conservation of sensitive areas. In South Africa, for instance, which does not possess abundant fresh water supplies, extensive areas of high rainfall mountain catchment terrain are conserved as wilderness areas.

It is becoming increasingly clear that subjecting marginal areas to even relatively light agricultural use may cause considerable environmental disturbance. Thus, unless the pressures are overwhelming, resource planners should carefully consider the possibility of protecting environmentally sensitive areas in a holding category such as a managed resource area. Alternatively, wherever possible, serious consideration should be given to protecting such sensitive areas as wilderness areas, so that the options of optimising physical benefits such as stabilised water supplies and the conservation of genetic resources, as well as aesthetic benefits for the maintenance of quality of life, may be preserved.

Examples of fragile landscapes which merit protection in this way on the Southern African sub-continent include the high mountain ecosystems containing the Afro-alpine and Afro-montane vegetation, together with many other mountainous or steep areas such as the escarpments of the Great Rift Valley. Most of these are important water source areas, which deteriorate rapidly, especially under primitive agriculture. In South Africa, it has been shown that water resources may be permanently impaired by such land use. Other marginal areas include the great swamps and the extensive tsetse infested 'miombo' areas of Central Africa. Priorities for wilderness areas could be those areas infested by tsetse fly, which are carriers of sleeping sickness.

Wilderness areas could also be considered as components of biosphere reserves and world heritage sites, two umbrella categories

Wilderness Areas of South Africa

Region	Name of Area	Date set aside	Area (ha)
Western Cape	Boosmansbos	1978	14 200
	Sederberg	1973/1976	71 000
Tsitsikamma	Groendal	1976	25 000
Natal	Mdedelelo	1973	29 000
	Mkhomazi	1973	54 000
	Mzimkulu	1979	28 340
Zululand	Ntendeka	1975	5 500
Northern Transvaal	Wolkberg	1977	17 500
Total	8 Wilderness Areas		244 500

Table 2

suggested by IUCN in 1978 under 'Internationally Recognised Affiliated Designations'.

The objectives cited for a biosphere reserve include conservation of present natural areas for comparative or baseline studies, both within natural and altered environments. Each biosphere reserve can be zoned to delineate a natural or core zone together with a manipulative or buffer zone, a reclamation or restoration zone and a stable cultural zone. The natural or core zone could consist of a dedicated wilderness area or a national park containing a substantial wilderness zone.

World heritage sites are created to protect features considered to be of world significance and will frequently include many previously designated protected areas, which could include dedicated wilderness areas. Wilderness area is fully compatible with this international category.

In South Africa, which was the first African country to establish wilderness areas, such areas may be proclaimed under the Forest Act No 72 of 1968. They are managed by the Directorate of Forestry of the Department of Environment Affairs. Areas declared under the Act enjoy some of the most secure legal status of any natural area in this country. At present, eight areas have been declared in various parts of the Republic, with a combined area of approximately 245,000 ha (see Table 2). A further ten areas are in process of declaration. These will protect a further 215,000 ha and result in a system totalling 460,000 ha.

The largest of the new areas, Baviaanskloof Wilderness Area, will protect approximately 150,000 ha of Cape Fynbos. This is a South African biome of great ecological importance. The Cape Fynbos stands as one of the world's six floral kingdoms in its own right. Although the smallest of the six kingdoms, it is estimated to contain over 6,000 endemic species out of a total of approximately 8,500 constituent species. The new wilderness area will play an important role in preserving a portion of this species-rich and diverse vegetation.

The first wilderness areas to be declared in the Republic were in the Natal Drakensberg. These are also to be significantly extended. They conserve the only Afro-alpine vegetation which occurs in South Africa, together with two other Veld Types. Approximately 1,800 species are conserved in the Drakensberg natural areas, of which an estimated 300 are endemics.

The Drakensberg wilderness areas and nature reserves, together with the game reserves managed by the Natal Parks Board, conserve some of the most scenic mountain areas of the country. The area has been described as one of the great natural spectacles of the African continent. This conserved area is considered to be of international significance, and has been proposed as a world heritage site.

In conclusion, I would like to re-emphasise the need for wilderness area to receive international recognition as a conservation category. IUCN should be requested to revise the present classification system for natural areas incorporating a category for wilderness. This would enable international recognition to be given to existing wilderness systems, as well as encouraging the declaration of additional systems. Many countries are in the fortunate position of having extensive wild areas which could be protected. Revision of the international system would encourage them to create further wilderness areas as part of their national system of natural areas. The category wilderness is also particularly suitable for the protection of environmentally sensitive areas.

Ekistics, Ecumenopolis and the Wilderness: Planning for a Global Ecological Balance

Gerald Dix

Cities of one sort or another have always been a part of civilisation, but the need to plan them correctly is now crucial. Tyuoni ruin, New Mexico, built ca. 1400

Amongst all the world's resources and environments, wilderness areas are probably facing the greatest pressures as humankind struggles to cater for the needs of bigger populations and increasing urbanisation. The resolution of potentially damaging conflicts of interests presupposes more than preservation: it demands instead rational practical policies related to regional and global needs.

The Declaration of the 1972 UN Conference on the Human Environment emphasised the importance of a balanced outlook, noting that "economic and social development is essential for ensuring a favourable living and working environment for man and for creating conditions on earth that are necessary for the improvement of the quality of life." Whilst "international matters concerning the protection and improvement of the environment should be handled in a cooperative spirit by all countries, big and small on an equal footing," environmental policies "should enhance and not adversely affect the present or future development potential of developing countries, nor should they hamper the attainment of better living conditions for all, and appropriate steps should be taken...with a view of reaching agreement on meeting the possible national and international economic consequences resulting from the application of environmental measures."

It is a long way from the bland but encouraging phraseology of an international conference attended by the like-minded of many nations to the formulation of policies and the preparation of plans that can gain the acceptance of those most concerned, the people whose homes and lives will be affected. Too often, since Stockholm, conservation arguments have been discussed in isolation from one another and frequently quite separately from the considerations not so much of economic growth but simply of survival.

It has become common practice to think of big cities and wildernesses as if they were independent of each other and at opposite ends of the development spectrum. But economic growth and conservation are not necessarily or even generally poles apart and opposed one to another. It may well be that in the tacit acceptance of the sentiment of the Stockholm declaration is to be found the key to the weakness, almost fragility, of many conservation and planning policies. This situation can only be remedied by considering the problems of the environment and of human settlements on a regional and global basis in order to see that, whilst the lessons of the past are properly taken into account, those countries struggling against adverse social and economic conditions are not put in a position where they have to pay the price of earlier errors occasioned by the excusable ignorance, or less excusable greed, of the first industrial nations. Progress will only be made when there is a greater understanding both of the possibilities for conservation and of methods of regulating environments.

There are five major categories of wilderness that can be distinguished, all still comparatively untouched but all likely candidates for intensive exploitation in the near future. To the extent that the consequences of their use are likely to be inadequately understood ecologically, they may be regarded as being 'under threat'. They are the skies, the polar regions, the major oceans and seas and coasts, the great forest areas and the deserts. Because they are still comparatively unsullied they deserve priority in consideration and action, although they may not all immediately appear equally important in relation to the needs of our urbanising world.

The skies are increasingly becoming filled with the flotsam and jetsam of space exploration and, at a lower altitude, the chemical pollution of two centuries of industrialisation. There are also a growing number of communications and spy satellites. That we are alternatively warned of the world overheating or of suffering a new ice age denotes an area of fairly comprehensive ignorance where there is need for research before it is too late.

The polar regions are already targets of further exploration, not for the reasons that attracted Peary and Amundsen but as possible sources of new mineral wealth in the last fairly unknown land masses.

The oceans and seas have long suffered the depredations of human beings. From time immemorial the sea has been both a source of food for those fortunate enough to live near it and a dumping ground for waste and refuse of all kinds. Until recently the scale of fishing and pollution was so small that no harm was done and the balance of nature hardly disturbed, but now the situation has changed dramatically, so that no part of the oceans is free from the possibility of action of one sort or another on a hitherto unknown scale, be it fishing, mineral extraction or the dumping of waste.

Even more vulnerable is the coastline, which in many instances suffers from pollution found in both sea and land, but which when combined is even more damaging. Special attention must be devoted to this zone of conjunction, as indeed it is in the system discussed later in this paper. There has been some progress over the avoidance of pollution in the seas—the Barcelona Convention, for example, in relation to the Mediterranean—but it has been slow, nations being reluctant to abide by agreements in the face of economic pressures.

Of equal international importance are policies concerning major wilderness areas on land that lie within the national boundaries and jurisdiction of one country or another, in many instances in the intermediate or less developed countries of the world.

Those that have caused greatest concern in terms of preservation in recent years have been the major rain forests, most notably that of the Amazon basin in Brazil. There, it is argued, once the forests have been chopped down, not only will the areas energetically cleared to provide land for farms to grow the food for an increasing population be subject to erosion but, so great is the scale of the exercise, the ecological balance for a whole sub-continent may be changed. This may well be so, in Brazil as well as in many other parts of the world where similar though smaller programmes are being undertaken. It could be serious for the world if it were, but criticism must be related to circumstances and to the way in which the cleared former wilderness is used—whether for financial gain for an individual entrepreneur, to supply timber for homes for the wealthy, or food for the undernourished. The future ecological situation must be carefully considered and weighed against other gains or losses in assessing a proposal of this kind. It may be wrong, though on occasion excusable, that through greed or ignorance areas or habitats of a scientifically particularly valuable kind have been destroyed in the past by countries now wealthy, but it would surely be morally indefensible to suggest that for that reason all similar surviving areas must necessarily be retained. In their attempts to preserve particular types of habitat, which may be rare or even unique, the world's ecologists and conservationists should not lightly deprive a poor nation of the opportunity to exploit its mineral or other wealth. This is not, of course, a new problem. At the turn of the century Winston Churchill, recently home from the Sudan, commented in relation to the Aswan Dam being limited in height and thus in capacity in order to save flooding some Pharaonic monuments, that "the State must struggle and people starve in order that professors may exult and tourists find some place in which to scratch their names."

The recent case of the Tasmanian hydro-electric scheme, though not in a developing country, demonstrated the difficulties in contemporary circumstances. The people and government of Australia's smallest state were trying to make the best use of their own resources to improve their lot in life, but the region proposed for development is reputedly one of only three large temperate wildernesses remaining in the world. Following a Supreme Court decision (on the scope of the Federal powers, *not* on the validity of the conservation or development arguments) the project has been abandoned, to the evident joy of conservationists the world over. Whether they are right or wrong is beside the point in relation to this paper, which is that Tasmanian industry and prosperity may suffer in the future because they earlier failed to utilise a God-given resource and they have now lost the chance to do so. The world may benefit, but will it compensate Tasmania? Who should pay the price for preservation? There are many other similar examples, often of development which goes ahead when, conceivably, for the general good it should not; and sometimes, no doubt, of development which is delayed or stopped to the detriment of humanity, even though an area of wilderness or a valuable habitat may be saved. Long-term gains and short-term costs are hard to evaluate, and a sublime future is of only academic interest to a society without the wherewithal to live long enough to enjoy it.

The conservation of wildernesses is often interpreted as the preservation of forests, a double confusion of little value. In this respect it may be helpful to accept President John F. Kennedy's definition of conservation as the wise use of our natural resources, which at least implies the possibility of beneficial change, and to regard preservation as a policy of no deliberate change—although, presumably, accepting that external factors, such as climatic variation, natural disaster or atmospheric pollution may have a moderating influence, however little direct action there may be. Further, it has to be appreciated that the world's major wildernesses are its deserts, which it is apparently possible to modify without incurring too greatly the wrath of the conservationist lobby, doubtless because whilst many remaining forests ap-

pear to be under threat from human activity, in the arid zones it is this activity and cultivation that is threatened by desertification.

In Africa and Asia in particular, vast deserts are marching relentlessly forward into the cultivated lands of nations that have growing populations but generally too few other resources to enable them properly to engage in the battle with the oncoming sand. Under much of the desert are aquifers, which, with the availability of greater expertise and rather more resources, could be used to supply water for cultivation. So too, in many countries, the sewage effluent of the larger settlements could be used to produce crops and sustain the tree belts necessary to arrest the advance of the desert. The United Nations Environmental Programme gave a lead with its 1977 international conference on desertification, but more research and experimental work is urgently needed, and first there must be a change of heart and an opening of minds about wildernesses and about the need to live in partnership with our environment, of which the wildernesses form but one element.

Our attitude towards wildernesses, as to so much of nature, seems often to be ambivalent, if not hypocritical, guided more by fashion than by any logical argument. But for survival—of nature, including human beings—we must try to clarify attitudes and avoid clashes of interest, for it is a question of balance. First we must agree, nationally or internationally, on policies about population and living standards, for in them lies the key to determining our relationship with our environment.

129

Consideration of the population factor in this paper has nothing to do with arguments about family planning or birth control but is concerned only with the realities of the anticipated world situation and its impact on areas of wilderness. In many countries populations are growing at annual rates of 3% or higher, the highest rates frequently being found in countries that are already amongst the poorest. Whatever future national, religious or personal attitudes about family size may be, a continuing growth of population is inevitable, to rather more than 5,000 million by the end of the decade and perhaps a further 1,000 million or so by the end of the century. Even then some of the most populous nations will continue to increase, perhaps for a further century or more. Most of this increase is brought about by reductions in death rates that are significantly greater than the almost universal reduction in birth rates, and as a result of greater life expectancy. It seems inconsistent to argue that birth control is an interference with nature, yet to accept unquestioned the prolongation of life and the consequences of the reduction or even elimination of disease that follow from advances in medical science.

In the long term a more significant and permanent influence on birth rates (and thus on eventual population size) will follow not so much from any family planning programme but from economic and social development and the achievement of reasonable living standards. Living standards, as well as population size, influence outlooks on the necessity for and the practicability of conservation policies. Any worthwhile conservation policy must be based on the fact that nature is not an artifact but a series of relationships, and that any change in one element inevitably produces consequential changes elsewhere in the system. As science is about transformations rather than creation, it is reasonable to look to scientific methods as a starting point in a search for a better basis for realistic policies for preservation, conservation and development. It is by natural evolutionary processes that new species and varieties of plant or animal are developed and old ones lost, as the ecological balance remains. If through preservationist zeal a dying breed is artificially stimulated to prolonged existence, we by our interference may inhibit the emergence of a new plant or animal. And, following a natural disaster, such as fire or flood in a primary forest, if we attempt to restore the *status quo ante*, we would no doubt—and despite our best intentions—upset the development of a new, though different, natural balance. What is important is not so much the recognition that the balance is being changed, but that too often we neither know nor understand the likely effects of our actions. Increasing research will help in this respect, but the world cannot wait until research is complete: it never is, and each new discovery merely exposes a further area of ignorance. Yet facts are better than dreams as a basis for planning, and so to increase our pool of knowledge we should

e k i s t i c   f o r c e s

	economic	social	political	technical	cultural	TOTAL
nature						
man						
society						
networks						
shells						
TOTAL						

e k i s t i c   e l e m e n t s

Ekistic Forces and Elements in the ekistic grid.

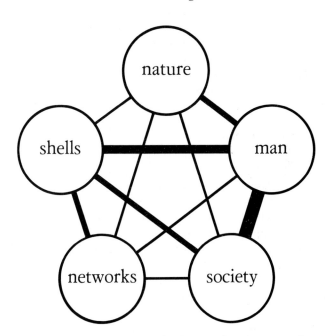

The Connection of Elements—internal cohesion of environmental components

Figure 1 **Ekistic Forces and Elements** in the ekistic grid and showing the way they are connected

monitor rigorously the consequences of all actions and policies, the better to understand their relationships. Ekistics provides a scientific framework for advancing our knowledge in this way.

Ekistics, the science of human settlements, was developed by Constantinos Doxiadis (1913—1975), Greek architect, planner, philosopher and humanist, in an endeavour to establish a system within which all environmental decisions could be taken.

Doxiadis was interested primarily in practicalities—in his case those concerned with human settlements and the relationship between settlements and nature. He accepted that with inadequate information risks would have to be taken and generalisations made, but he was anxious to establish a methodological framework which could be modified and refined in the light of experience and later knowledge.

He advanced the thesis that there are five elements in human settlements and five forces, or groups of forces, acting on them. The elements he identified were nature, the backcloth against which everything takes place; anthropos, the human individual; the society of human beings as a group, often organised but as often not; shells, the buildings and other structures in which we live, work and play; and networks, the roads and railways, air and sea routes, pipe lines, cables, and radio beams that enable us to carry goods and to communicate. The five forces or influencing factors were economic, social, political, technical and cultural. The elements and forces provide a good basis for the orderly examination of the influences on the structure of a town or region. Figure 1 refers.

From empirical study based on a wide international experience, Doxiadis was aware of the confusion caused by the lack of a consistent terminology and of any system to describe human settlements. He thought it necessary first to classify settlements in significant categories, then to build a model relating settlements of different kinds to one another and to their surroundings.

From the smallest community unit, the housegroup, through the neighbourhood, the small and large town, even to the megalopolitan scale and beyond, he found there was a fairly constant size relationship, by a factor of seven, between the different significant categories of size of settlement. Thus a group of six or seven dwellings would have a population of about 35 persons, the next larger group one of about 245, a neighbourhood about 1,700, a small independent town about 12,000 and the next larger one about 48,000. He classified a settlement of 4m population as a metropolis, and one of 200m as a megalopolis. These were fairly broad categories, intended to form the basis of a model that could be adapted to suit particular circumstances. They led directly to the construction of the Ekistic Logarithmic Scale and the Ekistic grid and later, as Doxiadis developed his 'logical and taxonomic frame for the classification of human settlements' to the

EPS Unit	Persons			
15	69	206	436	005
14	9	886	633	715
13	1	412	376	245
12		201	768	035
11		28	824	005
10		4	117	715
9			558	245
8			84	035
7			12	005
6			1	715
5				245
4				35
3				5
2				2
1				1

Ekistic Population Scale—persons in units of different categories.

ETS Unit	Square Metres					
18	000	000	000	000	000	000
17	135	750	000	000	000	000
16	19	392	857	000	000	000
15	2	770	408	000	000	000
14		395	772	000	000	000
13		56	538	000	000	000
12		8	077	000	000	000
11		1	153	850	000	000
10			164	836	000	000
9			23	548	000	000
8			3	364	000	000
7				480	570	000
6				68	650	000
5				9	800	000
4				1	400	000
3					200	000
2					28	059
1					4	084

Ekistic Territorial Scale—area for units of different categories.

Figure 2 **Ekistic Population Scale and Ekistic Territorial Scale**

more sophisticated Ekistic Population Scale, based on the number of inhabitants, the Ekistic Territorial Scale, based on area (Figure 2), and the Anthropocosmos model. These recognised the need for any effective system to include consideration of many other factors and, with later developments, could not only help our understanding of social, political and economic organisation and illumine possible courses of action we might take to improve our environmental situation, but could also be used for identifying gaps in our knowledge.

From his practice as a planner and his concern to understand and explain urbanisation and the system of human settlements, Doxiadis was prompted to enquire into the nature of cities of the future. "Are we going to go on living in the cities of the present which get increasingly worse with every day that passes because of their continuous growth, or are we going to live in those utopian cities which so many people talk about, but which never actually get built?" Being essentially practical, he wanted not only to find out the magnitude of the problem facing the world, but also to discover a realistic way of turning an impending crisis into an opportunity. He was firmly of the view that it was a scientist's duty to 'solve problems, not merely to grapple with them'. "He did not particularly welcome what he came to call ecumenopolis, the world city, nor yet the large areas of megalopolitan growth of America, Japan and elsewhere, but he regarded them as inevitable" and thought that if they were "it would be better to give them order and coherence, to ensure open space and light and air, to use our energies to care for the quality of life instead of wasting them fighting for the impossible."[1] The ekistic concept of ecumenopolis that emerged from a long-term research programme on the city of the future was not one of a limitless area of concrete and brick with roads and buildings stretching from horizon to horizon and beyond, but of a careful balance between human beings and nature, avoiding both extremes of density in urban areas and the unnecessary settlement of wilderness areas that, without proper policies and plans, might otherwise be imperilled. It was important that within settlements uses should be so arranged as to provide necessary open space and perhaps even areas of wilderness, and that the growth of ecumenopolis would be complemented by the simultaneous development of ecumenekepos, the global garden, to feed people at a better level than is now possible, overall, and also of an ecumenohydor, a global water supply system. This balance between people and their settlements on one hand, and their environment on the other, became of increasing importance to Doxiadis in his later years, for he was concerned to reconcile the needs of conservation and development in a Global Ecological Balance.

Doxiadis analysed prevailing conditions and ways of fulfilling anticipated global requirements under twelve headings, in accordance with their intensity of use and the degree to which nature had been modified. He defined zones ranging from the virtually untouched, save only for the occasional scientific expedition, to the intensively industrialised, and grouped these into four major areas as shown in Figure 3. This system of zones was applied to the use of the land, the seas, the air, and also, for the reasons touched upon earlier, separately to the coasts.

Figure 3 also shows the percentage of the world's land area that, as a result of Doxiadis' researches, it was suggested would be appropriate to consider under each heading. Zone one, classified as Real Wildlife, meeting a need for complete wilderness, comprises 40% of the whole land surface, remaining virtually in its natural state, with access restricted to scientists entering for research purposes. This zone includes many areas with virtually no or only limited animal populations and its title is to that extent misleading. The second category covers, by Doxiadis' calculations, 17% of the world's land, and is intended as an area predominantly preserved but available for visits for purposes of scientific observation, though not for commercial tourism. The third zone, Wildlife Embraced, comprising perhaps 10% of the land area, is the location of more but still limited human activity, although it includes areas occupied by a number of primitive tribes. Zone four, Wildlife Invaded, includes areas visited on a regular basis but with strictly limited machine access, and minimal destruction of nature. This area might form an admirable location for ecological education, observation and perhaps experiment, whereas zone five, Wildlife Conquered, comprises land controlled and exploited by human beings for forestry and commercial tourism, with hotels and similar facilities. These five zones, together constituting what Doxiadis called a Naturarea, cover 82% of the world's land surface.

Most human urban activities would thus be confined to rather less than a fifth of the land, with about a quarter of that for natural cultivation—that is, using evolving traditional methods—and another quarter for capital intensive factory farming and food production which would involve the drastic modification or perhaps even complete elimination of the natural landscape. The application of high technology and scientific discovery in this way should make possible the provision of a proper diet for those for whom such a thing is now an unattainable dream, whilst at the same time permitting the widest possible measure of nature conservation throughout the world.

In this scheme the remaining five zones are directly devoted to needs of urban dwellers, including recreation, low, middle and high density development and a zone for heavy industry and waste disposal. The low density zone would be predominantly residential, and the high density one devoted primarily to traditional town centre functions. It was assumed that the small percentage of land devoted to heavy industry and waste disposal would be arranged in a few large sites, which could

135

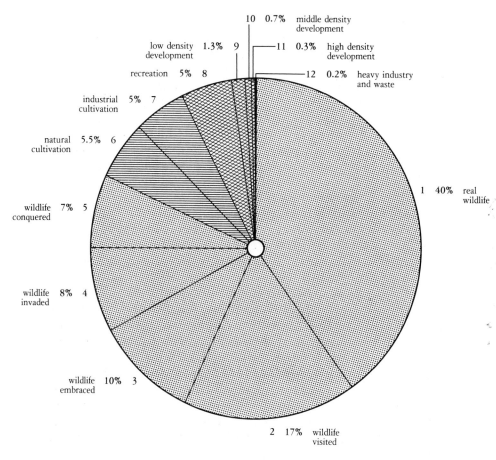

Figure 3 contents:

10 0.7% middle density development

low density development 1.3% 9

11 0.3% high density development

recreation 5% 8

12 0.2% heavy industry and waste

industrial cultivation 5% 7

natural cultivation 5.5% 6

1 40% real wildlife

wildlife conquered 7% 5

wildlife invaded 8% 4

wildlife embraced 10% 3

2 17% wildlife visited

Naturareas

Zone 1	As nearly virgin as possible
Zone 2	Visited by some humans but without permanent human installations
Zone 3	Humans enter and stay but without machines
Zone 4	Similar to Zone 3, but with human settlements
Zone 5	Nature prevails but humans enter with machines and can use the zone

Cultivareas

| Zone 6 | Natural cultivation in traditional ways |
| Zone 7 | Cultivation but with new methods allowing for higher productivity |

Anthropareas

Zone 8	Natural areas used as resorts, for sports, etc.
Zone 9	Inhabited at the lowest reasonable density
Zone 10	Inhabited, but at middle densities
Zone 11	Inhabited at the highest reasonable density

Industrareas

| Zone 12 | Every possible use for achieving the goal of the best industrialisation |

Figure 3   The Twelve Zones for Global Ecological Balance

be used economically, rather than a larger number of less efficient sites. Whilst in our present context our main concern is with the minimally developed areas, their protection will only be made possible if the overall balance is well understood and properly considered.

A similar set of zones has been proposed for inland water areas and rivers, and one for oceans and seas. The same principles apply in each case, differentiating between areas left in their natural state, and decreasing in extent with increasing intensity of human modification of the environment to water surfaces that are more or less completely modified by or from people's needs. While it may be asked how there can be any control over the sea, where pollution is carried by the currents and controlled by forces far beyond our command, in fact experience has shown, although so far only in a limited way, that when there is a sufficient awareness and concern, nations, individually or by agreement amongst groups, will act. When they do so, they must act, as with air zones, in a manner that not only coordinates with their own activities but, more importantly, accords with the demands of nature, harnessing its forces to our benefit.

The coast poses particular problems which can only be resolved in a satisfactory manner by having a special category of coastal zones and areas. For example, land appropriate for natural cultivation (in the Doxiadis classification) may be separated from an expanse of sea of particular ecological value that should be left untouched, unfished and undeveloped, by a coastal strip eminently suitable for recreation use. A coastal classification is needed that will reflect possible coastal uses compatible with adjoining sea and land zones. It should be emphasised, however, that the division of the world's surface between the twelve areas is likely to be markedly different in the various land, coastal and sea zones. Because of the needs of transportation, and the pressures of coastal use for human activities as urbanisation increases and ecumenopolis develops, the proportion of the coast within the seven Naturareas is likely to be lower than the corresponding percentage of the land. This should give no cause for alarm, however, for the system will help achieve a proper balance, and by using more of the coastline for our own purposes, we may be freeing land elsewhere from the possibility of development.

To define zones in the air may be well-nigh impossible at present, but to point to the need for some kind of consideration is surely necessary because of the lack of knowledge and because of the increasing possibility of planting permanent satellites in space. This may or may not be a good thing for the world, but it would in any event be useful to know the likelihood of the advantages or disadvantages to be gained by the invasion of the last great wilderness, in or beyond the biosphere. Nearer to Earth and closer to our own times, we should consider the impact on wildernesses of aircraft routes and of the intercontinental carriage by air currents of natural materials (such as sand from African deserts to northern Europe or Canada) and of human-created pollutants (such as the over-dramatised but serious phenomenon of acid rain) so we may have a better idea of what is acceptable and what is not, as well as of what is inevitable and what preventable.

Doxiadis emphasised that his work 'does not pretend finally to solve the problem of ecological and ekistic conflict, but rather to start the process (of resolving conflicts) in a logical and scientific way'. He was aware that as circumstances change, so must the allocation of resources and the disposition of effort to achieve what he accepted as a changing, evolving balance. His main point was that there must be such a balance so that our civilisation should not decline irreversibly, through ignorance, under the pressures of unconsidered urbanisation or unbridled preservation. Lacking proper knowledge it was not good enough, in his view, to say "Wait till we learn" and try to stop development, for that would not help anyone, least of all the poor of the third world: rather we must "have the courage to adopt the best approach on the basis of what we do know from science and history (for) we will learn from our experience and can ameliorate the processes for achieving a global ecological balance in the light of that experience."[2]

Many aspects of late twentieth century life have been characterised by extreme and over-reaction to events, apparently as a consequence of the increased speed of communications. An eloquent speech by an historical nonentity whose opinions are momentarily fashionable, an economist's estimate based on the forward projection of false assumptions, a good or bad forecast of production by a major company, or a strike or lockout can all lead to an immediate exaggerated reaction following a 30 second 'analysis' (sic) by one of television's innumerable universal pundits. The situation in relation to the environment may be little different, but for humankind, in the long term, potentially far more serious.

In recent decades we have moved in much of the world from a stage when development almost always meant construction of one sort or another and was automatically equated as being progress, with materials being used as though their supply was unlimited, to almost the direct opposite. Increasingly, cities seem to be regarded as pestilential to our morals, health and liberties, and the use of any natural material is seen as a sin. The surest way of discovering any merit in a broken-down and semi-derelict urban area is to propose its redevelopment, then wait for the chorus of protest. The quickest way to discover that a tract of land has characteristics that are unique or to discover the habitat of a hitherto insignificant insect is to propose that a new motorway or dam or airport should be developed or even, in many countries, that the land be brought under cultivation. It must be appreciated that every piece of land, be it natural wilderness or urban dereliction, is in some way unique, and our consideration of any change must surely be related to the probable impact of that change.

An environmental impact statement assessing each proposal in isolation is of limited value and may be positively unhelpful. Cost benefit analysis on its own would have precluded the building both of mediaeval cathedrals and the Sydney Opera House: an efficiency study would no doubt favour the cabbage rather than the rose. All major development decisions must be made on the basis not just of anticipated environmental impact, but also of the social, economic and other implications and interactions, locally and regionally, often nationally or globally. In short, a decision must pay heed to the elements and forces of Ekistics that Doxiadis clearly identified. The human element is important, for we are, I think, primarily concerned with a world for humankind. This is our world, and the ecological balance we seek, like the conservation policies we adopt, must surely be governed in the interests of human beings and their surroundings. Consistent beneficial policies are needed: Doxiadis' intention in developing the science of Ekistics, especially in its relationship with ecology, was to provide a basis for their evolution.

Much remains to be done. In reviewing *Ecology and Ekistics*, my colleague, Professor A.D. Bradshaw, pointed out that whilst ecology now has an ability to be predictive and thus to become formative of opinions, it is still far easier to predict the outcome of overuse of a sand dune system than of a city, despite the controls that planners can exercise. There is, as he says, a long way to go, for Ekistics does not yet relate closely to ecology as it is currently practised. There is certainly a need for better monitoring of proposals and for more responsive planning systems. Perhaps our first step should be to bring together people from some of the principal disciplines concerned, so that each may form a better understanding of the others' aims and of the difficulties that have to be overcome. Even more important is the creation of an atmosphere of understanding amongst politicians and people that all environmental issues are related.

Progress has been made since Doxiadis' ideas were first published, partly no doubt coincidentally, but certainly also partly because of the influence of his work. There are operative proposals for biogenetic reserves, for the reduction of pollution of the sea and for international cooperation. An omission at present, and perhaps one area for immediate cooperation, is the cost. As Doxiadis said, "If in becoming rich a European nation has done away with two-thirds of its wildlife, as it may have, it cannot insist that to maintain a global balance some African countries should retain every single part of their wildlife—and remain poor in consequence." And to suggest that some urgently needed cultivation to help provide food for starving millions should not take place, but that the site be preserved at 'any cost' because of its

ecological value, is equally unrealistic. This is particularly so in cases where, for example, the reduction in regional oxygen production occasioned by consequential forestry operations that may be required can be counterbalanced by oxygen produced from the development and planting for productive use of former desert areas. Which wilderness will contribute most to the future of humanity and the world?

There are other possible and probably more effective long-term ways of saving wildernesses and much else, and of encouraging economic development at the same time. For example, if we were to reduce the 30-60% loss of crops between field and table through insects and other pests, there would be less pressure to chop down trees or to cultivate deserts. The knowledge is readily available, but not generally applied. One stage further removed from commercial application are some ways of upgrading many of what we now regard as waste products. For example, it should be possible to produce clean water, fertiliser and nitrogenous meat analogue from sewage. Investment in bio-engineering, to advance these processes to the operational stage and to establish ways of growing animal protein foodstuffs in the developed countries (which could afford to do so), could lead to more home-produced food remaining in the less developed countries for their own consumption. The wise use of advanced technology in this and other ways could contribute significantly to the achievement of a continuing ecological balance, which to be effective must be realistic, scientifically sound and politically acceptable. Only if there is such a balance will it be possible for future generations to enjoy a beneficial urban life, or for there to be a wilderness.

Doxiadis' pioneering work has demonstrated ways of studying this balance and of examining environmental linkages. It has also demonstrated that if the world is to enjoy reasonable living standards and a reasonable environment we have no choice: a proper urban system is dependent on the development of a natural order. It is a future worth working for. For, as Doxiadis often remarked, if we do not try we can only fail; if we try we may fail, but we may succeed.

The wilderness is but one aspect of the world we inhabit. In our search for homeostasis, as we balance proper concerns for the preservation of wildernesses with ways of meeting the needs of humankind, and especially of the deprived, we know that nature goes its way without fear or favour, prejudice or rancour. Those who interfere might well bear in mind that in this, as in other contacts with nature, as they sow so shall they reap.

(1) C.A. Doxiadis (ed. Gerald Dix, 1977), Ecology and Ekistics, London, Elek, 1977. Editor's Foreword, p.ix.
(2) John Papaioannou, Ekistics Volume 50, Number 301, July/August 1983, pp.300-305.

◄ A lone sailboat is dwarfed by the Black Mountains in Arizona/Nevada, USA

Interfering drastically
with the nature without
creates, of necessity,
a disorder
of the inner nature.

C.A. Meier

WILDERNESS

Culture, Education
and Philosophy

Captions for colour pictures

Abruzzo National Park, Italy

Lake St Lucia, Natal, South Africa

Giraffe browsing in Umfolozi Game Reserve, Natal

Hippopotamus surfacing in an African river

Caledonian Pine, the symbol of wild Scotland

Cross-country skier above Glen Luibeg in January, looking up to Cairn Toul (left) and Ben Macdhui (right)

Dactylorhisa fuchsii, a common and sometimes spectacular plant of the hay meadows of the Hebrides

Red-necked phalarope (*Phalaropus lobatus*), Shetland Isles

St Croix National Scenic Waterway, USA

Pybus Bay, Alaska

Weld River rainforest, Tasmania

Puma (*Felis concolor*), in tropical forest of South America

Barrel cactus in bloom, Sonoran Desert, USA

Arches National Park, USA

Whither World Wilderness 2083?
A Look into the Crystal Globe

Ian MacPhail

You may wonder at my audacity in choosing as my title 'Whither World Wilderness 2083?' There is a moral to this: *beware of flattery*. When Ian Player invited me to speak, he said, "We want one of your provocative papers with an intriguing title." I fell for this and, without realising what I was letting myself in for, said, "My paper will be on World Wilderness 2083." Subsequently I experienced much anxiety until I had the idea of contacting some of the world's experts, asking them to look into their crystal globes.* What I have to offer you is, in the words of Montaigne, "A garland of other men's flowers, and nothing but the thread that binds it is my own."

Before we look into the future, it is important to look at the past, so here are some 'other men's flowers':

Pythagoras: For as long as man continues to be the ruthless destroyer of lower living beings, he will never know health or peace. For as long as men massacre animals they will kill each other. Indeed, he sows the seed of murder, and pain cannot reap joy and love.

Leonardo da Vinci: The time will come when men will look on the murder of animals as we now look on the murder of men.

Chief Seattle: There is no quiet place in the white man's cities. No place to hear the unfurling of leaves in spring, or the rustle of insects' wings. But perhaps it is because I am a savage and do not understand.

Count Leon Lippens, the Belgian conservationist: The destruction of a wilderness area is like demolishing Chartres Cathedral to grow potatoes on the site.

Sir Frank Fraser Darling: By the time the man-in-the-street fully understands the meaning of ecology it will probably be too late.

Aldo Leopold, American philosopher/conservationist: There is yet no ethic dealing with man's relation to land and to the animals and plants which grow upon it . . . . The land relation is still strictly economic, entailing privileges but not obligations. . . . Obligations have no meaning without conscience, and the problem we face is the extension of the social conscience from people to land . . . .

No important change in ethics was ever accomplished without an internal change in our intellectual emphasis, loyalties, affections and convictions. The proof that conservation has not yet touched these foundations of conflict lies in the fact that philosophy and religion have not yet heard of it. In our attempt to make conservation easy, we have made it trivial.

Finally, an anonymous flower: Greed will show quicker on a landscape than on a man's face—and so will kindness.

When we look into the future, it seems that we have two choices where wilderness is concerned. Dr. J. McNeely, in a recent paper formulating certain priorities arising out of the World Conservation Strategy, calls these two options 'Heaven Forbid' and 'The Golden Age'.

'Heaven Forbid' is doom-laden and utterly pessimistic. It suggests 'Wither World Wilderness' rather than 'Whither World Wilderness'. The paper on this option would be the shortest in the Congress and would read something like this: "Owing to lack of public support we regret that 2083 has been cancelled. Surviving in the nuclear wilderness will be the cockroach, the rat and the bureaucrat."

Most natural disasters—earthquakes, typhoons, hurricanes, droughts, famines, pestilence and floods—creep up on us and are unpredictable. I am a born optimist, and I believe that because the 'Heaven Forbid' option is predictable, it is also preventable . . . providing we have the determination and courage to do something positive about it. Perhaps the watchword of the 3rd World Wilderness Congress should be: *The predictable is preventable.*

Just as the predictable is preventable, it is also achievable, and I believe we can and must firmly grasp the 'Golden Age' option. Dr. McNeely describes it as follows:

In the 'Golden Age' option, everything will turn out well. The human population will stabilise, the best agricultural land will be used intensively,

146

with pests controlled by biological means and breeds constantly improved by genes from the wild. Marginal land currently being misused for transitory agriculture will revert to the wild, and allow wildlife populations to recover. We will develop alternative means of dealing with the functions of war, nature will be preserved in its pristine nature in natural parks, wild species will be conserved wherever they occur, and the urban-dweller will keep in touch with his wild heritage through travelling and television.

As I have looked into the future and how to achieve the 'Golden Age' option, I have been greatly helped by the experts I have consulted. What follows is a garland of these 'other men's flowers', with a few wild flowers of my own. I invite you now to project your imagination into the year 2083 . . . .

* * * * *

After much heart-trembling tribulation, and a series of perplexing and at times terrifying world crises, bringing humanity to the brink of the nuclear holocaust, people came to their senses and created the United States of the World.

I want you to imagine that my great grand-daughter, an eminent zoologist and adviser to the International Fund for Animal Welfare, has been asked to prepare background notes for the President of the USW's Keynote Speech at the 32nd World Wilderness Congress. This will be held during the first week of October 2083, at the Antarctic World Park Headquarters in Port Stanley in the formerly disputed Falklands/Malvinas Islands.

The Presidential brief will read like this:

Dear Madam President,

I am deeply touched that you should have chosen for your Keynote Speech at the 32nd World Wilderness Congress the title 'Whither World Wilderness 2183?' borrowed from my great grandfather's paper at the 3rd World Wilderness Congress held in Scotland exactly a hundred years ago. I remember him saying that in order to look into the future it is important to look at the past, and with this in mind I have prepared these background notes.

You will notice they are written on paper, which I have done deliberately to give you a 'feel' of the past. It was indeed a great day for wilderness when it was decided 60 years ago to give up using paper, and to use electronics for verbal communication. Although this saved millions of acres of trees, and paper is now used only for fine books and musical scores, it did not do very much to deter bureaucracy!

To provide a truly historical perspective, it is necessary to go back further than a hundred years, to 1871, when Congressman Clagett of Montana, USA, introduced his famous Park Bill which was adopted by 115 votes to 60, with 60 abstentions, in one of the most formidable and altruistic lobbying campaigns in US history. President Ulysses S. Grant signed the Bill on March 1st 1872. It read as follows:

That the tract of land in the territories of Montana and Wyoming, lying near the headwaters of the Yellowstone River is hereby reserved and withdrawn from settlement, occupancy or sale under the laws of the United States, and dedicated, set apart as a public park or pleasuring ground for the benefit and enjoyment of the people; and that all persons who shall locate or settle upon, or occupy the same or any part thereof, shall be considered trespassers and be removed therefrom.

Thus was created Yellowstone, the world's first National Park, and with it a growing awareness of people's basic need to commune with nature.

I would like to deal, now, with certain specific events nearer to us in time—events which, in spite of the human suffering involved, were to have a long-term beneficial effect on both humankind and wilderness.

Of all the great wilderness areas, the Antarctic was the most contentious, because of its potential mineral wealth. By 1990 what was then the USSR, with its slave satellites, had begun to get a taste of freedom under Olga Trotsky, the first Russian woman Premier. Her regime developed the freedom of the individual, the establishment of free enterprise, and a return to capitalism with free shares for all. Unfortunately this led to a series of World Power squabbles over the mineral spoils under the Antarctic ice, which nearly led to the outbreak of the Third World War and the horrors of the nuclear holocaust. In the nick of time, however, the world's leaders held an emergency summit meeting in Peking, and conceived the imaginative idea of setting up the United States of the World. Some of the world's most outstanding men and women were appointed as Governor of America (which absorbed Canada), of Europe (which absorbed Great Britain), of Latin America, and so on. Most appropriately Antarctica was declared a world National Park and peace reigned for some years.

The opening years of the 21st century were haunted by two explosive threats to peace, which hung like a sword of Damocles over the planet and suddenly fused in a horrifying way—the population explosion and the threat of the thermonuclear explosion.

The world population explosion became completely uncontrollable, leading to the Five Year Global Famine. The spectre of malnutrition, starvation, pestilence and death stalked both the industrial states as well as those formerly belonging to what was called the Third World. There were Famine Riots in all the state capitals, and skeletal Famine Marchers swarmed the rural areas in a desperate search for food. As the states began to revert to their old national status, the threat of nuclear war loomed again over the world. But, as has happened so often in the short history of the human race, outstanding men and women emerged from the survivors of the Famine, and common sense, goodwill and vision took control. The unthinkable was averted at the eleventh hour, and nuclear arms were destroyed and outlawed.

Gradually the population was brought under control. The two-children family became law, and the discovery of the male contraceptive pill resulted in a safe and reliable method of birth control. Inspired advocacy of its universal use was given by Her Holiness the Pope, who in her famous Papal Bull decreed that it was the duty of all Catholics to practise family planning.

The production of food was rationalised by strict controls and the prudent use of land. The dust bowls created before the Five Year Famine were returned to wise harvest, and the food resources of the sea were strictly controlled. Food was still in short supply, but nobody starved.

You will recall the experiments in utilisation of human protein. In those days of shortage it was compellingly argued that it was a profligate misuse of potential food to bury or cremate human remains. In spite of the skills of the food technologists and marketing experts, the repugnant idea never caught on. However, the universal revulsion it created was to have a very special effect on both people and wilderness. Slowly but surely people became vegetarians, with beneficial side effects on their health: the end of obesity, heart disease, etc. The billion dollar slimming industry was also ended. Years ago people had begun to find it distasteful in a still unequal world.

Will future generations' only experience of African elephants be through life-sized plastic replicas at Disneyland?

The greatest benefit to wilderness of the dietary revolution was that the large areas of land set aside for meat production were used more prudently. These included areas like the Amazon jungle where thousands of acres had been cleared to grow cattle for hamburgers, or like Botswana, where the semi-desert country was turned into real desert by over-grazing a gross population of introduced domestic cattle. The revolutionary change in people's diet also ended factory farming, which most people found unacceptable. So out of suffering came some good and positive long-term benefits. It was the beginning of 'reverence for life' and the end of our inhumanity to our fellow animals. It also marked the end of bloodsports—the killing of animals for so-called pleasure.

During the past hundred years a number of animals have gone the way of the dodo. It has been nothing like the numbers so gloomily predicted in the 1980s, but today we mourn the passing, forever, of the grizzly and polar bears, the tiger, the giant panda (ironically the symbol of the World Wildlife Fund) and the bald eagle (proud symbol of the old United States). On the credit side, many hundreds of new plant and bird species have been discovered.

The African elephant populations were seriously depleted, especially during the Global Famine. In some of the popular African parks they are augmented by realistic plastic and micro-circuitry replicas produced and maintained by the Disneyland organisation.

For many years nutritional scientists had pointed out that the world's population could be fed on soya beans grown in an area the size of Ohio (one of the old states of the USA). A revival of this idea triggered off what became one of the biggest and most challenging engineering projects of the 21st century. The World Corps of Engineers pointed out that Australia was the world's biggest island, but was surrounded by salt water. The challenge was how to make it into the vegetable garden of the world. A chain of nuclear-powered desalination plants was built around the whole coastline, creating a series of lakes, some as big as France. The desert bloomed, and an abundance of cereals, vegetables and fruits was made available. New wilderness areas were also created for people's delight and inspiration. The engineers then began an even more daunting and gigantic civil engineering project—to tackle the problem of water supplies which had been seriously depleted by over-population. The river systems of Canada and the former United States of America were diverted into different paths so they did not reach the sea for thousands of miles. Great care, however, was taken also to ensure a flow of water along the old river beds, so that the ecosystems of estuaries and other wetland areas were undisturbed. The success of this scheme resulted in similar engineering projects in the States of Europe, Africa and elsewhere, which provided water for human consumption, irrigation and hydro-electric power. Water was even piped from the State of Europe to desert areas in what used to be called the Middle East.

The Golden Age began. With it came a return to spiritual values, the unity of the Christian Church and the disbanding of missionaries, and the free worship of all religions. With this Age of Awareness and Enlightenment the four freedoms (first declared in the dark days of the Second World War by President Roosevelt and Winston Churchill) became world law:

Freedom from Fear
Freedom from Want
Freedom of Speech
Freedom to Worship

Ironically, one of the human problems which remained to be solved was created by the use of robots and microcomputers, which led to the one-day working week. The problem was the rational and enlightened use of leisure, and it became the main subject in the school curriculum. One of the many uses of leisure is to be found in wandering among the wonders of wilderness, pursuing a recreation which is more of a re-creation. Our forebears fought to preserve the wilderness, and today we carry the torch they passed on to us. In the wilderness, when we think about them, we might say, "If you seek their monument, look around you."

Madam President, these are a few background notes for your speech. To end it may I suggest that you reiterate my great grandfather's words at that other Congress, a hundred years ago:

THE PREDICTABLE IS PREVENTABLE... OR ACHIEVABLE.

* I would like to thank Sir Peter Scott, Sir Peter Kent FRS, Thor Heyerdahl, Professor Peter Jewell and Dr. Keith Eltringham of Cambridge University, Sir Vivian Fuchs FRS, Gerald O. Barney, eminent American researcher on world problems, Dr. J.G. Mosley, Director of the Australian Conservation Foundation, Mark Halle and Dr. Thomas E. Lovejoy of the World Wildlife Fund, Eddie Brewer, Director Wildlife Conservation, The Gambia, and Major Ian Grimwood, winner of the Third J. Paul Getty Prize for Wildlife Conservation.

Wilderness and the Search for the Soul of Modern Man

C.A. Meier

Wilderness is nature in her original condition, undisturbed and unadulterated by human beings. Does that mean Paradise? Ever since the original sin, Paradise has been forbidden to us, but, according to Jewish tradition, God has relocated Paradise to the end of time—which makes it eschatological, a utopia, goal or *apokatastasis tōn pantōn* (re-establishment of everything). The implication in this is that Paradise—and wilderness—was originally in order, and that human interference has created disorder. How has this come about? Here we are confronted with the age-old problem of the opposites—nature/culture; matter/spirit; evil/good—with humanity placed right between them and having to cope with the tension between them.

In Genesis we are told to make use of everything present and to multiply. We have certainly done so, even to the extent of creating the atom bomb and the population explosion. We have abominably abused the liberty given to us, to the point where we may soon extinguish ourselves by behaving as if we ourselves were the Creator. We are suffering from hubris to an extent that cannot go unpunished.

On the other hand, in humble obedience to that original commandment, we have only made use of the laws of nature, exploring, for instance, physics, chemistry and biology as best we could according to our limitations. Where then is the mistake or sin? My humble answer, arising from fifty years' experience with disordered human beings, is that we have become intoxicated with all the frantic 'progress' in the outer world, we have become lopsidedly extraverted and have forgotten our soul. Lost in the outer, we are estranged from our soul and our own inner nature.

But we have paid for it. Neurosis has become the plague of our days, the penalty for our hubris. Interfering too drastically with 'nature without' of necessity creates disorder of the inner nature, for the two are intimately connected.

To understand this, we need to look briefly at the history of some of the ideas which have preceded today's concept of wilderness preservation, and to delve into the essence of philosophy, psychology and medicine. The connection between 'nature without' and our inner nature has long been part of our philosophical tradition. According to the presocratic Greek philosophers, the universe was one big organism with its many organs functioning in perfect Harmony. Humankind was only one of these organs. For Parmenides, the universe consisted of two components, love and hatred, attraction and repulsion, which cyclically changed from one to the other in due course of time. This view tacitly presupposed the existence of what was later called *sympatheia tōn holōn* ('sympathy of all' or what has been called 'holism') and the inter-relatedness of all things in the cosmos, an idea which found its fundamental place in the philosophy of Poseidonius.

This philosophy, in which humanity is peacefully contained in something very much bigger than ourselves, prevailed for many centuries and focused principally on the relationship between the macrocosm and the microcosm. The human being was conceived of as a small cosmos, containing everything in the world right up to the stars—for indeed, if this was not so, how could we ever understand anything out there? Epistemologically, Plotinus taught that our perception is only possible through Sympathy between Subject and Object; while Sextus Empiricus said that perception, cognition and understanding are possible only through an outflowing of the macrocosm into the microcosm (us). Porphyrius taught that the soul, when it encounters the visible, recognises herself in it, as she carries everything within herself and the All of things is nothing else than the soul.

Another aspect of the relationship between the macrocosm and the microcosm which brings us closer to modern psychological problems is the thorny question of the relation between the psyche and the soma, Psyche and Physis, Soul and Body, which to my mind inevitably leads us to the religious question.

Since Poseidonius the macrocosm and the microcosm have never been conceived of as a pair of opposites, but rather as complementary

aspects related by the aforementioned Sympathy. Poseidonius himself saw this relationship including the macrocosm within the human being; while for Iamblichus it was precisely this relationship which justified the operation of the priest:

In all theurgical operations the priest sustains a twofold character; one, indeed, as man, and which preserves the order possessed by our nature in the universe; but the other, which is corroborated by divine signs, and through these is conjoined to more excellent natures and is elevated to their order by an elegant circumduction, this is deservedly capable of being surrounded with the external form of the Gods. Conformably, therefore, to a difference of this kind, the priest very properly invokes, as more excellent natures, the powers derived from the universe, so far as he who invokes is a man; and again, he commands these powers, because through arcane symbols, he, in a certain respect, is invested with the sacred form of the Gods. *

The priest therefore brings the macrocosm (divine actions) down into us, the microcosm. However, in working with this idea we have to be careful not to become inflated and so lose awe and respect for the macrocosm, or nature.

The relationship between the macrocosm and the microcosm became a fundamental notion of Renaissance philosophy. In it the microcosm was seen as the mirror of the macrocosm, to the extent that the perspective was even inverted: the world became a *makranthropos*, or *megas anthropos*, and the human being was therefore a concentrate

154

of everything of importance in the cosmos. This idea increased the danger of self-inflation. Pico encapsulated it thus: "For if man is a small world, then the world is a big man." John Scotus Eriugena (ca. 820) said something similar: "Man is the inclusion (or end) of all, since everything is in him enclosed." And according to the Swiss Paracelsus: "Everything was created in One; macrocosm and man are one." This basic conviction probably accounts for his worldwide success as a medical man, for he always tried to bring about harmony between the macrocosm and the microcosm, the loss of which, according to him, accounted for his patients' sickness.

With the Renaissance came the dawn of the natural sciences, and as we focused more and more on exploring the external world, the harmony and balance between the microcosm and macrocosm began to suffer. In our attempt to discover more about the external objects in our world, we began to analyse and dissect them, sometimes, if they happened to be living creatures, even killing them as a result. As the natural sciences developed, respect for nature as a whole disappeared and we lost our original fear of her. We no longer brought sacrifices to her, and began to see ourselves as dominating her, to the extent that today our knowledge of the laws of nature has led us to the construction of the A-bomb, and to a domination of nature that is in many ways destructive.

But this has not been without effect on our inner nature (microcosm), for in the process we have lost something valuable, healthy and sane, and the price we pay for it is anxiety neurosis. The dangerous aspects of nature which kept our forebears watchful and humble, and which have now almost disappeared, have turned inward, and the whole of Western society is rapidly approaching a physical and mental cracking point as a result of the dangers within.

This is a very serious matter, for if 'wilderness without' disappears completely, it will inevitably resurrect powerfully within, whereupon it will immediately become projected, enemies will be created and so forth. Its terrifying aspects will take revenge for our neglect, lack of reverence and ruthless interference with its beautiful order. For wilderness is by no means chaos: it is most admirably ordered and organised, quietly obeying the laws of nature. As long as it is not interfered with too badly, it functions beautifully.

Ostanes, a famous Persian-Egyptian alchemist authority said in the 4th century BC: "Nature enjoys nature; nature vanquishes nature; nature rules nature." There is a depth of meaning in these few lines, for if we let nature be as she is, she will enjoy herself like a virgin; and so she will always be victorious and self-regulated; and she will religiously obey her own rules.

Modern terminology calls this Cybernetics, meaning self-regulating. But what if nature is no longer left to regulate herself, if she is too badly wounded and interfered with to be able to recover? The repercussions of this sacrilege in the psyche of a single human being are unpredictable, but one thing is certain: as a result of this unrelenting process of destruction, we are in great danger of losing our humanity.

One of the basic laws of physics is that action = reaction. If we interfere with 'wilderness without', something will inevitably happen to us as a reaction, ie, to 'wilderness within', or vice versa. And if we damage 'wilderness without' too badly, 'wilderness within' would really go 'wild'.

This is because there is a dichotomy in human beings: on the one hand we are an intrinsic part of nature, and on the other hand there is something different in us which seeks to understand the One. We have to learn to live with both aspects of ourselves and to cope with the tension between them, respecting the subtle balance. For centuries Christianity has emphasised that a mature person should be freed completely of his or her carnal being. But such a person turns sour, for, like 'nature without', our inner nature also does not tolerate too much interference such as repression, askesis and so forth. In order to remain sane we have to keep the balance as best we can.

How is this to be practised? I am a psychologist, and so am not able to give technical advice on matters of conservation, but I can intimate how psychology may help. First, we have to admit frankly that in spite

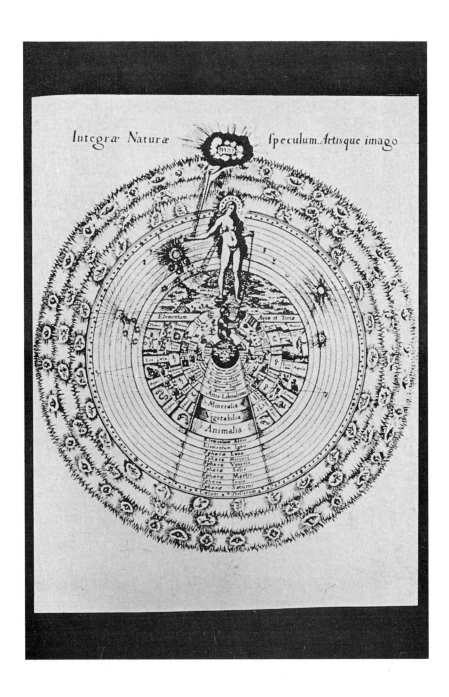

of our Culture we are still mammals, ie, *natural* beings. Culture tends to forget this aspect of ourselves and its archaeological and prehistoric existence in our unconscious psyche. However, everything of which we are unconscious in ourselves is automatically projected. To illustrate this we have only to think of our primitive fear of creatures like spiders, mice, snakes or tigers, most of which are perfectly harmless if unmolested.

The powers in the unconscious are so overwhelming that we tend to project them as far away as possible. An example of this is the way in which people today are increasingly turning to secular astrology, projecting their fate on to the stars in this time of growing insecurity on the planet. Scientifically it is inconceivable that specific stars could have extremely personal effects on the lives of Tom, Dick or Harry. But when we look at this from a psychological perspective, a different picture emerges.

We have created constellations out of purely statistically distributed single stars, endowing them with mythological names, such as Andromeda or Orion, and populating the sky with a vast collection of gods and myths. These images are archetypal, which means they correspond to certain pre-existing images and processes in our collective unconscious which we simply project on to the stars. This is not altogether harmless, since projection is a psychological action which consequently has its *re*action on us. In this way the archetypal images represented by these benevolent or malevolent stars or constellations affect our behaviour, however unconscious we may be of them, and thus they constitute our 'fate'. If we remain unconscious enough of them, the archetypes go to work and the boomerang of projection hits back.

Archetypes are frighteningly contagious, as can be seen in many mass movements in history—for instance, the Huns, Vandals, Turks, the French Revolution, Napoleonism, Hitler and the Kremlin. Identifying with an archetype can produce the megalomania that you are the ruler of the world and something close to God Almighty.

The archetypes are within us, and some of them represent the *chthonic* part of our soul, by which we are linked to this Earth, nature and wilderness. We are fascinated as well as afraid of these archetypal components of nature, and seek to know more about them. We climb mountains, and explore the dangerous and hostile areas of Earth—the Arctic and Antarctic with their icy coldness and darkness, the desert with its heat and dryness, the impenetrable jungle, the sea with its frightening storms and unfathomable dark depths. But these areas can all also be found in the depths of our own unconscious, and the tragedy is that with all our increasing knowledge and domination of 'wilderness without', we still cannot tranquillise the inner wilderness.

Some years ago I heard from Richard Wilhelm the story of the rain-maker of Kiao Chow, an event which he personally witnessed and which beautifully illustrates both the establishment of a harmony between the macrocosm and the microcosm, and also the way in which we, the microcosm, are capable of contributing to this harmony.

Wilhelm lived in a district in China which was experiencing a terrific drought and was threatened with famine. The local rain-makers tried to produce rain, but to no avail, so finally they sent for China's most famous rain-maker, who lived far away in Kiao Chow. When he came, he asked only to be left by himself in a lonely place in the wilderness, with one person visiting him daily to bring him his meals.

After a few days without rain the local people became impatient and sent a delegation to ask him why there was no success, but he simply sent them away. The next day it started snowing (in mid-summer!) and then the snow turned into pouring rain. When he came back to the village, people asked him why it had taken him so long. He declared: "When I came to this district I immediately realised that it was frighteningly out of Tao, whereby, being here myself, I was naturally also out of Tao. All I could do therefore was to retire into the wilderness (nature) and meditate, so as to get myself back into Tao. But I can tell you it needed hard work."

With that he returned to Kiao Chow, happy as a lark.

This whole event may of course be dismissed as sheer coincidence, as such outer events described may happen in full accord with the laws of nature once in a blue moon. But from a purely meteorological perspective, snow in mid-summer is highly improbable.

Psychologically, the event can be seen as follows: the magician comes to a place which is physically out of order and thereby becomes out of order himself (being contaminated, introjecting, taking the macrocosm into the microcosm), so that he becomes part of sick nature. He then makes an effort to put himself in order (Tao) again, which is hard work, but eventually he is successful, nature herself is healed and it rains, ie, the boomerang hits the target.

To sum up, psychology sees us as metaphorically living in the upper floor (consciousness) of a house which is supported by the lower floor and eventually by its foundations, the cellar. The lower floor and cellar represent the unconscious, the Earth, Mother Nature and, when in its original condition, the virgin nature with which we live in a sort of *participation mystique*, and it is here that the archetypes live.

The archetypes or Instincts are the psychological aspects of the biological facts, the patterns of behaviour by which we live and are lived. Inasmuch as we are unconscious of them, they are projected and experienced as if they were in the macrocosm. Although this part of the psyche strictly belongs to us, the subject or microcosm, we experience it in the form of outside objects, creating, for example, werewolves, weird places filled with demons, wells populated by nymphs or djinns, and so forth. In other words, our soul is divided up into many partial 'souls' or fragments. In this sense, wilderness is really the original biotope of the soul.

With the development of consciousness in our Western civilisation, these fragments are slowly integrated. But it is important to remember that a total integration—or what Jung called Individuation—is a vain desideratum, for the unconscious is as inexhaustible as nature. This is our 'wilderness within'.

The correlation of the microcosm and the macrocosm is itself the best justification for wilderness preservation. In order to remain sane and healthy we need to preserve the balance and harmony between the two, and it is ever so much better to preserve 'wilderness without' than to negate 'wilderness within', which inevitably means that it goes rampant and becomes projected on our fellow beings, friend or foe. Apart from analysis, I know of nothing better for the maintenance of harmony than to keep 'wilderness without' alive and unspoiled. Those of you therefore who are working for the preservation of wilderness are not only acting idealistically or ideologically, but are also making a vital and substantial contribution towards the health of humanity globally.

* *Iamblichus,* On the Mysteries of the Egyptians, Chaldeans and Assyrians, *ed. Thomas Taylor,* London 1895.

Seekers, Eye-Jugglers and Seers: Ways of Viewing Wilderness

William Pitt Root

What I want to address in terms of the concept of my talk are items that involve some of the crucial differences between being an observer and a witness. There is no such thing as a poet who is an observer. People who are called poets are often observers, but in the act of committing true poetry they are witnesses—as many of us are. The witnessing of a poet happens to come out in words which other people sometimes hear or read. The witness is the committed observer—the one who will stand up and say not merely "I have seen" as in a court of law, but "I have been moved", as in the courts of heaven.

The American poet Robert Frost once remarked that the education of a poet is quite unlike that of a scholar. He said scholars can more or less follow a set path, whereas poets abhor guided tours, preferring rather to walk out into the fields and forests, wandering as their minds wander, and it is only upon returning home that they must bend to the task of plucking burrs from their trouser cuffs or skirt hems. It is these burrs, said Frost, which constitute the poet's education—the things that stick to them as they pass through life. Thoreau once said he had travelled widely at Walden Pond. In these past few days I have travelled widely too, by listening both to formal talks and informal conversations, and in doing so I have gathered up many burrs.

So I am largely going to abandon the notes I have made up for an orderly and progressive talk in order to address some of these burrs. Burrs, of course, are seeds designed to adhere fiercely and to germinate once conditions are correct for them. Occasionally the conditions for germination are extraordinary, apparently inhospitable, rude even. For instance, a forester from Montana and I were speaking earlier about some of the conditions necessary for a certain kind of pine forest to regenerate itself and how public abhorrence of forest fires had, in fact, retarded the growth of certain forests which require burning to rejuvenate. The poet Gary Snyder notes that there is an alternative: if that particular species of pine cone is eaten and passed through the guts of a bear, that process also will germinate the seed. Process, any process, is complex.

A contemporary American poet, William Stafford, who is something of a sage, once wrote: "Purify the pond and the lilies die." A pond is a pond is a pond, but here it is the natural world as well. Nor does the natural world stay out-of-doors in some abstract external wilderness. The head of pediatric surgery in Galveston, Texas, once told me how, in the old days of the open-air operating theatre, post-operative infections were virtually unheard of. However, once the inevitable 'improvements' were made—overhead vents sealed and rooms constantly sterilised by chemicals and so on—infection rates rose dramatically and the dread staph infection appeared, which occurs only under hyper-sterile conditions and is so difficult to cure. Purify the pond and not only will the lilies die but those who appreciate the lilies may be afflicted too. One knows from the Old Testament, if not from the barnyard itself, where lilies spring from most ardently: it is the dungheap. And not only poets and farmers, but scholars as well are drawn to consider such matters. The coprolite, which is fossilised dung, is among the most informative and ancient of texts. There are periods of prehistoric time which, in certain regions, are otherwise wholly lost to us, except for the evidence contained by the coprolite. From its contents can be deduced an entire spectrum of botanical and biological species. When we read the best texts well, we are inevitably reading parables, of course. And the lesson of dung and the lily is an invaluable one.

Poetry, like wilderness itself, never arises out of hyper-sterile conditions. And neither poetry nor wilderness can be defended out of such a perspective. In matters of this sort, matters of values, the equivalent of hyper-sterile conditions is objectivity—objectivity purged of subjective elements; testimony distilled, cleansed and purified of non-quantifiable elements until it is rendered up as facts which are turned into numbers which are fed by specialists into computers where they are further rendered into realms more ethereal and insubstantial than any poet would ever dare to dream. This process is usually defended as one that liberates debate from the confusion of conflicting values and unreasonable passions. But human debate has always been intended to resolve such conflicts and has always been conducted with passion as one of its touchstones of sincerity. The result of such objectivity is not so much to remove the touchy element of values as it is to remove it to a level reserved for specialists. These specialists are most often technocrats in the service of special interests wealthy enough to hire them, influential enough to wield them like the new Class weapons which they are. And we, the people, are in effect excluded from the fray before it has even begun. It is not, in fact, a situation where subjective values have been removed—only the subjective values of unaffiliated individuals. Which is to say most of us.

Objectivity has its role, but it should be a limited one. If we see politics as an arena which we should concede to objectivity and to facts-and-figures thinking, we are, in the long run, conceding our purposes as conservators of wilderness and wilderness ways. Because, objectively speaking, the governments, corporations, developers and merchandisers have the goods on us. The statistics we can muster are often no more than scraps from their big tables; more importantly, they should be relegated to the secondary position they most properly occupy in the world-wide wilderness crisis. Our concerns are not dollars-and-cents matters, they are matters of values, of passion and spirit.

Poetry does not have a notoriously successful role in politics, in spite of the fact that poets have been called 'the unacknowledged legislators of the race'. Many treaties with Native Americans in the USA were signed with the coda that such-and-such conditions 'shall be so as long as the sun does shine and as long as the grass does grow'—a poetic way of saying 'forever'. Poetic and optimistic, as it turns out. Someone once figured out that the average life of these treaties was eleven years. Often that was long enough, because by then the Indians involved had been weakened to the point of not being able effectively to resist the swelling population of Whites. Rarely if ever are treaties with indigenous peoples anywhere broken to the advantage of those peoples. Nor is it just in the US or only in the past that the clashes between aboriginal peoples and our own civilisation result in such tragically wasteful violations. Nor can we rest secure that the trajectory of our civilised behaviour toward indigenous peoples is safely contained in history books, from which we may learn our old errors. In Tasmania, for instance, where *physical* natural resources have burgeoning support, the *human* natural resources, the aborigines, are sorely neglected; indeed, the official policies toward them are still based primarily upon the demonstrable absurdity that the last aborigine in Tasmania died in 1876, hence there cannot possibly be a 'problem' with them.

Bureaucratic thought and language, like air and water pollution, seem to fall inevitably as shadows from all our institutions of progress. I am not against progress but, as an artist whose primary natural resources are language and spirit, I am inevitably aware that certain kinds of progress are, as E.E. Cummings has said, 'a comfortable disease'. In some cultures the terms 'poet' and 'prophet' are interchangeable, which I find instructive. One task of a poet is simultaneously to regard the past and the future, bringing them to bear as a vision of the present. This requires not only vast amounts of information but considerable intuition, for deciphering and shaping. Through intellect we may know things and the principles of things, but it is through instinct that we apprehend the spirit of things, especially in relation to ourselves, our spirits. William Butler Yeats says poems must be dug from 'the rag-and-bone shop of the heart'. By 'heart' he means the repository of our own and our race's history. Or, if you will make the jump with me, the dungheap of the past and the instinctual drives that govern our conscious lives.

The heart is our inner wilderness—our most fundamental raw material, our dungheap and our chief source of psychic 'burrs'. And it is liable to the identical processes of redefinition, manipulation and exploitation that threaten our outer wilderness: the forests, deserts, plains, mountains and jungles we all understand must be preserved. Our struggle to preserve the natural geographical wilderness corresponds to, and *must be seen* to correspond to, a need to preserve those elements of ourselves which respond to the wilderness just as vegetation responds to rain. A part of these concerns must be an actively compassionate regard for indigenous peoples everywhere, for they are the fuller incarnation of those very aspects of ourselves we are here to protect. The fate we have come to over centuries they must confront in short decades, and they must do so for the most part without the benefit of material and philosophical cushions.

'The rag-and-bone shop of the heart' is not a lovely image. It implies the damage of wounds and the dailiness of commerce. Our Earth and its inhabitants are wounded and scarred, and the wounds are many and deep. Few poets now are recognisable as descendants of those 'blithe spirits' of the past. Few are easily made happy by the world they find around themselves these days, though fewer still would ever concede that joy is not the natural condition of the human spirit. And when I say 'poet' I mean not simply my fellow practitioners of that art but the poet and lover of wilderness in each of us.

Now whether we look back to the Greeks, to Oedipus the King, who had to know the truth before he could become the master of his tragic fate as the blind seer; or to Freud, Jung or Laing, all of whom counsel us to return to our wounds, our traumas, in dreams and memories coded and dramatised for us by our blind obsessions and neuroses or our plain flatout foolishness; or to Jesus who said over and over that to enter the Kingdom of Heaven one must become as a child again; or to the Stone Age people of the South Seas who heal some maladies of the spirit by literally re-enacting birth—always the message is clear and consistent: truly to go forward, we may first have to go back.

As it is with the individual, so it may be with the culture. Our modern world, the Western European world in particular, is a tower of Babel, the United States even more so than Europe since we rest on European shoulders for the most part. But Europe too stands on yet older, firmer shoulders—not only of Rome and Athens but of Egypt and Mesopotamia, cultures which stand in turn on even older and firmer shoulders which recede into prehistoric times we can only barely grasp in the dim light of our excavations. We are imperilled by our hubris which supposes us to be somehow the fruit which may prosper without roots. Or, to return to the Babel metaphor, we are trying to build our 99th floor without fully acknowledging our foundation—the Earth itself upon which the entire enterprise must finally rest.

I am speaking not only of wilderness the place, but of wilderness the way. Hand in hand with preservation of the place must be preservation of the ways in which it has been lived in, naturally—for virtually all wilderness areas have been lived in. Those ways are best known by the dwindling aboriginal cultures themselves. Only a sorry second-best is to be discovered by the too-specialised scientists, praiseworthy as many of them may be; indeed, the best of them are the first to admit such a sentiment. Holistic interdisciplinary practices are entirely to be applauded and everywhere encouraged so long as they are responsibly exercised, but not even they can begin to restore the context of reverence in which the artefacts and folkways they discover are so firmly mounted. We must show reverence to the elders of our species, many of whom still share this Earth with us and do so all too often in positions that are powerless and despised.

Just what is it that these aborigines have to offer us, and how is it relevant or even important to 20th century people? One of the things it has to do with is the essential nature of human beings, specifically in relation to our seemingly inevitable belligerence toward one another. From our recent history, we derive our fatalistic tendencies to despair not only of our future but also of our past, projecting onto our ancient forebears an image in keeping with our notion of ourselves as basically

savage and brutal. Just how unfortunate this travesty of the human image is we may begin to glean from examining a few of the extant groups, until recently uncontaminated—culturally speaking—by our own ways. The Eskimo people, for instance, had neither a word nor a concept for 'war' until we gave them ours. Contrary to the dramatic contentions of Robert Ardrey, who tried to prove that humankind is descended from a killer-ape of sorts, we find over and over again, especially in the past ten or twenty years, group after isolated group of people still living as pre-Iron Age, even Stone Age peoples, in places like the Kalahari desert or the Malaysian islands, who demonstrate incontrovertibly that early people lived (and in some cases still do live) in elemental harmony with the world, preferring peaceful ways when possible. The so-called 'dream people' of Borneo lived amongst their hostile neighbours (popularised as the 'head-hunters of Borneo') not only without warfare but virtually without crime—two conditions that no modern culture could ever boast of. According to one anthropologist who lived among them and studied them, they are the most emotionally mature people on Earth today. And the 'gentle Tassady', as they are called, survived in total harmony with their environment for countless millennia, enjoying the company of any creature who chose to consort with them in their village until the trader who discovered them introduced them to cooked flesh, ending in one hour the balance there which had begun before the first stone was carved for the first pyramid. As such a simple instance shows, these people and their ways are an endangered species, too. Yet, without knowledge of and full respect for their authentic cultural genius, we will soon join them in extinction—first spiritual extinction, then physical extinction which, by then, may not be much resisted. That degradation has, in fact, begun for us. It is what we are here to resist.

I do not wish to fall into the trap of over-romanticising early people. The myth of the 'noble savage' is fallacious when made into an article of general faith and is no less misleading than the image of the club-wielding brutal Neanderthal man. Some human strains have treated their environment unwisely and have paid the price of extinction. The Anasazi of Arizona, for instance, vanished over a thousand years ago, leaving, in the form of old garbage pits, evidence that they began by eating all the big animals on what were then plains. They decimated species after species, their prey growing smaller and smaller in successive layers of their dumps until at last they were eating desert rats and finally disappeared. Modern humans have no exclusive option on environmental folly. But what we do have that the Anasazi, for instance, did not have...is the example of the Anasazi.

Some of what I say may seem simplistic, but I prefer to argue that it is elemental. Two stones sitting on the desert may at first glance resemble one another. But if you kick one it flies off, and if you kick the other you stub your toes ferociously, because it is the tip of a buried mountain. The elemental is that in the human spirit which most resists change. It is that complex of aesthetic, moral and religious impulses all of which are profoundly rooted in the same dungheap fertilising the surface of our one and only Earth. To value what is universally precious in ourselves, we must recognise and take heart from our antecedents, our aboriginal brethren. They are our oldest surviving family. To destroy them or to let them be destroyed is to let our deepest taproots be hacked off.

I am going to read to you from a document unlike most documents we know, and yet the very qualities which distinguish it from the documents we know typify it as coming from the race which gave it to us. This comes from Chief Seattle, in 1854, in response to an offer to give reservation land in exchange for the land of Chief Seattle's people. I will read the beginning of this speech twice, first omitting some words, then including them. He opens saying, "Every part of this earth is sacred. Every shining pine needle, every sandy shore, every mist in the dark woods, every clearing and humming insect is holy." This is beautiful, and yet it is still incomplete. When we read it whole, as it was written, we see what else is required: "Every part of this earth is sacred *to my people*. Every pine needle, every sandy shore, every mist in the dark woods, every clearing and humming insect is holy *in the memory and experience of my people*." As a culture, we cannot yet add those key phrases which make the vision whole and give it its wonderful authority.

Chief Seattle ends his speech with these remarks, which are the conditions upon which he concedes that native ground to the Whites: "You must teach your children that the ground beneath their feet is the ashes of your grandfathers. So that they will respect the land, tell your children that the earth is rich with the lives of our kin." He talks then about Whites perishing, and he says, "Finally the destiny of the White man who has come to dominate us is a mystery to us, for we do not understand when the buffalo are all slaughtered, the wild horses are tamed, the secret corners of the forest heavy with the scent of many men, and the view of the ripe hills blotted by talking wires. Where is the thicket? Gone. Where is the eagle? Gone. The end of living and the beginning of survival."

Chief Seattle was a seer, a man who looked past the faces of people and the glittering appearances of our proud culture and looked hard and deep into their hearts instead. His view of the wilderness was not our view, but the view we aspire to. "Whatever befalls the earth," he said, "befalls the sons of the earth. Man did not weave the web of life: he is merely a strand in it. Whatever he does to the web, he does to himself." Surely what we are here for is the attempt to reverse this process foreseen over 130 years ago with such terrifying clarity not only in its details but in its consequences—the end of living and the beginning of survival. That is an irreducible kind of poetry because it is forged of passion and image as well as idea. The visions of the seers on our Earth—be they ancient Hebrew or modern Englishman transplanted to London from Missouri, be they Native American or new American with the vision of a Democratic Vista, be they Kalahari Bushman or contemporary Ugandan or Sudanese or Greek—have an awful and remarkable consistency in what they see and what they say.

What they say is that the universe and everything in it is alive and responsive, and nowhere are there objects devoid of life. Even Pythagoras, who approached poetry by means of mathematics, declared, "Astonishing! Everything is intelligent!" The French poet Gerard De Nerval wrote:

Free thinker! Do you suppose you are the only thinker
on this earth where life blazes inside all things?
Your liberty does what it wishes with the powers it controls
but when you gather to plan, the universe is not there.

Look carefully in an animal at a spirit alive;
every flower is a soul opening out into nature;
a mystery approaching love is asleep inside metal....

The great German poet Rilke, writing about the mineral gold, says:

The ore feels homesick. It wants to abandon
the minting houses and the wheels
that offer such a meagre life.
And out of factories and payroll boxes
it wants to go back into the veins
of the thrown-open mountain,
which will close again behind it.

Over and over the seer-poets from all ages and places who look simultaneously into the inner and outer wilderness show us that it is the wilderness which is wise and incorporates balance, and people who are foolish and who suffer when they fail to follow that model in wilderness which they may always return to and be restored by, if they are willing to be made wise and whole again. And I mean the mountains and deserts of the spirit as well as those of the earth, for they correspond to one another with an immaculate and universal delicacy. Sir Thomas Browne wrote, "We carry with us the wonders we seek without us: there is all Africa and her prodigies in us." But without a real Africa outside us, we would lose the means of portraying, by metaphor, what is within. And humankind, without metaphor or image, without an outer wilderness to provoke and stir and order what is within, would soon bear less resemblance to us than we bear to the Bushmen, as seen through Bushmen eyes.

Not all people and not all poets are seers. This has been the case in the past as well as the present, as attested to by the prevalence among many cultures of the tales of the eye-juggler. Among the Kalahari Bushmen, for instance, the baboon is cast into this role and is said to like to take out its eyes, the primary organ of consciousness, and play with them. In similar legends in North America an Indian will be playing with his eye—not in a frivolous but in a sacred manner—when he is seen by a stranger, often a White man in later versions of the story. The White man will of course want to do it too. But he ignores the warnings involved—namely that the eye, held high in the hand, should only be used to look in the four sacred directions—and lo and behold, he finds he cannot fit his eye back into his head. He is lost.

Eye-jugglers are addicted conceptualisers who abstract ideas from the world and then play with them, becoming addicted to them to such an extent that to exert the power that concepts make possible they cannot return to their hearts. They cannot get their eyes back into their heads, and so play with ideas blindly. They look through ideas instead of through their eyes. Here is an example of a poem by such a one, from *An Essay on Man* by Alexander Pope:

Lo, the poor Indian! whose untutor'd mind
Sees God in clouds, or hears him in the wind;
His soul, proud Science never taught to stray
Far as the solar walk, or milky way....
To be, contents his natural desire,
He asks no angel's wing, no seraph's fire;
But thinks, admitted to that equal sky,
His faithful dog shall bear him company.

The American writer James Fenimore Cooper, one of the first hero-isers of the Native American, is another such one. Cooper probably makes more mistakes in his books about the natural world than any other writer has ever made in as many pages. For instance, at one point he has his character tracking someone who goes into a stream to conceal his tracks. So what does our vexed tracker do? He diverts the stream from its bed and doggedly pursues his hapless quarry! Cooper's books are riddled with such instances, mercilessly pointed out by Mark Twain in an hilarious essay. Many of the fallacies are of this sort, in which an idea or concept becomes so remote from its origin that the thinker imagines the thing itself is susceptible to the same manipulations as the concept is. That is eye-juggling. These are amusing instances, but the same dynamic enforms George Orwell's Newspeak and the mischief of politicians who persist in discussing such matters as limited nuclear warfare. It is the eye-juggler who estimates the value of a forest or a park in terms of board-feet or the number of tourist

171

Southwest desert (USA) with native inhabitant at work
Tribal people throughout the world are a precious and important part of wilderness and society

contact-hours. Eye-jugglers do have visions of a sort. Unlike seers, their visions are abstract and objective and their purpose is commonly to exploit.

To have real vision you must be able to see; ironically, to see you have to stop looking. The distinction is that when you look you have some kind of intention in mind. You look for or you look at, always maintaining a distinct distance between yourself and what you observe. This is where the third way of viewing comes in, the way of the seeker. When you seek, you are looking *for*. You look at something with the idea of discovering something else by means of it. You look at a tree and say, "That's about 200 board-feet," or "That's as pretty as a picture," or "It looks like a dancer in the wind." In each instance the viewer, in seeking, is superimposing over the tree some projected image or idea, manipulating the reality rather than comprehending it. We here might bristle at seeing a tree in terms of board-feet, but what about as a dancer? Yet once that kind of manipulation has begun, no matter now harmless the original impulse, the process has a way of feeding into further, less harmless categories of manipulation or exploitation.

An example of this is the set of mind which developed during the Renaissance and which viewed wilderness as something raw, something to be improved upon, something to be turned into, for instance, gardens—such as the great gardens of England and France. The belief behind the impulse to transform wilderness into a garden is benign enough. The great gardens of the world were often modelled upon ideas of how the cosmos is formed, a cosmic geometry. But a garden is a manipulated landscape over which we exercise the ultimate shaping and moulding power, which, if you really love wilderness, is a disfiguring power. The extent to which this notion has hold of our imaginations is shown by the term we use to describe great wilderness tracts in America. We call them parks, which suggests they are domesticated and tamed and made suitable for human use. A wilderness park is an oxymoron, a contradiction not only in terms but in values.

Another example—a kind of metaphor or parable—of this set of mind is that of Claude's mirror. Claude was a popular Renaissance painter of idealised landscapes. The elements which formed a taste for a novelty such as Claude's mirror played an important part in the education of the aristocracy which would imprint not only the Renaissance era but also much of subsequent Western European culture.

During the Renaissance the classic works of Virgil, Ovid and other Latin poets had been 'rediscovered' and formed the core of the curriculum for young gentlemen from England, France and so on who went to study in Rome. The bucolic or pastoral element in these works was strong and influential, but the landscapes recalled by these poets, mostly from their childhoods, tended to be highly idealised ones, as much of the work was written while the authors were in a state of exile from the places they depicted. Their appeal to the young gentlemen, similarly exiled from their own homelands, was understandable. However, there was little realism among the Latin poets and painters. I don't mean there should be, only that the scenes are picturesque and lovely rather than awesomely, ruggedly, dangerously beautiful, as true wilderness tends to be. Montaigne introduced the term 'landscape' in his essays around 1580, using it to describe the background painting for a dramatic production. So these young gentlemen were imbued with that version of what a natural setting should be: not a wilderness but a landscape, idealised not only by the Latin classical poets but by the contemporary Roman painters who used the classics as models for their scenic paintings.

The students who came to study these works came mostly by coach, passing *en route* through the Alps but doing so, according to contemporary records, with the shades firmly drawn against the view of the ominous terrain, the wilderness we now find so inspiring. They found it frightening and unfamiliar, something that harboured kidnappers and rogues. And this is where Claude's mirror comes in. The device named after this landscape painter was a curved mirror which the gentlemen carried when travelling. The surface of the mirror was ground in a manner that made the reflections in it appear to be darkened, as if by a coat of varnish, in a style typical of Claude's canvases. Upon seeing a likely prospect, the traveller would ask the coachman to stop, would step out of the carriage, turn his back on the scene and hold his mirror up in front of him so he could view the landscape behind him, a scene which instantly became...a landscape by Claude! This is, of course, the forerunner of our polaroid cameras, but it is also a highly artificial way of viewing the terrain. That it required viewers literally to turn their backs upon what it was they wanted to see is, in itself, highly suggestive.

How have we become so far removed from natural wilderness? I will not pretend to have a complete answer, but I will point out this much. Many of our greatest conceptualisers have also been highly inspired people—such as Pythagoras, for instance. But he had a side which has survived into our culture and a side which has not. The maker of concepts has survived, in the form of ideas received from him; but the inspired figure who said, "Astonishing! Everything is alive and intelligent!" is not passed down so easily. That living presence of nature was once common knowledge in our culture, as it still is among many remote peoples. Genius is not a matter of IQ, but of awakened spirit. Genius was one of the three household gods of the ancient Romans, and it was the spirit that was one's own preserving presence. Not intelligence, but spirit, that ignites when one is inspired. The term 'inspiration' comes from breathing in, not merely air but spirits in the air. The twin for that term, the Greek 'enthusiasm', means taking a god into oneself, a god's spirit and power. One takes in the spirits around one, and gives them back into the world as inspired actions or visions which we receive enthusiastically.

Here are some familiar lines from Wordsworth, which are indicative of one of the breakthroughs of the Romantic movement. In these lines from *The Prelude* we see Wordsworth cracking Claude's mirror, revealing a wilderness which, because it is imbued with a power not of his making and not under his control, must therefore be capable of threatening him, conjuring in him a sense not of simple loveliness but of awe:

One summer evening...lustily
I dipped my oars into the silent lake,
And, as I rose upon the stroke, my boat
Went heaving through the water like a swan;
When, from behind that craggy steep till then
The horizon's bound, a huge peak, black and huge,
As if with voluntary power instinct,
Upreared its head. I struck and struck again,
And growing still in stature the grim shape
Towered up between me and the stars, and still,
For so it seemed, with purpose of its own
And measured motion like a living thing,
Strode after me...
. . . .
...after I had seen
That spectacle, for many days, my brain
Worked with a dim and undetermined sense
Of unknown modes of being...
...No familiar shapes
Remained, no pleasant images of trees,
Of sea or sky, no colours of green fields;
But huge and mighty forms, that do not live
Like living men, moved slowly through the mind
By day, and were a trouble to my dreams.

In this passage, the poet is *seeing*, not merely looking, and though what he sees disturbs him at the time, as the unknown usually will, it is through this crack and others which he is brave enough to peer through that a new way of viewing wilderness begins to emerge.

The concluding section from a piece of mine called *Light In A House of Mirrors* is my response to the La Push area of Washington's coast where there are tall rock stacks that have a very eerie presence. Although there is a kinship with the spirit of Wordsworth, this prose passage is based upon a Native American legend, and is a confirmation of his vision which is parallel with it rather than derivative from it:

Once there was more land, higher than now. The waters grew jealous, gathered their tribes and conspired. Men knew this and the greatest planned to flee inland, leaving the others—the sickly and the weak—to form a wall to hold back the waters. So there they stood, and the waters were delayed before they rushed inland. Today we can see the heads of the old ones at the shore here, vast, moss-haired, silent—for these were the runts, the least of their race—and we feel dwarfed beside them. For the greatfathers, who were saved, shrivelled among the safe places far inland. The heroes still stand guard at the edges. We call them stones so we will not remember. They no longer speak to us, who are neither their sons nor daughters.

If in this passage and the earlier one from Wordsworth there is a sense of ominous oppression in response to the enormous powers of nature, both human and non-human, that is not necessarily the case. Here is Walt Whitman, in *Song of Myself* (which is really a song of the human spirit possible in us all, aroused to a natural condition of joy) describing a sunrise as it has never been described before:

To behold the daybreak!
The little light fades the immense and diaphanous shadows,
The air tastes good to my palate.
Hefts of the moving world at innocent gambols silently rising,
freshly exuding,
Scooting obliquely high and low,
Something I cannot see puts upward libidinous prongs,
Seas of bright juice suffuse heaven....
The mocking taunt, See then whether you shall be master!

Dazzling and tremendous how quick the sunrise would kill me,
If I could not now and always send sunrise out of me.
We also ascend dazzling and tremendous as the sun,
We found our own O my soul in the calm and cool of the daybreak.
My voice goes after what my eyes cannot reach,
With the twirl of my tongue I encompass worlds and volumes
of worlds....

This is the poetry of the grandeur and magnificence witnessed by the visionary seer of the wilderness, the one whose spirit responds in kind to that glory it beholds. "Speech," he says, "is the twin of my vision." It is the vision which makes him a seer, the speech which makes him a poet, and the poetry which makes his spirit contagious among us all. We come to such a poet as we come to the wilderness itself, to have refreshed and confirmed in us again and yet again the knowledge of our own true stature which is not subject to the erosions of abstraction and exploitation so long as we are willing to resist them—and so long as we have the wilderness to empower us with the spirit to resist effectively. In the service of such a cause, neither the poet nor the politician may stand aloof. We must join hands with each other by joining voices whenever and wherever we can.

Song of Returnings

All the bones of the horses rise in moonlight
on the flatlands and hillsides, dropping
from trees, squeezing out from
under rocks, disengaging themselves
from the earth and things that live from the earth
and the scattered uniforms assemble
> *to the sounds of bugling come back from the stars*
and what has rotted into dust reforms with a furious sound
> *of whirlwind tearing the faces of the astonished living*
and gold flows molten from the mouth of Cortez
> *and returns to the stones and the water and the air*
and the redwoods collapse back into cones
and Christ is pried from the cross and flogged and spat upon
> *and let loose among fishermen who scatter to their ships*
> *and enters his mother's womb and enters into the stars*
and Babylon reassembles and Sodom and Gomorrah reassemble
and David sings then babbles in his mother's arms
and all living things return to their sources
and the waters return to their sources
and the sun returns to the source
and the vast darkness returns
and all things are
and are not.

The Essence of Nature

Dorothy Maclean

I have always loved nature and being outdoors. Because of that love I was later in life given the task of harmonising with the essence of nature. While this may be a little unusual, it is not new, and many speakers here have addressed that subject. I would like to quote a few of them.

'Man is not fulfilled until he understands the essence of nature'—'The human mind can blend with the great mind, and there are no limits to knowledge'—'The potential of man is unlimited'—'Wilderness is the original cathedral, the original temple, the original church'—'Perception, understanding, is only possible in the flow from the macrocosm to the microcosm'.

To some, these ideas may sound just beautiful or poetic, even impractical. They are the types of ideas I have explored and tried to bring into my everyday living, and I have found it is the practicalities of life that have taught me most. My exploration began in earnest at a very difficult period of my life when I was divorcing my husband, the person I loved most, so he could live his own life more fully. I was trying desperately to love unpossessively and finding it very difficult. But at that time I had a peak experience of knowing—not hoping, not believing, not just having faith—but *knowing* that God was within.

This completely changed my life, so much so that even friends who I met the next day noticed a difference in me. So powerful is it to touch just the fringes of our own divinity. This experience gave me a tremendous background to go on from, and later when I was living alone a thought kept coming to me: "Stop, and listen, and write down." At first I paid no attention, but it was so persistent that I eventually did as it suggested. And I found myself in touch with this still, small voice within, which gave me the most wonderful inspirational thoughts. I would put them into English with the aid of a dictionary and a thesaurus beside me.

This led me into a tremendous period of going into the dimensions of the human soul and of exploring what great beings we are in our inner selves. I always emerged from these experiences a happier and more loving person. This blending and teaching always brought me back to everyday living; it never took me out of it. It led me to try to do everything in my daily life in the consciousness of that oneness that I was experiencing within.

After many adventures and learning experiences, I found myself in this caravan park at Findhorn in Scotland with Peter and Eileen Caddy. One morning in May 1963, during my normal morning meditation, I was told I had a job to attune to nature. "Well," I thought, "this is a wonderful opportunity to go for a walk." But when I told Peter about it, he said I should help with the garden. He was having a lot of difficulty trying to grow vegetables in sand. So the following morning I asked about this in meditation and was told that I was indeed to help with the garden, but I was to realise that everything in nature had an ensouling intelligence, and my job was to attune to and harmonise with that intelligence. My immediate response was to argue because I didn't think I could do it. I had no idea of who these intelligences were or how to contact them—and in any case how could I attune to something I didn't even know existed?

However, I had had ten years of inner attunement by then, and I had learned to trust it. So a few weeks later, when I found myself in a very deep meditative state, I thought I would attempt attuning to these beings of nature, whatever they were. As Peter needed help with the garden, I decided to try with a vegetable—in this case, my favourite vegetable, the garden pea. I tried to tune in to the essence of that, and to my surprise I got an immediate response in thought and feeling which as usual I translated into words and put down on paper. The being said it had been going about its business and it wished human beings would go about their business the way it did, because we were great beings of light and we weren't using our potential.

When I shared this experience with Peter he immediately gave me a long list of questions to ask about the garden, and in fact he kept me busy for about two years. They were ordinary gardening questions, and

I am not going to go into detail about that here, because it has all been written up elsewhere.

From my very first contact with the essence of the garden pea, I realised that I was contacting not an individual being behind a particular plant, but rather the group soul of a species. The only word I had for this in my vocabulary was angel—or the Sanskrit term 'deva', which means 'shining one'. I experience these beings not as form, but as an energy field. They hold the archetypal energy and pattern for growth on the planet, from plant growth to human growth, and in that sense they are, in a way, our parents. I also came to realise that I was tuning in to a knowledge that every culture and religion has talked about in the past, including Christianity, which has a whole science of angelology that is not even translated from the Latin.

The angels gave us facts and practical advice about gardening, but they didn't tell us what to do. I believe that was deliberate, for two reasons. First, I found that these nature beings do not have free will. They are at one with the whole rhythm of divinity and have always stayed in the Father's House, so to speak. I think the other reason is that they want us to make our own decisions, because the human way is to learn by our choices, and if they told us what to do we would just be robots.

Through my inner contact with the angels, I began to understand many things. For instance, when I attuned to the intelligence of the species we call wild violet, I found that the power and authority evoked by one tiny flower in the grass of the sand dunes was greater than that of the most cherished garden flower, simply because it was wild. The being told me the reason for the plant's power was that it had found its niche and was doing what it was meant to be doing. It said when we humans found our own place and purpose, we would be just as powerful.

From the angels I also learnt about my human self. Whenever I tuned in to them I would partake of their qualities and it was like a tuning fork effect—I would feel, for instance, their sense of joy and would resonate with it and so become a more joyful being myself. I realised that I must have those qualities within myself or else I couldn't recognise them outside myself—just as faults I see in others must also be within myself for me to recognise them. I realised that we human beings contain all the angelic qualities and capabilities; in fact, we too are angels, every one of us, although working differently to the angels themselves.

As each new plant was brought into the garden I would welcome the angel of that species. I got quite a shock when I first tuned into a tree—a little cypress seedling, one of several we were planting as shelter around the garden. All the messages I had received from the different angelic beings behind the species were helpful, philosophical, loving and to the point, but this one had a very different feeling. The angel had a definite message to give, and I share it with you here:

We come in with a lordly sweep, for we are not just the small trees you see in your garden, but denizens of the magnificent spaces of great hills in the sun and wind. We put up with being hedges, but always in our inner being is the growing towards the open sun-kissed places where we stand out in clustered grandeur. You feel in us an almost intolerable longing to be fully ourselves. We in the plant world have our pattern and destiny worked out through the ages, and we feel it quite wrong that we and others like us are not allowed to be because of man and his encroachment. Trees are not so much doers of the world as be-ers. We have our portion of the plan to fulfil. We have been nurtured for this very reason and now in this day and age many of us can only dream of the spaces where we can fulfil ourselves. The pattern is ever before us, out of reach, a dream that we are forever growing towards, but which seldom becomes reality. The planet needs the likes of us in our full maturity. We are not a mistake on the part of nature; we have our work to do.

Man is now becoming the controller of the world forests, and is beginning to realise that these are needed. But he uses silly economic reasons for his selection, with no awareness of the planet's needs. He should not cover acres with one quick-growing species, which, although admittedly better than none, shows ignorance of the purpose of trees and their channelling of diverse forces. The world needs us on a large scale; perhaps if man were in tune with the infinite as we are and were pulling his weight, the forces would be balanced. But at present the planet needs more than ever just what is being destroyed—the forces that go through the stately trees. We have been vehement. Here are these facts of life and no-one to listen to them. We have rather dumped this on you: though you feel at one with us, you feel unable to help. You are only looking at it from a very limited view. We know that the very telling of this to you does help—that a truth once in human consciousness then percolates around and does its work, and we feel the better for communicating. Let us both believe that the Almighty One knows all this better than both of us, and that something is being done.

Whenever I tuned in to a tree, I got a variation of this theme—the need for trees on the surface of the Earth. For example, the angels told me trees are the skin of the Earth, and that if more than a third of the skin of any being is destroyed then that being perishes. They said they have a job to do in their maturity, to do with the channelling of forces. And just as a child cannot do the work of an adult, so an immature tree cannot do the work of a mature tree. In many forests trees are often cut down before they are allowed to mature and to develop their canopy. The tree angels also said they had a special gift for humans in this troubled and chaotic day and age—they can give us mental stability. For this reason, they suggested that we build large forests beside our cities.

I showed my tree messages to Richard St. Barbe Baker, the Man of the Trees, when he visited the Findhorn Community, and he said he had come to exactly the same conclusions through his own knowledge and experience of forestry.

Later, when I was living in America, a workshop was arranged for me with men of the Washington and Oregon Forestry Service. After hours of busing and backpacking, I arrived after dark in the canyon where the foresters were working. After eating I had to talk around the camp fire. I couldn't see anyone as I told them what the trees had been saying to me, and when I finished there was total silence and everyone quietly went off and got into their sleeping bags. I spent most of the night wondering if they thought I was quite mad or whether they were so awed they couldn't speak. But during the following two days I spent in the canyon each man came up to me individually to thank me for what I had shared. They said they had joined the forestry service because they had understood these things as children, but had forgotten them, and they were grateful I had helped them remember.

There are of course other, less happier stories. I visited the groves of redwoods in California, where a little plaque says these groves have been set aside in perpetuity. I looked up and could see that the trees were already dying—dying because we have destroyed and polluted their climate, put roads through their area and dammed the rivers that feed the alluvial soil they need.

Another important area of contact for me has been with the mineral kingdom. My first experience of this was when I decided to tune in to the being of a very pretty pebble I picked up on the Findhorn beach. As the mineral kingdom in our human classification is of a lower nature than the animal and vegetable kingdom, I thought I would get a very unevolved angelic being, but instead I got the greatest being I had yet contacted. It stretched across universes, and I called it the Cosmic Angel of Stone. I would like to share its message with you.

Yes, I whom you have contacted am concerned with vastly more than your planet, for I contain or am connected with mineral life existing in various stages throughout creation. Nature is full of paradox, and when you seek contact with what you consider a lower form of life, you in fact contact a more universal being. The mind of man codifies and formulates, which is within its right and purpose, but forgets that all is one and that God is within all, and that basic substance, seemingly most devoid of sensitive consciousness, is held in its state of existence by its opposite, too vast for you to do more than sense its fringes and know that it extends beyond your present imagination. You realise too that dense matter is influenced in its make-up by stellar energies.

It was the beauty of this particular stone that drew you to me. Beauty is of God, beauty is working out on all levels; consciousness of beauty brings you into contact with any part of the universe. You are contained in it just as I seem to contain universes within myself. The more you appreciate beauty the more you are linked universally. It is good to seek it on high levels, for then your consciousness is expanded. You feel right now that you can only look at every pebble with the deepest reverence and worship because it is part of my vastness. We are glad that in this way you have been shown a very little of the glory of God. The glory of God is everywhere, stretching from the furthest reaches of the universe to the little grain of sand, one and the same thing, held in eternal love and timeless with life.

Yes, of course it would be good for you to attune to me if you work with stone—reverence all life, emanate my patience, unfold the mysteries of God and even of pebbles. Do it as a learner of life, a revealer. Let your dominion be

182

over yourself, and let your expanded consciousness seek God's life in all things, for indeed it is and, as you have learned, in the most surprising things. The colour and sparkle of a stone is wonderful, but more wonderful is consciousness which brings about these outer manifestations and grows cosmically. We are all part of one life, no higher or lower. Praise God in the vastness of all life.

Our relationship with the mineral kingdom is one in which we have much to learn. The next experience that made an impression on me was when we in the Findhorn community borrowed a bulldozer to flatten a piece of ground on which to put a print shop. I had been away for the day and when I came back I felt very upset about the churning up that the bulldozer had done. I felt it was all wrong, and it seemed that the nature forces were withdrawing. So I contacted a being which I had made a connection with earlier, the Landscape Angel. It seemed to be in charge of the whole area.

The Landscape Angel asked whether we had thought of warning the plants that were going to be bulldozed. Had we thought there might be beings living on the surface of the earth and that we would be destroying their homes? Had the person who drove the bulldozer thought of doing it with love, and specifically attuning to and becoming one with the machine? The answer to all these questions was no. We apologised and, because of our ignorance, we were forgiven and the nature forces returned. It seems that when we do destructive things in ignorance, the nature realms will accept that as a temporary step, but not when we learn and become more knowing, which is our destiny. We cannot be forgiven as long as we know. And we are now coming to the point where the planet is giving us feedback on our ignorance, and we have to act on it.

Another experience I had with the mineral kingdom was when I went to California and lived in an apartment in the last building leading to a deserted little valley in the Sierras. Of course I tuned into the angels there, and for the only time ever in attuning to them there was a sense not of joy but of frustration. This was because of our treatment of the soil, particularly in North America. We have come in and raped the land, paying no attention to its value. This is in contrast to the previous treatment of the land by the North American Indians, who had a wonderful contact with it, and these angelic beings had been used to having sympathetic humans there. It is also in contrast to the treatment of land in Europe, where people and nature have grown up together very closely. You can see this by how the roads and buildings in Europe are often bonded together. People have listened to nature and have taken the land into consideration. They have tried to keep it in good heart, through various ways of treating the soil, letting it lie fallow and so forth. This was not done by the White people in North America, because there was so much land they did not feel it necessary. And what the angelic beings may have known that I did not was that the bulldozers were to come into that area the following year.

There are a few points I wish to make which I think are relevant to this Congress. First, nature has a soul level, just as we humans have. On that level, we are one. On that level, both we and they are all-knowing. Second, we humans contain in our make-up all the life of the planet—mineral, vegetable and animal qualities, as well as our human and divine qualities. Third, it is practical to function from that all-knowing level of nature. The original Findhorn garden was an example and became known for its vibrant and abundant plant life.

I think we in the Western world need to stop and listen. We cannot become aware of our higher dimensions if we are too busily focused on the outside all the time. We have to stop and listen to nature because that is where we can learn. But we need to listen to silence too. We need to listen to both the sound and the silence of nature.

I believe we can find the answers to all our human and environmental problems from that inner level of ourselves. Unless we have a contact with the higher nature of ourselves we are not going to bother to try to find answers, because it is only from a higher consciousness of the need and the wholeness of nature that we are then going to be able to use our minds to find solutions.

We are divine beings and have the capacity to create heaven on Earth. We have created something of a hell. My experience is that even the nature angels consider our present creations as part of our learning process. They see and believe in our capacity to remedy our mistakes. They see that we are great beings of light, and they know we can find answers by using our minds. Our minds are the instrument of our intuition, and as we work from the higher level of ourselves we can work directly with the angelic realms.

One more point is that wilderness is necessary. In the wilderness, nature forces are at their strongest. We need wilderness areas to help us remember who and what we are. The purity of nature awakens the purity within ourselves. The peace and beauty and life of nature is essential for our well-being, and any scheme that takes us to the wilderness can take us to God and make us whole.

the intellectual faculties of the left hemisphere of the brain, with its masculine organising power and its pride in controlling and even 'conquering' nature (a terrible phrase). But the price we have to pay is enormous. It is the atrophying and going dormant of the organs of perception associated with the right hemisphere of the brain, the feminine, sensitive, intuitive faculties which can apprehend the living oneness of life and spirit. Blake, that great visionary poet, tells us of this price when he talks of the "wrenching apart of the perceiving mind and what we perceive from their original indivisible unity, to produce an externalised, fixed, dead nature and a shrinking of our humanity from the boundless being of the Imagination, into the mortal worm of 60 winters and 70 inches long."

We have shrunk and withered like an uprooted plant, and have lost the 'being' within nature. But listen now to Wordsworth in the great poem *Tintern Abbey*, describing how, as a boy, nature to him was all in all.

...the sounding cataract
Haunted me like a passion: the tall rock,
The mountain, and the deep and gloomy wood,
Their colours and their forms, were then to me
An appetite....That time is past,
And all its aching joys are now no more,
...other gifts
Have followed...and I have felt
A presence that disturbs me with the joy
Of elevated thoughts; a sense sublime
Of something far more deeply interfused,
Whose dwelling is the light of setting suns,
And the round ocean and the living air,
And the blue sky, and in the mind of man:
A motion and a spirit, that impels
All thinking things, all objects of all thought
And rolls through all things....

But you are still out in space. Now look at the Earth holographically. You know that when a holographic plate is shattered, every fragment contains the whole three-dimensional picture. When Professor Carl Pribram was lecturing once in America, he suddenly stammered and checked in the reading of his paper as the thought hit him—"My God, what if the whole universe is a hologram!" If indeed it is, it follows that every human mind is a tiny bit of the shattered plate. This reminds us of the myth of Osiris, the god who was cut up into a thousand pieces, to be set together by the goddess Isis. However, while the holographic plate is inert, we human beings, a little lower than the angels and crowned with glory and honour, have the unique task of carrying the divine gift of free will in order that we may become in time co-creators with God. We are that part of nature which can become consciously creative and therefore can, to some small degree, re-create the photograph in the cosmic hologram.

It must be a source of excitement for the angelic world to watch the planet Earth as human beings begin to be creative and overcome their destructive egoism and violence. For we are called on to realise, in time, the true archetype of the human being, that first concept formed in the divine mind before matter came into manifestation. We were the measure of all things, made in the image of God, with the ability to carry and focalise Thought, Will and Love; spiritual beings entering the temple of the physical body in order to experience and overcome the limitations of matter and the sense world. This of course involved for the time being the losing of the realms of spirit and the experience of separation and loneliness, cut off from the divine.

But we are now passing through the phase of separation. We are living in the time when humankind stands on the threshold, when our self consciousness can take a quantum leap into cosmic consciousness. In this training ground of Earth we are reaching a stage when, so to speak, we are preparing to enter the university. This is the intense excitement of our generation. We have recovered the concept of oneness. With our intellects, we have dissolved matter into energy. Our leading scientists now approach the next step, which is to realise that energy is alive, that it is an ocean of life, being and intelligence poured out from the divine source.

This is, of course, not new. We are recovering the vision of the mystics of all ages, the ageless, ancient wisdom both of the Orient and of our Western mystery traditions. The so-called Hermetic Wisdom, deriving from the Egyptian initiate, Hermes Trimagistus, laid down as first principle that the universe is mind, not mechanism, and that everything manifests the law of correspondences—as above, so below; as in the macrocosm, so in the microcosm. The human being is the microcosm reflecting the macrocosm; in essence a droplet of divinity and therefore immortal and imperishable. The essential being, the I, always was and always will be, and cannot possibly die, since it is an attribute of God. This immortal self is housed in the perishable body, truly a fantastic temple for the spiritual entity to operate in the heavy density of matter. This concept is of paramount importance in our death-ridden culture, and in this turn-about in consciousness we see that humanity is not an accident of chance natural selection, but is one of the great purposes of God.

We are now grasping the holistic world view, first put forward in the 1920s by Jan Smuts of South Africa. 'Holism' implies, by its spelling, that the whole is holy. We are recovering this concept, held virtually by every culture but our own, and central to the secret knowledge of

the mystery traditions. Therefore look again at our Earth in its beauty and conceive that it is truly a living creature, a being, an organism with its own breathing, bloodstream, glands, sensitivity and intelligence. We are an aspect of the intelligence of the planet. Furthermore, we must see that humanity is itself an organism, integrally part of the whole of nature. Ours is the first generation which could grasp this thought. Teilhard de Chardin's noosphere is a living body over the face of the Earth and we are each cells in the one great body. When cells in our physical bodies choose to ignore the programming of the whole and go off on their own, we call it cancer. Similarly, when human cells in the body of Earth act out of egoism, greed and violence, and go off on their own reckless way, the Earth itself becomes cancer-ridden. The disease is far advanced, though not necessarily terminal.

We are polluting the planet, physically, mentally and morally, to the extent where we could bring about the extinction of our civilisation in the years ahead. But a change is taking place. More and more human beings, cells in the body of humanity, are stopping in their tracks, appalled at what the rightful stewards of the planet are doing to their mother the Earth. They are pausing, awakening, attuning and re-orientating. This is what Teilhard called 'homing upon the Omega point', lifting ourselves above the murky atmosphere of emotion and egoism surrounding the Earth into the clear light of heaven, and realising our true nature. The great hope is that when a critical number of people have consciously taken this step, a new understanding could shoot through the world. For when individual human beings freely take this step in attunement, it is immediately possible for the powers of the angelic world to pour through them to cleanse and purify our polluted planet and to harmonise all life. Teilhard called it 'the wild hope that our earth is to be recast'. There was never such a time to be alive!

Now it is time to come back to Earth. Take a plunge into the atmosphere, and turn once more with the Earth, seeing the stars appear to swing around you. Now dive back into your waiting body. This is almost an alarming experience, for you are undergoing something like the drastic limitation involved in birth, descending from the widths of space into the sense world. And this could be a relief. As T.S. Eliot wrote: "Humankind cannot bear very much reality." The Earth, to you, is now flat and stands still, and the sun begins to rise and the moon to set.

What has all this to do with the preserving of wilderness in the living Earth? Because we are part of the Earth, we are not mere onlookers observing nature. We *are* nature, and we represent an evolutionary point where nature becomes conscious of itself. As Wordsworth and the great poets of the Romantic Movement realised, nature is not fulfilled until human beings, the crown of creation, take the step in

◄ Sitka Totem (Alaska)

consciousness to grasp the Idea, the Being within the tree, the plant, the bird, the mountain. This gives new meaning to the statement in Romans 8: "The created universe waits with eager expectation for God's sons to be revealed," and to the opening of St. John's gospel: "In the beginning was the Word, and the Word was with God, and the Word was God...All things were made by him." First came the Divine Idea, the archetypal creative Thought, to be realised later in substance. The Divine Idea is present everywhere, expressed into nature's forms, but this world of being and spirit is invisible to the physical senses. It is through the eye of the mind that it is apprehended. The mind, as droplet of the eternal mind, can, to use Blake's words, "open the eternal worlds, open the immortal eyes of man inwards into the realms of thought, into eternity, ever-expanding in the bosom of God, the human imagination."

Now consider also the deeper significance of the magnificent achievements of the younger generation in the so-called adventure sports, in which great feats of enterprise, endurance and skill are accomplished in exploring the world. You do not need any particular mystique to enjoy mountaineering, skiing or gliding; your motive may be fun and sheer excitement. But if you start thinking holistically and realise that we are the point of consciousness of Earth, a deeper meaning is revealed in the great sports and their exploration of nature. Through us, Earth herself is taking a step in her consciousness of the elemental world. In hang-gliding and free-fall, we relate closely to the element of air. In skin-diving, canoeing and surfing, we identify in consciousness with the element water. As we climb on rock and snow or explore great caverns, we relate to the element earth. The planet is waking up through us, for we are her point of advancing consciousness. When Wordsworth walked the Lake District in love of its beauty, he was awakening nature herself. Nature is not fulfilled until we take this step in consciousness. Her dormant spirit awakens as humanity recovers the Hermetic vision and begins to live by it.

This factor is not taken into account in our politics, economics or even ecology. There is of course no need for this mystique, but those people planting trees, stopping pollution and preserving the beauty of landscape and wilderness are all serving Gaia, the goddess of Earth. The so-called 'alternative lifestyle', which grows directly out of holistic thinking, is concerned with living in a way that serves the living Earth. It is conservation, with spiritual vision.

Holism implies, indeed, that there is a power of higher intelligence which could actually bring about molecular change to depollute the planet, but this will not happen without our invocation and cooperation, since we are instruments of freedom. Ours, however, is the initiative, and our age is one of real science fiction in which, through a time of change, almost anything is possible. Glory be!

To close I give you a poem which I dedicate to Sir Laurens van der Post, a great and distinguished man. It is by a great mountaineer, Geoffrey Winthrop Young, who lost his leg in the First World War and then climbed the Matterhorn with an artificial leg. Such was the scale of the man. His poem is called *Envoi*.

I have not lost the magic of long days:
I live them still, dream them still,
Still am I master of the starry ways,
And freeman of the hill.
Shattered my glass, e'er half the sands had run—
I hold the heights, I hold the heights I won.
Mine still the hope that hailed me from each height,
Mine the unresting flame;
With dreams I charmed each doing to delight;
I charm my rest the same.
Severed my skein, e'er half the strands were spun—
I keep the dreams, I keep the dreams I won.
What if I live no more those kingly days?
Their night sleeps with me still.
I dream my feet upon the starry ways;
My heart rests in the hill.
I may not grudge the little left undone;
I hold the heights, I keep the dreams I won.

The Bible:
An Ecological Perspective

Gordon Strachan

I bring you unofficial greetings from all the heretics within the Church—from all those who, despite official Church attitudes, are passionately concerned about the preservation of the environment. As a member of the clergy of 20 years standing I want to say to you on behalf of the ecclesiastical establishment, *mea culpa*. I want to confess before you that the Church has sinned grievously over the centuries by being the main instigator of the split between nature and grace, matter and spirit. Sir Laurens van der Post has asked: what is it uniquely in us in the West that has made us so brutally savage towards nature? I can tell you: 2,000 years of dualistic Church indoctrination.

Professor Lynn White's famous essay *The Historical Roots of our Ecological Crisis* traces this dualism back to the seventh century. I trace it back to the third, to St. Cyprian, the man who was canonised among other things for saying "There is no salvation outside the Church." Cyprian also said, "He can no longer have God for his Father, who has not the Church for his Mother." He formalised what the Church had been coming to believe for 200 years: that Mother Nature and Mother Earth had no place in the Christian religion, and that their place had now been taken by Mother Church.

From earliest times, Christian theology did not believe that God's grace extended to creation. There was no covenant of grace for nature. She was excluded, outside the scope of redemption. Theological orthodoxy, with a few exceptions, could be stated like this: "When you are born, you are in a state of nature, which is a state of darkness. You share that darkness with the whole of creation. Then, through the preaching of the Word, you receive the good news that Christ has saved you from your sins, that you have been redeemed from your lower nature and from nature as such, and have been received into the realm of grace and light." The unique dispensers of this truth were the Church Fathers. What they said was 'gospel'. The one thing you could not do, on pain of excommunication or even death, was question the Church's doctrine of the Church. It was all-mighty, all-powerful. It was effectively the third person of the Trinity, the Holy Spirit being identical with the spirit of holy Mother Church.

The Church justified the exploitation of nature by quoting texts from Genesis where God said, "Fill the earth and subdue it; and have dominion over (it)", as if these were representative of the whole of the Bible's teaching about creation. Indeed, as far as nature was concerned, the command to 'subdue the earth' came to be synonymous with the Christian message. This text, more than any other, has justified the contempt with which Western people have treated their fellow species on this planet. It is so deeply ingrained in our consciousness that many conservationists honestly believe that the whole of the Bible must be rejected because of its anti-nature teaching.

But this is not the case. The Church was quite wrong ever to suggest that these texts were typical of the biblical position as a whole. They come from a time when the Israelites were learning to be farmers after being hunter-gatherers and, in such a context, it was appropriate to speak of subduing the earth. But even if we admit that these texts are, on the face of it, anti-conservationist, they are very few in number compared with the many which speak of God as the creator of and carer for all things, of humankind as the stewards of his creation, of the heavens declaring his glory and the Earth his handiwork, of nature itself revealing the divine character as in the parables of Jesus, of even the sparrow's fall being noticed by its maker, and of the numerous injunctions in the Law and the Prophets to live in harmony with the land and to treat it as a potential Garden of Eden.

If we can 'deschool' ourselves from traditional Church indoctrination and go back to the Bible itself, we will find that it is very much *for* the conservation of nature, both in its cultivated forms and in the wild. We will find that it is for stewardship, not subjugation. Indeed, so much is this the case that it is possible to say that a new gospel of harmony with creation awaits those who have the diligence to find it.

I would like to offer one brief example of what I mean, and I choose the paradigm of the Temple, which is central to the Bible. I am thinking especially of Solomon's Temple (figure 1). The measurements of this temple, the focal point of Hebrew religion and national life, correspond to the ratios of the perfect musical intervals which, according to ancient cosmology, were the microcosmic expression of a macrocosmic harmony. The furnishings of the temple—the seven-branch candlesticks, the table of shewbread, the altar of incense, the cherubim, the palms, the cypresses, the flowers in bloom and the Ark of the Covenant—were symbolic representations of the main features of the Garden of Eden—a model of the natural harmony which was supposed to obtain throughout the land of Israel. The seven-branch candlesticks represented the trees of life; the table of shewbread, the bread of life; the altar of incense, the fragrance of the forest; the other trees and the cherubim, the perimeter of the Garden; and the Ark of the Covenant, the presence of the Lord God in the midst of his creation (figure 2).

This ecological interpretation of the structure and contents of the Temple of Solomon has been consistently omitted from the Church's teaching. Yet it recurs throughout the Bible, as in the visionary temple of Ezekiel and the New Jerusalem of St. John's Revelation. This New Jerusalem has always been portrayed by artists as a city full of towers and streets and numerous houses. This is as true of Gustave Doré in the 19th century as it is of Lufft (figure 3), Cranach and Durer in the 16th. Even the recent Bible translation, *Good News for Modern Man*, portrays it sparkling with urban glory. Yet if chapter 21 of Revelation is read carefully there is, apart from the reference to one golden street, no urban imagery whatsoever. The walls are crystal, as are the foundations; the gates are pearl, and on the inside there is absolutely nothing except the Tree of Life and the River of Water of Life flowing down from the throne of God and of the Lamb. It is not a city in any urban sense at all. It is only a city in the original meaning of the Greek word *polis*, that is, a 'representation of the cosmos' and a 'replica of the universe' as Lewis Mumford says in *The City in History*. Like the Temple from which St. John derives much of his symbolism, the New Jerusalem is a paradigm of creation not of a spiritual metropolis or holy conurbation. It is an image of the Garden of Eden within a crystal cube

196

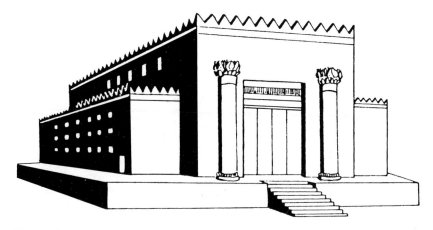

Figure 1

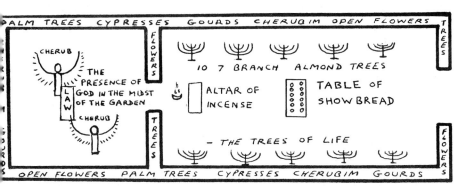

Figure 2

which, according to Hebrew cosmology, represented the firmament of the created universe.

The Temple was the most important spiritual centre throughout much of the history of the Bible. When we realise it was built as a model of the cosmos, a microcosm of the universal harmony, we begin to glimpse the cosmic dimensions of our Christian heritage. This is the dimension which the Church has denied us, and which we must claim for ourselves.

The Bible can help us find a spiritual justification for our quest to preserve this beautiful planet from the destruction which now threatens it. But it will only yield its rich treasures once we begin diligently to undo the theological damage of centuries. The whole of nature is *within* the Temple. All creation is *within* the New Jerusalem.

Figure 3

The Garden of Eden is the central image of humankind's relationship
to nature throughout the Bible. We must stand our traditional notions
on their heads and turn our ecclesiastical teaching upside down. Only
then will we find that Revelation 9:4 which says: "They were told not
to harm the grass of the earth or any green growth or any tree" is
much more typical of the whole biblical attitude than "subdue the earth".

At the 2nd Wilderness Congress, Sir Laurens van der Post said,
"Wilderness is the original cathedral, the original temple, the original
church." I don't think he learned that from the Bible. I think he learned it
from life, from his experience of the wilderness, and from wide reading
in the wisdom of other cultures. But had he known, he could have
found it in the Bible too, and I want to tell you that it is there. The
Temple of Creation is a central message of the Bible waiting to be
rediscovered and put into practice. If all Christians around the world
could find that truth and live by it, we would take a big step towards
solving our ecological crisis and preserving wilderness for posterity.

Human Rights within Natural Law

Carolyn Tawangyawma

Right relationship with nature has always been the foundation of the lives of traditional people

My sisters and brothers, I bring greetings from the elders of the Traditional Community of Hotevilla Village, of the Sovereign Hopi Independent Nation. I wish to place before you a message of awareness about the danger to humankind's survival on this Earth. I bring this message under the banner of the Great Spirit, the Creator of the universal plan and of the instructions and of everything given to Hopi and all people on Earth. The things that have been given to us are very precious. We are to protect and use them wisely, and to share them in order to keep harmony among all people. However, humankind has forgotten this, thus making the search for peace extremely difficult. We fear that humankind has gone too far and forgotten too much to be able now to find this peace.

Over the ages the ancient Hopi have seen and experienced many things, such as the changing from an old to a new world order because of a dreadful disaster resulting from humanity's mindless action in forgetting the Creator's divine laws. This has happened to three previous world orders, which have then been destroyed. It is sad that humankind seems never to learn from its past history. Now, once again, we have failed to live by the divine laws, and so gradually land and nature are becoming unbalanced. Technology is rapidly eroding our ancient culture and tradition. The wild life and forest are diminishing rapidly, while the precious water and air are becoming unhealthy to drink and breathe. The changing climate also symbolises a grave warning.

We can correct these faults by retracing our steps back to divine laws. This is a difficult step, because we are tempted on all sides by material values. The moral values we once followed have now become make-believe, but if we correct our ways we could turn the course of the future. Our prophecies foretold that the time might come when someone with a very clever mind would seek out the secret of nature and defy its laws. Much discovered from this would benefit us, but most of it would also have a dangerous side. Because nature has its own mysterious protection, humankind would eventually harvest misfortune. It has become clear now that what was prophesied were many of the products of modern science and technology such as medicine, drugs and weapons.

Meanwhile, the Hopi who turn against their original vows are unbalancing the earthly cycles that control the seasons. Because Hopi land is a spiritual centre of the Earth, this change will affect the entire Earth. According to our ancient prophecies, Hopi land will be the first to feel the effect. We will know the imbalance is coming about when our planting month is delayed by cold weather or when frost comes before our crops are mature for harvest. Both these events happened this very year, so our harvest will be less. Already wild life is beginning to disappear, while most summer insects are not returning with the seasonal cycles. We see these events as signs of some great change or new turn of events coming soon, but only the Great Spirit knows the exact time. Perhaps this is fulfilling a Hopi prophecy of a great purification of the present world order. No one knows what form this will take. It can come in peaceful ways or in the form of a terrible catastrophe. We Hopi are ready for the outcome. Whatever it may be, we all deserve what will be given.

In Hopi land, disharmony within our communities is becoming serious. Although all the villages are closely related in certain ways, such as in our ceremonial cycles and in the spiritual structure of our thoughts, our local matters are not alike. Our villages are independent from each other, and we do not interfere in other villages' affairs. Each village has its own leaders.

Recently, as a step towards removing the puppet government set up by the United States, there has been a movement to unite all the Hopi villages. All except Hotevilla agreed to unite. In the Western European concept, political unity is a means of power. But we in Hotevilla see this as a weak and possibly dangerous approach. We have decided to maintain our purpose based on a concept of spiritual unity and on the code of laws of our village. We hope that further efforts to relieve the Hopi of the burden of colonial rule will proceed with caution regarding this sensitive issue until it is clear what the result will produce. If the original basis of society can be kept alive within the Hopi nation and elsewhere, it will become the way of life for the world as a whole, as it was in the beginning.

The way one nation treats another serves either to strengthen or to destroy the spiritual basis for peace in the world. As long as America continues to oppose the spiritual way of life we call the Hopi way, serious wars are bound to result throughout the world. Contrary to the opinion of many, the greater the military force of a nation, the greater the danger to that nation. Peace can only come to the world through an honest, non-violent relationship with the indigenous people, who are the caretakers of all life.

Sacred Lands are a Source of Balance

Joan Price

Hotevilla Village

Water under the ground has much to do with rain clouds. Everything depends upon the proper balance being maintained. The water under the ground acts like a magnet attracting rain from the clouds; and the rain in the clouds also acts as a magnet raising the water table under the ground to the roots of our crops and plants. Drawing huge amounts of water from beneath Black Mesa in connection with the strip-mining will destroy the harmony, throw everything we have strived to maintain out of kilter. Should this happen, our lands will shake like the Hopi rattle; land will sink, land will dry up. Rains will be barred by unseen forces, because we Hopis have failed to protect the land given us, as we were instructed. Plants will not grow; our corn will not yield and animals will die. When the corn will not grow, we will die; not only Hopis, but all will disintegrate to nothing.

Excerpt from Statement of Traditional Hopi in 1968

The fluid nature of wind and water is an eternal and dynamic order that connects us all together. We can no longer classify our experience of wilderness by means of political boundaries that have emerged out of a technological, industrial culture. Wind and water patterns span many

Traditional craft designs often reflect the patterns within nature, as in these cloud motifs on Hopi pottery

cultures, national boundaries and diversities of humankind. Wind and water form their own boundaries, by surrendering to the form of the earth, and are not subject to human management. These natural boundaries are like invisible walls that divide forces in a dynamic balance—a standing balance between heat and cold, density and space, and positive and negative electricity. They link us all together in natural power.

The scientific study of the fluid dynamics of wind and water patterns has added a complex mathematical dimension to our understanding of the environment, one which reveals the limits of science as an absolute way of knowing. The fundamentally unpredictable aspect of nature and climate defies scientific and technological control, yet displays global relationship and order within all life.

We are currently experiencing a global crisis, the magnitude of which has never before been encountered in the industrial mind. We have lost touch with the natural order, and need to find a knowledge to guide us back into harmony with nature and amongst ourselves. Technology has created ecological disasters, and the use of technological knowledge to resolve these disasters has in fact created a greater crisis. The natural world needs a reorientation. The Earth is alive and speaking through us. She wants us to rely on her own nourishment, provisions and organisation, and to come into harmony with her.

Ancient cultures which have lived with the Earth for thousands of years, from Buddhist to Native American, have a long and close communion with the forces of nature. Wind and water patterns have been instrumental in shaping their social conduct, giving rise to a set of natural laws governing people in accordance with the cycles of nature. Some of these laws include:

1. The absolute right to rely on nature and to develop a culture in the community that reflects the natural order.
2. The right not to divide the land, or the people from one another, by bringing in a technological, industrial value system which cannot guarantee harmony with nature for seven generations to come.
3. The right to use land and yet not simultaneously retain it (a right given by the Creator and not a political body).

These rights are fundamentally different from those of the prevailing culture, and are at the same time fundamentally harmonious with the natural order.

I believe we must transcend the mentality which expresses through the words and language of the industrial, technological world. In comparing the natural and eternal patterns of wind and water with images of the Native American cultures, I have found that the symbols of motion used amongst Native Americans have anticipated scientific knowledge by centuries. These symbols are about balance between forces. If we let them sink into our inner mind, we may be able to tap their power for transformation. I believe we must internalise the order of nature in order to transform the problems we experience among ourselves. Wind and water are powerful forces which transform Earth energy into balance. These forces are part of our spiritual nature. In every ancient language, the word spirit means wind or breath, and a deeper understanding of these environmental forces will give us greater insight into our spiritual nature. We have much to learn from the ancient cultures which still exist! They know that the Earth is alive and that it desires peace and purification, and that this can happen only if we attune ourselves to its sacred order.

More than a Pretty Picture: Photography as a Tool in Wilderness Conservation

Theodora Litsios

'The Three Brothers', Yosemite Valley, by Carletin Watkins

The link between photography and wilderness conservation in the United States goes back over 100 years. In the 1860s and 70s, both the emerging art of landscape photography and the new idea of national parks were coming into their own. Photographs by Carletin Watkins, George Fiske and William Henry Jackson, although over a century old, continue to inspire us with the beauty of the areas they depict. Their impact was even stronger 100 years ago when photography was a new and unique medium. The fact that many of the scenes captured by these early photographers can still be seen in very much the same state today is a reflection of the success of their work. Their photographs and those of others were instrumental in communicating to the US public and its leaders the uniqueness and beauty of areas that were in danger of being destroyed in a young nation's eagerness for expansion and profit, and they helped prompt Congress to enact laws to preserve these wilderness areas for public use and appreciation by the creation of national parks.

In the 1860s and 70s the government was promoting development of the land as quickly as possible. Acts of Congress, such as the Homesteading Act, made acquisition of land easy and inexpensive. White explorers, settlers and seekers of gold were discovering in the western United States a land of varied landscape rich in natural resources. Unlike the native Indians, to whom the land was sacred and not something one could own, many of these new settlers saw the land as a commodity to be used to the greatest economic advantage. The great abundance of natural resources fostered a careless attitude toward nature and the land. Forests were brutally logged, and land was mined and exploited in many ways with little regard to long range effects

Artists, on the other hand, were finding a landscape through which they could express the prevailing attitude of the day toward nature. The belief in the right to own and use the land stemmed from the view of nature as a gift from a generous God to his people. It was seen as the hope for renewal and a better life. Landscape artists such as Albert Bierstadt painted scenes of glowing beauty and drama in the European tradition. These beautiful paintings, very popular at the time, were not always accurate portrayals of the landscape. Bierstadt was known to make mountains steeper and peaks sharper, to resemble more closely the Bernese Alps that he had loved and painted as a young art student in Europe.

But it was through photographs that the average American became acquainted with the land west of the Mississippi. The development of the collodion or wet plate photographic process in the early 1850s not only allowed photographers to work out in the field away from the studio, but also resulted in unlimited numbers of prints being able to be produced from the glass negatives. By the late 1850s, photographers were taking this new process to the far reaches of the wilderness in the west.

However, the new collodion process was still a difficult and complex one, requiring great dexterity. The photographer had to clean a glass plate and coat it with the collodion, a viscous substance made light-sensitive by immersion in a bath of silver nitrate. The plate then had to be exposed while still wet, as the coating's sensitivity to light diminished as it dried. After exposure the plate had to be developed, dried and lacquered. The immediacy of the process required that a portable darkroom be on hand, and pack mules carried the glass plates, chemicals and other supplies for these early landscape photographers.

It was after seeing some of the first photographs to be taken of Yosemite valley that a young San Francisco photographer, Carletin Watkins, ventured to this remote area and began his love affair with the valley through photographs. He discovered a wilderness area of magnificent and awe-inspiring beauty. Seeking to reflect these aspects of the landscape, he built a camera that produced images on glass plates that measured 18″ by 22″, much larger than the plates used by most photographers at that time.

By 1863 both Yosemite and Watkins' photographs were becoming increasingly well known. Since its first settlement in the early 1850s, Yosemite's beauty had been extolled by early survey parties, painters such as Bierstadt and photographers such as Watkins, Edward Muybridge and Charles Weed, and it was attracting more and more visitors. But with the popularity came an increased concern that the area could too easily be exploited and destroyed. The first inkling of this came as early as 1853 when two promoters had a 315 ft sequoia tree cut down from a grove near Yosemite, stripped the bark to a height of 116 ft, and had it shipped East and put back together to show as a curiosity. Many people thought it was a fake, and others were enraged that such a grand product of nature should be destroyed to be shown as a public curiosity.

Concern over Yosemite's fate was beginning to grow, and in 1863 a group of Californians led by Frederic Law Olmstead, a leading landscape architect, urged the preservation of Yosemite and the great sequoia trees. One leader of this group, Israel Raymond, wrote Senator Conness of California urging protection of this area, and sent along some of Watkins' photographs to increase the power of his message.

The impact was significant enough to motivate Senator Conness to introduce a bill into Congress in March 1864 that made Yosemite Valley and the nearby grove of sequoia trees a state park of California. In June that year, at the height of the civil war, President Lincoln signed a bill that stipulated that the State of California accept the grant upon the express condition that 'the premises shall be held for public use, resort, recreation and shall be inalienable for all time.'

With the close of the Civil War in 1865, the US focused its energies on exploring its western territories, with both private and government sponsored surveys studying various areas of the west. One private survey, a group of Wyoming citizens with a military escort led by General Henry Washburn, explored a particular area of the Wyoming Territory known as Yellowstone. Their curiosity had been piqued by stories of amazing sights such as bubbling mud pots, geysers, huge canyons and waterfalls. Their survey proved these stories to be true, and a member of the party, Cornelius Hedges, along with David Folsom, a previous visitor to the area, conceived the idea of preserving the area for public benefit. Joined by another survey member, Nathaniel P. Longford, they wrote articles and gave public lectures describing the wonders of Yellowstone and calling for its preservation. One of the people who attended a lecture was Dr. Ferdinand Hayden, director of the US Geographical Surveys of the Territories. He became interested in Yellowstone and was granted $40,000 by Congress to conduct an official survey of the area.

Hot Springs on Gardiner's River, Yellowstone, by William Henry Jackson

Realising that the public was sceptical of the existence of such a fantastic landscape, Hayden took along an artist, Thomas Moran, and a photographer, William Henry Jackson, to document their discoveries. Jackson, who took along 400 glass plates, chemicals and other necessary supplies, became the first person to photograph the wonders of this remote wilderness area, sometimes producing 20 photographs a day—quite a feat considering each took 30-40 minutes to create.

The information and images with which they returned in the winter of 1871 were powerful indeed. Armed with this new evidence, Hayden worked with those who were trying to convince Congress to pass a bill preserving Yellowstone. He distributed Jackson's photographs among the senators, who were immensely impressed by them. Major Chittenden wrote: "The photographs were of immense value. Descriptions might exaggerate, but the camera told the truth; and in this case the truth was more remarkable than exaggeration... They...convinced everyone...that such wonders existed, that they should be carefully preserved for the public forever." Congress agreed, and in December 1871 a bill was introduced to preserve almost two million acres of the Wyoming Territory. The Yellowstone Act was passed in February 1872, and the first National Park was created.

This established a precedent, and in 1916, when the National Parks Act was created by Congress, 37 national parks and monuments existed. This Act established a policy toward the management and preser-

Hetch Hetchy Valley, Yosemite, by J.N. LeConte, Jr.

vation of these scattered and independent parks with the creation of the National Park Service.

It was also in 1916 that a young photographer was taking his first images of Yosemite National Park while on vacation. In the next few decades the name of Ansel Adams was to become synonymous with great landscape photography and a concern for wilderness preservation. Adams was studying to become a concert pianist, and pursued photography as a hobby. Yosemite was his favourite subject, and his appreciation of nature grew along with his technical ability. Soon he was giving all his creative energy to photography, and his growing concern for wilderness conservation led him to become a member of the Sierra Club. In 1936 the Sierra Club sent him to Washington DC to promote their plan for the creation of a national park in the Kings River Canyon and the high country of the Sierra Nevadas that surrounded it. They knew Adams' photographs of the area would be a powerful means of communication. Adams carried his portfolio through Washington showing it to senators and cabinet officials and addressing a conference on national and state parks. Although there were no immediate results from this trip, on his return Adams was offered a great commission—Walter Starr, a longtime member of the Sierra Club, offered to subsidise a book on the Sierra Nevada mountains as a memorial to his son, Walter Jr., who had died in the Sierras while creating maps.

Adams worked hard on what he loved best, creating images that expressed the grandeur and beauty of nature. The book, *The Sierra Nevada: The John Muir Trail*, was published in 1938, a creation of the highest quality. This impressive volume was distributed to many Washington officials and did much to help establish the Kings Canyon National Park, which was finally created in 1940. In a letter to Adams, F.A. Silcox expressed an attitude that was probably shared by other Washington politicians: "Although I never visited the High Sierra country, these pictures give me a feeling of the stupendous beauty of this country such as I didn't think possible while sitting in a remote office. These beautiful photographs certainly impress on one the value of the objectives for which you and other members of the Sierra Club have been fighting for many years, the preservation of the natural environment of the High Sierra."

Not all battles for wilderness conservation are successful. Sometimes the only remaining evidence of the lost beauty of an area are the photographs that recorded its grandeur before its destruction. Such is the case with Hetch Hetchy Valley, sometimes called Little Yosemite Valley. Although part of Yosemite National Park, this valley was doomed in 1913 when an act of Congress gave approval for a dam to be built to create a reservoir to supply San Francisco with water. The conservationist John Muir and others fought a long and hard battle to stop the needless destruction of this valley, but in 1923 the gates of the O'Shaughnassy Dam were closed and the Hetch Hetchy Valley slowly flooded.

Many people grieved this loss and hoped it would serve as an example of the needless destruction of a wilderness area. But such lessons are too quickly forgotten and in 1963, only 40 years later, history repeated itself when Glen Canyon, a magnificently carved canyon of the Colorado River, was also buried under water by the building of a dam which many believed to be unnecessary.

We are fortunate to have Eliot Porter's photographic record of Glen Canyon as a poignant testimony to its beauty. In 1961 and 62 Porter made several trips to this canyon, which was already destined to be flooded. His photographs were published in a book entitled *Glen Canyon: The Place No One Knew.* The tragedy of this loss is clear when one sees these photographs for the first time. If, like myself, you view them before reading the text, the heartbreak is greater when you discover that this spot you have just fallen in love with no longer exists.

As both the world and its wilderness areas seem to shrink, activities such as logging, mining, blasting for oil exploration and other commercial exploitation around many of the national parks have left them greatly endangered. In the last ten years, the buffer zone of a few miles around the parks has diminished rapidly. Aerial photographs show how logging up to the very border of the parks has become common practice, and make us painfully aware of other threats—such as a proposed coal mine eight miles north of Glacier National Park, geothermal development near Yellowstone that threatens Old Faithful Geyser, and a proposed high level nuclear waste dump less than two miles from Canyonland National Park.

From the first photographs ever taken in wilderness areas, to the more recent ones showing threats to our national parks, photography continues to be a powerful tool in the battle for wilderness conservation. As a means of communication it has repeatedly brought powerful images of wilderness areas to people who have never seen or experienced nature in this way. Consequently more people have been able to preserve these remote and often threatened areas. As the battle for wilderness preservation continues, so will the important role that photography plays in working toward continued success.

Wilderness Vision Quest

Michael Brown

As a psychologist trained in a discipline called Psychosynthesis, I conduct internationally a wide variety of seminars and workshops, personal growth and professional development programmes. One of the many programmes I have created is called the Wilderness Vision Quest. Since 1976 I have led groups of people on this camping and backpacking experience. Through an intimate encounter with nature, I help interested people grow in their appreciation of the natural world and, through the careful use of tools for self-discovery, explore and develop some of the valuable human resources which lie dormant in all of us. More than 400 people have taken part in this programme, gaining a sense of recreation and renewal by living lightly on the land and attuning to its wonders. The comments and reflections which follow are informed by, and flow from this work.

There are a large number of organisations in the United States today that guide people on experiences of wild country. Outward Bound, the National Outdoor Leadership School and Wilderness Odyssey stress physical challenge and high adventure as a means by which to conquer and let go of negative self-concepts, break through psychological barriers and enhance self-esteem. The American Rivers Conservation Council offers canoe and raft trips down splendid and pristine waterways as part of their educational and conservation efforts. The American Forestry Association offers horseback trips and trail rides in the wilderness of our western states. The Smithsonian Institution offers group excursions to Alaska, among many other places. The National Audubon Society and the National Wildlife Federation offer programmes on bird watching, plant identification, and the study, observation and protection of endangered species.

But what is wilderness and why does it so capture our imagination? The term 'wilderness' evokes different images for different people, but I believe the urge to officially designate areas as wilderness and to protect these areas from mining, timbering, grazing and other uses, is an outer expression of a universal inner need: the need to hold and honour, within us and out in the world, some small part of life as sacred. Thoreau once said, "In wilderness is the preservation of the world."

Wilderness provides us with the opportunity to witness ecosystems as they evolve outside human influence, to witness a primal state of cooperation, balance, harmony and wholeness. Each part of the land contributes indispensably to the whole, from the smallest microorganism to the giant redwood trees in the oneness that truly is life. The struggles of life, death and rebirth can be found on every square foot of natural terrain, and all the lessons of transformation as well: caterpillars changing into winged butterflies; verdant life bursting forth from the floor of charred and burnt-out forests; the ruffled grouse charging us with outspread wings to protect her young and draw us away from them; trees still reaching up toward the light even when struck by lightning, upturned by wind and water or smashed by other falling trees.

It is time to speak openly and with a clear voice about the spiritual dimensions of our contact with the natural world. It is time to focus deliberately on and work consciously toward the constructive discovery, exploration, healing, enrichment and growth of the human spirit. Arthur Carhart, in *Timber in Your Life*, said, "Perhaps the rebuilding of the body and spirit is the greatest service derivable from our forests, for of what worth are material things if we lose the character and the quality of the people who are the soul of America?"

There is an almost exponential growth in the number of people who are turning explicitly to the environment for a deeper sense of naturalness, simplicity and solitude, and a tangible spirituality grounded in the mysteries of nature. We all know we are moved by the beauty and wonder of nature, and yet few of us can really articulate how or why. We need to develop a new language of the spirit, be conscious of and able to speak about the values we derive from our wilderness adventures if we are to secure and then preserve the last few remaining truly wild regions on the planet.

Few of us know how gently but with intention to approach the mysteries and wonder of nature; to truly find simplicity in the wilds; to set the stage for an experience of the eternal, the infinite, the ineffable. Almost without exception, those organisations that do lead people into wild country simply wait for or hope that special and memorable experiences will occur. These are the moments we most remember. But we can consciously and deliberately move toward these dimensions through the careful use of specific methods and techniques for expanding and heightening our awareness. Through a combination of physical activity, light diet, exposure to the cycles and rhythms of nature, and carefully selected individual and group processes, we can intensify our experiences both of the wilderness and of our inner lives. We can learn to create the physical, emotional and psychological readiness to hear the voice of nature, be touched by wonder, develop our imagination and intuition, and have the energies of inspiration move powerfully through us. We can move closer to a primal sense of the unity of all creation and, for our effort, be regenerated and renewed at the deepest levels.

This is a healthy and holy movement: a response to the inner urge toward excellence and well-being that can become so eclipsed in urban living. In fact, we *need* to experience and deeply explore the natural world on our quest for wholeness. Jose Arguelles said, "If nature is a harmony and man a part of nature, then man himself must be innately harmonic. The laws governing his mind and body reflect and partake of the functioning of greater nature." We live in bodies that are exquisitely wired by evolution to perceive and respond to subtle shifts in colour, temperature, sound and movement. We are natural creatures living, to a great degree, in unnatural and unmoving environments, disconnected from the weaving, pulsing, throbbing web of life. We have to do something fairly radical to kick-start ourselves into full operation once again, but we must do it in a way that also honours the inherent wholeness of our body, feelings, mind and spirit.

On the Wilderness Vision Quest I teach participants a wide array of methods and techniques for deepening their appreciation of the natural world and for facilitating the process of self-discovery. Through my work in Psychosynthesis I have developed an eleven step process which I call 'Creative Explorations of Inner Space'. This process is effective in a variety of settings, and for a variety of purposes. Allow me to outline how I employ it on the vision quest. You can even use it on your own after reading it here if you are interested in giving it a try. However, such inner journeys are often much easier to experience under competent supervision.

CREATIVE EXPLORATIONS OF INNER SPACE (CEIS)

Step 1: **Preparation.** On the Wilderness Vision Quest, I spend a couple of days preparing the participants for the CEIS. Each morning begins with an hour of gentle stretching and body movement in the form of Hatha Yoga. We work in our journals several times a day, recording our experiences and documenting the aspects of the land which excite, stimulate or inspire us. We take only four pounds of food to eat for a period of a week, to lighten up in our bodies and move closer to our true emotions. Preparation is a critical and important step to take when we decide to have contact with deeper aspects of our inner lives.

Step 2: **Deep Relaxation.** When it comes time for the CEIS, I begin with about five minutes of deep relaxation. I direct the participants to simply close their eyes, breathe deeply a few times, and let go of their stress and/or tension. This helps them detach from the external world and tune into their inner lives.

Step 3: **Reflective Meditation.** We have already made a list of the various aspects of nature which have been fascinating to us. In this step we choose the one fascination which means the most to us. We write about this fascination in great detail: what it is; in what niche it finds its expression; its size, shape, colour; what it means to us and how we feel about it. We take about 15 minutes to reflect consciously on these dimensions.

Step 4: **Receptive Meditation.** Now we sit with eyes closed, quietly and in a receptive mode, allowing deeper thoughts and feelings to surface and enter our conscious minds. The more subtle aspects of our fascination rise into our field of awareness and, when they do, we record them in our journals. We take about 10 minutes for this.

Step 5: **Visualisation.** We close our eyes and breathe deeply a few times. Then we allow an image or mental picture to form in our mind's eye of that which is our fascination. In other words, we call up this aspect of the natural world in imagination, thus engaging this important psychological function. The images that come to mind are often quite startling. Seldom are they an exact representation of the outer form. Since the imagination is the holographic function of the psyche, it takes a great many variables into account all at once, and the image which appears is a composite picture of what we know, what we see, what we feel and its meaning to us. It takes only a few moments for this image to appear in visualisation.

216

Step 6: **Symbolic Drawing**. Now we open our eyes, take out our journals and draw a large circle on a blank page. This circle becomes a frame in or around which we make a drawing of our inner image. We use oil pastels, coloured felt-tip pens, magic markers and other material with which to make the drawing, and we take as much time as we need to draw it. Some people are finished in ten minutes; others take half an hour. It is not uncommon for me to spend up to three hours making a symbolic drawing, but then I have been at this a very long time and derive tremendous satisfaction from the process. I tell participants not to be concerned with the artistic value of the drawing. Intellectual judgements or perfectionistic criticisms will prevent the symbolic drawing from occurring in a fluid and authentic manner.

Step 7: **Cognitive Analysis**. Now we analyse our drawings, writing in detail what we see and how we feel about the artistic expression. What are the differences between the inner image and the outer symbol? What do the colours and shapes stand for? Now that the image has been externalised, what further thoughts or reflections come to mind? What is the meaning of the drawing? The answers to all these questions are recorded in our journals.

Step 8: **Symbolic Dialogue**. We close our eyes once again, take a few deep breaths and bring back the image into our mind's eye. When we can visualise the image clearly, we ask this question directly to the image: "What do you have to teach me at this moment in my life?" Focusing on the inner image and asking this question helps us access very deep levels of consciousness. Nature speaks to us through the voice of our intuition in a language of poetry and wisdom. As these messages enter our conscious minds, we write them down beneath the drawing in quotation marks. This symbolic dialogue can be repeated once or twice again in the course of about 15 minutes, to extract the maximum cognitive learning.

Step 9: **Symbolic Identification**. Now we stand up with our eyes closed, breathe deeply a few times, and recall the inner image. Visualising the image clearly once again, now we let ourselves go imaginatively. We let our awareness slip into the living reality of the fascination with which we are working. We become the fascination in our bodies, letting ourselves dance, move, gesture, assume various body postures appropriate to this unique expression of the natural world. We also let whatever sounds, noises, or spontaneous music that seems appropriate flow through us. The longer we allow ourselves to experience this symbolic identification, the deeper we move in rapport with the creative intelligence of the universe. Our own blocked channels of energy open up, new circuits establish themselves (if but for a little while), and we explore some of the latent but quite potent human potential within us. When we are finished, we return to our journals and record our experiences.

Step 10: **Grounding**. As we begin to wind down the CEIS, we reflect on everything that has happened. We wonder how we can apply the insights, energies and wisdom we have received to our everyday lives. We choose one real aspect of our ordinary lives that might benefit from the application of this material, and write about it in detail.

Step 11: **Closure**. The last step in the CEIS process helps us return to ordinary levels of awareness. We take the time to share our experience with another person or with a small group of people. We speak of our experiences in depth, and we listen to the experiences of others as we all try to bridge the gap between ourselves and each other, and between ourselves and nature. A very powerful bonding occurs through this process, with others and with nature. Our fascinations on the land continue to be important teachers for us after this. We learn to pay special and close attention to what fascinates us on the land, realising that any part of nature can become the gateway to profound states of awareness, insight and energy.

As we slow down to observe and reflect on these facets of nature, we begin to internalise their messages. Just as we need mirrors with which to see our own faces, we also need the mirror of these natural processes in which to catch the reflection of our inner selves. We are drawn to or fascinated by various aspects of nature because they resonate with essential aspects of our inner lives. Within each of us are pains to be healed, experiences to integrate, talents, abilities and potentials to be actualised.

As we learn how to observe and then participate this fully with nature, we leave behind those patterns and beliefs that keep us feeling so separate and alone. We discover the unity of life and the importance of our special part in it. Empowered by this perspective and these experiences, we can return to our daily lives changed in a positive way, open, responsive and alive, and more able to align our actions in the world with our deepest values.

The Use of Wilderness and Environmental Studies across the School Curriculum

Don Richards

Young students exploring Lake St Lucia, Natal, as part of their course work

Fred Polak, author of *The Image of the Future*, presents an interesting and frightening parallel which humankind, and especially those involved in education of any form, should take cognisance of:

> Imagine an Indian tribe which for centuries has sailed its dugouts on the river at its doorstep. During all this time the economy and culture of the tribe have depended upon fishing, preparing and cooking the products of the river, building boats and appropriate tools. So long as the rate of technological change in such a community stays slow, so long as no wars, invasions, epidemics or other natural disasters upset the even rhythm of life, it is simple for the tribe to formulate a workable image of its own future, since tomorrow merely repeats yesterday.

> It is from this image that education flows. School may not even exist in the tribe; yet there is a curriculum—a cluster of skills, values and rituals to be learnt. Boys are taught to scrape bark and hollow trees, just as their ancestors did before them. The teacher in such a system knows what he is doing, secure in the knowledge that tradition—the past—will work in the future.

> What happens to such a tribe, however, when it pursues its traditional methods unaware that six hundred kilometres upstream men are constructing a gigantic dam that will dry up their branch of the river? Suddenly the tribe's image of the future, the set of assumptions on which its members base their

present behaviour, becomes dangerously misleading. Tomorrow will not replicate today. The tribal investment in preparing its children to live in a riverine culture becomes a pointless and potentially tragic waste. A false image of the future destroys the relevance of the education effort.

This is our situation today—only it is we, ironically, not some distant strangers, who are building the dam that will annihilate the culture of the present. Never before has any culture subjected itself to so intense and prolonged a bombardment of technological, social and info-psychological change. This change is accelerating and we witness everywhere in the high-technology societies evidence that the old industrial era structures can no longer carry out their functions.

Yet our political leaders for the most part propagate (and believe) the myth that industrial society is destined to perpetuate itself indefinitely. Like the elders of the tribe living on the river bank, they blindly assume that the main features of the present social system will extend indefinitely into the future. And so most schools, colleges and universities base their teaching on the notion that tomorrow's world will be basically familiar.

The Global Report to the President of the USA in 1980 stated:

If present trends continue, the world in 2000 AD will be more crowded, more polluted, less stable ecologically, and more vulnerable to disruption than the world we live in now. Serious stresses involving population, resources and environment are clearly visible ahead. Despite greater material output, the world's people will be poorer in many ways than they are today.

The Bali Declaration of October 1982, linking conservation with sustainable development and the rational use of the world's natural resources, states:

Earth is the only place in the Universe known to sustain life, yet, as species are lost and ecosystems degraded, its capacity to do so is rapidly reduced, because of rising populations, excessive consumption and misuse of natural resources, pollution, careless development and failure to establish an appropriate economic order among people and among states. The benefits of nature and living resources that will be enjoyed by future generations will be determined by the decisions of today. Ours may be the last generation able to choose large natural areas to protect.

How are we preparing our children? If our future citizens are to value wilderness, then they must not only know what it is, but must also realise the intricate part it plays in the scheme of things. I believe children should be introduced to the concept of wilderness and exposed to the reality of it as soon as possible—for otherwise we shall continue to develop future citizens on an assembly line of education like a string of sausages, environmentally illiterate and insensitive to the concept of wilderness and to the necessity for its conservation and preservation, not only for its own sake but for the survival of humankind.

Piaget, the noted child psychologist and researcher, maintains that from about the age of eleven, children begin to be able to evaluate the world around them without relying on information gathered from concrete objects. According to Piaget, they are now ready to begin learning abstractly, gradually developing the capacity to reason through the use of hypotheses. When given information, they can start making logical deductions without first turning to concrete examples.

Hence it is reasonable to presume that eleven upwards would be the suitable age to introduce children to 'wilderness' and its role in humanity's survival.

Human beings are part of the environment, both depending totally on it and also affecting it. By understanding our use and misuse of the natural and human-created communities in which we live, we can better deal with problems that face us.

Environmental studies is not a subject, but a method of education based on the idea that the world around the pupil is his or her natural classroom. Environmental learning can be as simple as looking around at your own surroundings to see what they include and what is pleasant and unpleasant about them. The ultimate objective of an environmental programme is to enable us to think reasonably and understandably about our environment—to see patterns of cause and effect which make sense. Environmental learning is a practical and common sense way of schooling. Instead of studying make-believe situations and solving make-believe problems, the student is faced with real-life ones. No-one can be taught environmental awareness; it must be experienced.

In preparing children to understand the need for wilderness areas, we can use wilderness itself as an outside classroom. Here children can both identify problems and identify themselves with these problems, and try to solve them as they are faced with them. They can research and learn how to process their research. They can learn to think for themselves as they become aware of their surroundings, and so see that they must become responsible citizens of planet Earth by contributing to making this world a better place to live in.

A BLUEPRINT: THE TREVERTON PROGRAMME

An exciting educational venture has begun at Treverton Preparatory School in Mooi River, Natal, South Africa. Environmental studies have been introduced across the whole curriculum at the Standard Five (11-12 year old) level. Tuition and practical work in all the normal school subjects—including science, geography, history, mathematics, English, Afrikaans, art and religious instruction—take place in the outdoors, and then later in the classroom, where pupils consolidate what they have learnt.

The central theme of the study is the Mooi River from its source in the Drakensberg Mountains to its confluence with the Tugela River. The many varying ecological habitats and systems provide ideal

Howick Falls forms a spectacular and environmentally interesting study for emerging naturalists

subjects for study and comparison by multi-racial groups of boys and girls in the Standard Five classes. The study area embraces three major wilderness areas in Natal and Zululand, and these are not only used to promote an understanding of the normal school subjects in the curriculum but also serve to make the pupils vitally aware of the need for wilderness areas—which results in environmentally literate citizens.

Members of a class are divided into groups which camp out at different study points along the river and in the wilderness areas, where they do research. They then complete a two-week consolidation period back at school, when they prepare projects and teach-backs on the results of their research. In this way the whole class benefits from each group. Prescribed text books are interwoven into these environmental studies, and the normal tuition throughout the year is all related to what students have learned in the field.

This environmental approach to education is a scholastic one which enables students to study and learn through real-life situations, backed up by normal teaching practices. As they get to grips with the environment and especially with wilderness areas, they discover their place in it and their responsibility to it. They also discover they are an important link in God's creation.

The study areas covered are: 1) the school and its environment; 2) the Giants Castle Game Reserve—a study of the Bushmen; 3) Mooi River town—an urban study; 4) Fernwood—a study of the source of the Mooi River and its environment; 5) Zululand—a study of the culture and history of the Zulu people plus bushveld ecology and estuarine ecology; 6) Rosetta—a study of the upper-middle Mooi River and its environs; 7) Durban—a study of the early history of Natal, early settlers, plus study of fish, reptiles, docks; 8) Pietermaritzburg, the capital of Natal; 9) the Mooi River falls area; and 10) comparison of all study areas and conclusions.

I will give an example of just one of the study areas here—the Giants Castle Game Reserve. Here the aim is to study the history and culture of the Bushmen in relation to the ecology of the Giants Castle area; to learn about geographical concepts such as plateaus, peaks, valleys, watersheds, sponges, etc; to learn about the geology of the area and link this with its plant life; to show pupils that wildlife areas have to be wisely managed and conserved in all respects; and to show pupils that areas such as Giants Castle are needed by people to reflect on God's wonderful creation.

Preparation for study in this area involves drawing up an outline of work schedule. A preliminary reconnaissance of the area is made, pre-study, on-study and post-study worksheets are worked out, accommodation, food and transport arranged, and necessary materials and reference books collected.

To introduce the study, a tape on the history and culture of the

Bushmen in the Giants Castle area is borrowed from the Natal Parks Board and played to the class. Pre-study worksheets are given out to the children. We discuss the basic geology of the area, as well as the basic vegetation in relation to the geology. On arrival at the rest camp at Giants Castle, or when necessary during the study, on-site worksheets and reference material are handed out.

The pupils are divided into groups, and each allocated a different assignment. Group One is assigned the history of the Giants Castle Game Reserve; Group Two, the wildlife of the reserve; Group Three, a study of the Bushmen; Group Four, the geology and ecology of the Drakensberg, as well as its importance as a water conservation area; and Group Five, the management of the Reserve.

In addition to working on their particular assignments, all groups also do field work on the whole area, studying plant and river ecology and the Reserve. A project in the Afrikaans language is also set.

Once back at school, each group writes up a project on their assignment and gives a teach-back to the rest of the class.

Group One (the history of the Reserve) cover the early people—the Bushmen; the Langabalele Rebellion; and the formation of the Reserve, including the pioneers of the Reserve. Audio-visual displays accompany the teach-back.

Group Two (wildlife of the Reserve) produce charts, drawings and sound recordings, and graph game counts. Food chain and habitat displays accompany the teach-back.

Group Three (a study of the Bushmen) give a teach-back on the history and culture of the Bushmen, accompanied by visual and audio displays.

Group Four (the geology, ecology and importance of the Drakensberg as a water conservation area) produce models and overhead transparencies of a cross-section of the geology of the area, a cross-section of the vegetation belts, and a map and model of the Reserve.

Group Five (management of the Reserve) cover management techniques employed by the Natal Parks Board, using models, overhead transparencies and slides of conservation modules and methods.

In evaluating the students, the work done is recorded and progress in writing, language, maths and other skills is noted, as are special talents. Note is also taken of pupils involved in a narrow band on the project, so they can be involved in other areas. The projects are marked. All material used in the projects and teach-backs is collected and stored for exhibitions (such as Parents' Days, conferences and symposiums) or for reference.

During their year of total involvement in the environment, the children emerge as young people whose attitudes and values have changed. They have not only received a true education, but also have become caring people, caring for others, for their environment and for the wilderness they have grown to love.

The environmental education programme has now extended into the rest of the school. In the Standard Six year, each child completes a mini-thesis and spends two periods of five days in the year doing research with experts in whichever field they have chosen. In the High School, a very active outdoor pursuits programme has been instituted.

We have to look to the future, and we believe that this form of education immerses the student mentally, physically and spiritually in their surroundings, enabling them to gain a deep understanding of our dependence on our environment and our responsibility to it as the custodians of God's creation. There is hope that our wilderness areas will be in good and capable hands.

The Value of Wilderness for Young People of Today and Tomorrow

Karen Blair

Wilderness areas are one of the greatest assets we have in which to train young people to understand themselves and their world

In considering the theme of this talk, I obviously do not have the background of a person with many years' experience of wilderness. Consequently, I am simply going to speak about my work for the Duke of Edinburgh's Award, and to share some thoughts on how it has affected me as a young person and why I feel wilderness areas should be maintained for the young people of tomorrow's society.

The Duke of Edinburgh Award Scheme is an international programme which became known as the Duke of Edinburgh's Award in 1956. At present it operates under a variety of titles throughout the world. It is an organisation within which young people between the ages of 14 and 25 can take part in a wide variety of activities which give them enjoyment, excitement and satisfaction. Its founder, Prince Philip, Duke of Edinburgh, describes it as a 'do-it-yourself kit for education in the art of civilised living'. To gain the award, according to Commander Peyton Jones, International Secretary of the Scheme, participants require qualities of 'self-discipline, perseverance, enterprise and effort'.

Wilderness can be defined in different ways, but the definition I like is that found in the 1964 American Wilderness Act: "An area where the earth and its community of life are untrammelled by man, where man himself is a visitor who does not remain." In the light of this definition, only areas such as the polar regions, deserts in Africa, rain forests in Australia and jungle areas in South America can be classified as wilderness. Due to the proximity of human beings, there are no true areas of wilderness in Britain. The Duke of Edinburgh Award Scheme expeditions therefore take place in wild country, in areas such as the Highlands and western isles of Scotland, the Lake District, the Peak District, mid-Wales and Snowdonia.

Through my involvement with the Duke of Edinburgh Award Scheme and with Outward Bound courses I have attended from college, I have had fairly extensive experience of Britain's wild country. I was also fortunate enough to be brought up in Peru, where I was to some degree able to experience the wilderness areas there. On several aeroplane flights I have viewed the vast expanse of dense jungle areas and the forbidding, cold, snow-peaked tips of the Andes which stretch for miles without any sign of life. In Peru I made a study of the Jagua Indian tribe, one of the few remaining primitive tribes who inhabit an area near Ampiyaw river, about 146 miles down the Amazon river from Iquitos.

One of the reasons wilderness areas are important for young people is because of their aesthetic value. In wilderness areas, one leaves behind all aspects of civilisation and the considerable amount of human-created ugliness, and is instead surrounded by naturally created beauty. As the senses become attuned to the surroundings, one learns to observe the vegetation, trees and plant-life, or perhaps the barren and rugged beauty of rocks, mountain peaks, streams and waterfalls, marshes and moorland. Areas vary in appearance with the seasons and the time of day. The beauty remains, irrespective of weather conditions which affect the landscape in a variety of ways.

These areas also provide us with an experience of peacefulness and tranquillity away from the hustle and bustle and pressures of modern living. By communing with, responding to and delighting in nature's different moods, one is able to relax and enjoy life at a slower pace. Our senses of sight and sound become quickened and more acute, helping us to develop an appreciation of the environment. For example, the nocturnal sounds I encountered in the jungle were frightening but intriguing. Worries too can be supressed, because nature provides us with something else to think about.

Nature can also be comforting and friendly. The poet A.E. Housman, for example, who introduced nature into many of his poems, felt he was able to communicate with nature, and regarded it as a companion which could relieve him of his suffering. In his poem, 'In my own shire, if I was sad', he depicts nature as a friend which can comfort him when in trouble, something humankind is unable to do because of its own troubles.

Another reason wilderness areas are important for young people is because they can provide adventure, which plays an important part in character building. Facilities for Outward Bound courses in Peru are limited, although the natural environment is ideal. However, there is scope for organisations such as scouts, brownies, guides, rangers and the foreign-run Scripture Union which holds camps on the coast and in the jungle for both privileged and underprivileged youngsters. It was through these organisations that I first savoured and developed a desire to further my experience in this field. Peru has a tremendous amount to offer, particularly where mountaineering is concerned, and in recent years the Cordillera Blanca has become a popular goal for expeditions from all the major climbing countries.

My final two years of schooling took place in Britain, where my earlier experiences in Peru encouraged me to take part both in the Duke of Edinburgh's Gold Award Scheme and in the Physical Education course I am now following. Both of these have helped build my enthusiasm for the wonders that nature provides, and convinced me of the need to preserve them for future generations.

Some of the activities in which I have participated are rock-climbing, abseiling, mountaineering, canoeing and camping, all of which involve elements of uncertainty. In rock-climbing, for example, tension and nerve are involved as one faces anxiety about whether the rock can be negotiated safely, before deciding to commit oneself. Self-confidence and good judgement are strengthened. As confidence grows, commitment follows and the challenge is faced. The element of risk is over only when the feat is completed, and the reward is great physical and spiritual satisfaction.

The rewards from any adventure situation are most important, and vary according to the activity being undertaken. For example, in rock-climbing I enjoy both the breath-taking scenery viewed from the heights and the great feeling of achievement, satisfaction and elation at reaching the crest I have aimed for. In mountaineering, the essence of achievement lies in relief at arriving at the destination after combating the weather and terrain with a map and compass. And in canoeing, there is the magnificent sensation of riding the powerful current and the thrill of moving with the force of water as well as the feeling of trying to control and dominate it.

By taking part in such activities, people learn to appreciate the environment and to cope with unexpected situations. They also gain much valued human qualities such as concentration (for to relax your vigilance could have drastic consequences), determination and persistence. I remember hiking and camping in a force ten gale on a wet

Physical strength and endurance, such as can be gained from rock-climbing and canoeing, are among the important qualities which can be acquired through wilderness experience

and stormy night. Thoughts of giving up crossed my mind, but the idea of allowing the weather and terrain to defeat me made me all the more determined to continue. Initiative and self-reliance are also developed, for if you do not check the weather and gather sufficient provisions such as firewood and food, then it is you who suffer. Faith and trust grow as you learn to care for, encourage and rely on other individuals as well as on material things such as a rope in rock-climbing. Cooperation is another quality fostered by outdoor activities. The ability to recognise, value and use the differing talents among members of a group, as well as to deal with others and use their ideas and suggestions, is an important step towards learning to live effectively. You also learn that fears and difficulties can be overcome, and that you can achieve things if you really do try. I have become aware that there is no such word as 'can't', because 'where there's a will there's a way'!

At the same time, taking part in such activities and being subjected to forces of nature like the weather and the power of water makes one humble. This is particularly important today when modern technology has become so powerful that it can lead some people to a sense of omnipotence. Being in a wild environment produces a respect for and understanding of the world that exists beyond human control.

Outdoor pursuits can heighten awareness and allow young people to test and discover their powers and potentialities, to learn true values, and to experience new things away from the crowded influences of city life, radio, television and above all from the great temptation to watch and receive instead of to do. Taking part in activities is vital, for as Wordsworth once said, "It is in moments of feeling and excitement that one's deepest lessons are learned." Every teacher knows that it is only by capturing the interest and engaging the emotions of young people that they can effectively be taught.

Wild country areas can also be a challenge and stimulus for the older generation. I was inspired recently by a documentary film, *Miles to Go*, which showed women of all ages experiencing high risk activities in the wilderness areas of America and facing challenges different from those encountered in everyday life.

I have personally gained a great deal from being in wilderness areas and taking part in high risk activities there. I hope to continue to gain experience and to encourage others to do so also. It is vital that we strive to preserve those areas in which rivers, seas and mountains meet to provide a natural challenge and training ground where the young people of tomorrow can be helped to gain the human qualities valued in society and to experience wilderness. There is no point encouraging young people to explore wilderness areas if there are no wild places left for them to find.

Wilderness: A Way of Truth

Laurens van der Post

When we contemplate the future of wilderness today, we see it as a place without human beings, where people go only as visitors. But we forget that there was once such a person as the 'wilderness man'. The original wilderness contained not only plants and trees and animals, but also people.

When we talk about primitive people in the world today, we are not really talking about them in the sense of *first* people. Most of our ideas of primitive people are based on what we have observed of great indigenous cultures which are already well advanced on the way to civilisation. The American Indians, for instance, were far more in communion and communication with their instincts than we are, but they were by no means primitive. They were already very sophisticated people. People like the Navajo and Hopi had their own forms of civilisation. The Navajo were great sheep people, while the Hopi were agricultural people who went in for husbandry. They had already crossed the great divide and tamed a part of nature for their own uses. The great black societies of Africa are also people of very vast and sophisticated forms of human organisation.

But Africa did produce a first person. And this first person has haunted my life from the time I was born, because I had a nurse who was one of the last survivors in my part of Africa of the first people. I owe her a tremendous amount, because through her the private person in me, the child in me, took wing.

In later life I had the privilege for about three and a half years to be in constant contact with these first people of Africa, the Bushmen. When we contemplate them I think we realise the horror of what we have done—that in destroying wilderness we have destroyed 'wilderness man'. In a way, that is the greatest loss of all, because this person could have been our real bridge to knowing wilderness and nature in the way in which it is known by the Creator and in which it should really be known.

I would like to tell you a bit about these people. It is not a romantic vision because, obviously, they had their faults too, and they were very human faults. But they were faults, in so far as I could observe them, that had no unnecessary complications to them. They were faults that were in proportion and that were incorporated and kept in position by the great necessities of nature, by the totality of their way of life. They committed themselves to nature as a fish to the sea, and nature was kinder to them by far than any civilisation ever was.

The one outstanding characteristic of these people as I knew them, and which distinguished them from us, was that wherever they went, they felt they were known. The staggering loss of identity and meaning that we in the modern world experience was unknown to them. As St. Paul says, "Then shall I know as even now I am known." This sense of being known has completely abandoned us in the modern world, because we have destroyed the wilderness person in ourselves and banished the wilderness that sustained them from our lives. And because of the absence of this wilderness person in ourselves, we are left with a kind of loneliness, an inadequate comprehension of what life can be. We have become the greatest collection of human know-alls that life has ever seen. But the feeling that our knowing is contained in a greater form of being known has gone.

One of the most extraordinary things to me about these first people was their lack of aggression. I asked them if they had ever had war, and they said, oh yes, they had fought and were known as very great fighters. But except for when they fought against the Black and the White people, they had only had one war among themselves. I asked, "Was it an awful war?" And they said, "It was a terrible war." I asked, "Were many people killed?" And they said, "One man was killed." That was enough. One man. It didn't have to be numbers. In this terrible world in which we live today, we think things only matter if we know them in numbers. We talk about the sum of human misery. There is no such thing in the wilderness. The sum of human misery is really an abstraction, because misery is never more than what one person can feel. It is inflicted on one person at a time. This misery was enough for them. And I asked, "What did you do?" They said, "Well, we decided that those of us who had done the killing should never meet again because we were not fit to meet one another."

So they drew a line across the desert. And for centuries they had not crossed that line, in case they should take life again. They held the life of one person to be so precious. I asked them, "But how can you draw a line in the desert?"—because one side of it looked to me very much like the other. They always thought that I was singularly stupid and uneducated, and, of course, I am, in their terms. I was a baby, not even in the kindergarten class. And they said, "Well, you see, no two dunes are alike, no two plants are alike. It is part of our education to know what dunes and what plants are the dividing lines, and we never cross those dividing lines."

So there went a people to whom life was full of meaning. They always moved in small companies, and the groups I knew best never exceeded 23 in number. That was the entire community, and everyone was a clear-cut individual with their own individual gifts, making their individual contributions to their little society. There was none of the smearing and blurring of personality that we get in the mass societies of the West and of Asia. Yet to them, everything was family. They had no captains or kings, and the highest title they could bestow was to call somebody a grandfather or grandmother. The stars were part of the family too. The star Sirius, for instance, the great dog star, was grandmother Sirius to whom they prayed. They would say, "Oh grandmother Sirius, who sits there with a heart of plenty and so full of light, give us who do not have so much, some of your plenty." And they believed it happened and it helped. The whole of the cosmos was a family. They had an extraordinary feeling of kinship that burnt like a flame and kept them on course, that kept them warm and full of meaning. I have seen a woman at night hold her little boy up to the stars. I asked, "Why the stars?" And they said, "Don't you know the stars are great hunters hunting there in the outer dark? She is asking the stars to take from her son the heart of a little child and give him the heart of a star instead."

The sense of communion that these people had with the cosmos came out above all in their stories. There was nothing about which they did not have a story. There is one story that I want to tell you, because I think it sums up the importance of serving the truth, even if one has only a part of the truth which one can fulfil in one's own lifetime.

This is a story of a hunter. The people in the groups I knew all hunted, but there was always one man who was better at it than most. Often he also happened to be the musician. They had musical instruments shaped like a bow and the hunter who shot so well with his bow was often the one who also played beautifully on this wonderful bow stringed instrument.

The story goes that one day this hunter was out hunting and became very thirsty. He came to the edge of a pool—it was in the rainy

South African Zulus in traditional dress

Bushman Rock Art, Giant's Castle, Natal, South Africa. Original inhabitants of wilderness, 'first people', left an important and valuable legacy in their stories and art

season—and bent down to drink some of the water. And as he looked into this pool which was deep blue with the midnight blue of an African summer's sky, he suddenly saw in the rippling mirror below him the reflection of a great white bird. He looked up quickly, startled, but the bird had already gone. But from that moment on he wasn't the same. He lost all interest in hunting. The people, because they loved him, tried desperately to revive his desire for hunting, but it had totally abandoned him. One day he said to his people, "I am sorry; I am going. I am going to find this bird whose reflection I saw. I have got to find it." And he said goodbye and vanished.

The story goes that he went all over Africa, all over what they then naturally thought of as the entire world. And whenever he came to places where there were people, he would describe the bird to them and ask if they had seen it, and they would say, "What a pity you didn't come last night, because the bird was roosting nearby." So it went on and on until, toward the end of his days when he was quite an old man, he came to an enormous mountain right in the heart of Africa. He asked the people at the foot of the mountain if they knew anything about this bird. And they said, oh yes, it came to roost every night on top of the mountain. So he climbed the mountain and when he came close to the top he found the summit was a sheer cliff which he couldn't scale. His strength was worn out and he knew he could go no further. He stood there looking into the red and scarlet sunset of Africa and thought, "I shall never see this white bird whose reflection is all I know." And he prepared himself to lie down to die.

Then at that moment a voice inside him said, "Look." He looked up and, in the dying light of the African sunset, he saw a white feather floating down from the mountain top. He held out his hand and the feather came into it, and, grasping the feather, he died.

When the Bushmen told me this story, I asked, "What sort of bird was this?" And they said, "The bird has many names, but we think of it as the Great White Bird of Truth."

Here we have an example of the instinctive symbolism of people who are spiritually 'aware'. The imagery comes naturally out of their being, putting them on the trail of truth, yet with a humility that does not try to grasp it all at once. Some of us here at the Wilderness Congress would like the whole of our wilderness dream at once. We are impatient, and feel if we don't get it immediately, we shall never get it. But in this story just the reflection of the bird, not even the bird itself, was enough to send a man on its trail—and one feather from that bird made his life worthwhile and allowed him to die content.

The processes of history work slowly. There are no short cuts in creation. Things happen by the planting and sowing of seeds, and do not appear all at once. We must have the humility of spirit to recognise how small, in a sense, is the success we can achieve in a single lifetime.

We can't do it all. But what we can do is set things in their right direction, and I think that is beginning to happen. And as we do that, since life is universal and we don't control it, something far greater than ourselves begins to work. This puts at our disposal, late as the hour is, time enough for the right things to happen. There is always time enough, no matter how desperate it is, for the complete thing to happen.

I would like all of us who are pursuing wilderness to take this in, and to know that if we follow in the way of the 'wilderness man', we too shall grasp a feather of truth. And that one day, one day that indeed will come, we shall be able to contemplate the whole bird in its entirety.

I would like you to reach out and believe this. I would like to make a pact with you that our wilderness dream will come true. The Earth today is wounded and sore. But our pursuit of the wilderness dream will bring about not only the protection of the wilderness such as we have it today, but also the rehabilitation of the Earth, with people able to live in the wilderness state of communion with it, following the White Bird of Truth.

This will come. Nothing can stop it, for nothing can stop a dream that is true. If you go back into the history of humankind, you find that in all the great cultures—the Greek, the Babylonian, the Chinese, the Japanese and our own—everything begins with a dream. Think of the dreams in our own Bible—of the tremendous dream of Jacob's Ladder, for example. Think of the dream which started the great Greek Homeric saga of the *Iliad* and the *Odyssey*, when a god sent a dream into the head of sleeping Agamemnon as he lay by the black ships on the great plain of Troy. It all starts with a dream. Until we can say at last, "Pass, world. I am the dreamer that remains, clear-cut against the sky." That is a quotation from a poem by a friend of mine.

We cannot, today, recreate the original 'wilderness man' in shape and form and habitat. But we can recover him, because he exists in us. He is the foundation in spirit or psyche on which we build, and we are not complete until we have recovered him. Life not only involves being conscious of the moment in which we live, but also involves a vision of the future. And before we can live properly, before we can face the future, we have got to remember. There is a phrase that occurs over and over again in the *Upanishads* which says, "Oh man, remember." We have got to remember the needs and hunger of our instinctive, intuitive natural self. It needs our consciousness, because without our consciousness it has no life. But without its prompting, our life has no meaning. In the modern world, we have become so engaged in doing that we have become divorced from the aspect of ourselves which gives us being.

The real task of every generation is to make what is first new and contemporary. The first people, the wilderness people, were not com-

236

plete. They needed something more which they were in search of, and there was an enormous act of evolution that had to occur. But in the lop-sided way in which the so-called civilising process takes place, one part that was glaringly lacking was pulled out of the wholeness and developed to the exclusion of others. In the process of developing it, we fell into the heresy of thinking that that was the lot, and of course it isn't. What we need to do now, in very simple mathematical terms is to make the first the last, and to bring it up to where we are. We still carry around with us the world of nature within. We need to match that to the world without, to make the world without more and more an expression of the world within.

The reason we exploit, damage and savage the Earth is because we are out of balance. We have lost our sense of proportion. And we cannot be proportionate unless we honour the wilderness and the natural person within ourselves. That is where the balance comes from. Our greed and aggression and corruption by power comes from cheating that first person within ourselves out of his natural inheritance, as Jacob cheated Esau. The whole great progression of evolution as represented in the Bible is based on a monstrous act of deception which passed for intelligence. It *is* a form of intelligence and has to be seen symbolically, and I do not want to suggest that that development is invalid. It *is* valid, but we should recognise that it is not the whole story. Somewhere, beyond the walls of our awareness, the Esau side, the wilderness side, the hunter side, the seeking side of ourselves, is waiting to return.

By grey crags
the old, blue-headed,
red-stemmed Scots Pine
holds the wind in its sail,
long enough
to bring forth song
or tell the tale of great deeds
long, long ago,
when it was young.

Finlay MacRae

WILDERNESS

Focus on Scotland

A Message from the British Government

George Younger

The River Affric

It is the strong conviction of the United Kingdom Government that the natural environment of this country is a precious asset. By the definitions that some people use, we may not have much wilderness, but we have large areas of virtually uninhabited territory and great opportunities for outdoor recreation of all kinds.

As new needs arise, further changes in the Scottish landscape are inevitable, and it is important that proposals for development ensure the maximum benefit to the community while also avoiding significant damage to the environment in which that community lives. In Scotland a well-established planning system provides for careful consideration of development proposals which have serious implications for the environment. A unique system of national planning guidelines sets out policies for the conservation of such precious assets as good farm land, outstanding landscape and sites of special scientific interest. The guidelines also indicate preferred areas for major industrial development and mineral workings. We are also in the course of considering—with local authorities, conservation bodies and development agencies—guidelines for skiing developments which will take into account

◄ The Central Highlands—The Cairngorms National Nature Reserve

both the development potential for downhill skiing in Scotland and the need to avoid conflict with other uses of the land such as for wildlife or landscape conservation or for walkers and climbers.

I see no necessary general conflict between the social and economic development of the Highlands and the protection of the landscape and wildlife of the area. The development of the oil industry is a particularly good example of how resource development on a major scale can be achieved without significant damage to the beautiful wild areas for which Scotland is so renowned, but with substantial advantages for the well-being of remote and fragile communities in these areas. Over a period of ten years, nearly 100,000 new jobs have been created in developments largely or partly related to North Sea oil (many of them in the Highlands and Islands), 3,000 hectares of land have been used for terminals and processing industries, 2,000 kilometres of pipeline have been laid underground and 14 separate communities have been involved. Most of this development occurred within a very short space of time. Between 1970 and 1975 applications were considered for all five major gas and oil terminals, all the service bases, the four overland pipelines and some eleven platform yards together with 54 other developments. All these were approved rapidly without major objections and without the need for a public inquiry.

This was largely achieved by anticipatory planning. Aerial survey, information gathering and site assessments were carried out on the coast from 1972-74. Coastal Planning Guidelines were prepared recommending preferred conservation and development zones for oil and gas related development. When the actual applications arrived, working parties were set up between the oil companies, the local authorities and nature conservation interests early enough to influence the choice of location and to agree to methods of monitoring the environmental impact. Later an oil development forum of conservation agencies and amenity interests was set up to give them a better understanding of the need and opportunities for development and to offset ill-informed criticism of potential dangers or impacts that in many instances were avoidable or even non-existent.

To give some examples of the developments that took place, several of the major sites were in previously undeveloped areas of nature conservation, landscape or wilderness interest. At St. Fergus on the coast of Grampian where a large gas terminal was built, the sandy coastline is of considerable ecological interest, particularly the dune and wild fowl habitat. Informal early discussion with nature conservation experts and local amenity groups resulted in a site being chosen, with the agreement of the oil companies, which allowed the area to be protected. Subsequently a dune management group was set up with representatives of the developers, planning authorities and nature conservation bodies to monitor compliance with the planning condition that the whole dune system—which had to be pierced to allow the pipeline through—should be managed as a conservation area. A similar working group at Nigg on the Moray Firth enabled the platform yard there to be sited in such a way as to avoid damaging a neighbouring wildlife site of national significance on the foreshore.

At Shetland, the most northerly group of islands in Britain, with a population of only 17,000, six different oil companies made commercial finds some 50 miles offshore. Six different pipelines and terminals would have destroyed the physical and social environment. The Islands Council obtained technical advice on the most suitable location for one major terminal and secured powers to acquire the land and control of the harbour. They then entered into negotiation with the oil companies for one association of the companies to set up the terminals as a joint venture. The result has been the construction at Sullom Voe of the largest terminal in Europe, capable of handling 1.4 million barrels per day and costing £1.2 billion. This was built in a manner which has attracted well-earned plaudits from environmental interests. The cooperation which was built up between the oil industry, the local authorities and conservation interests allowed the oil industry to develop rapidly to meet the economic opportunities, yet without significant detriment to the natural beauty of the areas in which it is operating. Where various parties share an understanding of each others' objectives and a willingness to cooperate in reconciling them, substantial necessary development can be accommodated and welcomed without serious damage to the environment. I believe the development of the oil industry in Scotland has demonstrated that this can be done.

Others can describe the extensive pattern of nature and landscape conservation areas in this country, covering 667,000 and one million hectares respectively; the nature reserves established by the Nature Conservancy Council and voluntary bodies; and the cooperation between local authorities and Government agencies such as the Countryside Commission for Scotland, the Highlands and Islands Development Board and the Scottish Tourist Board, which have provided in Scotland a widespread system of country parks, long distance footpaths, mountain, forest and water recreation areas.

With regard to the World Conservation Strategy, the United Kingdom Government fully recognises the importance of this Strategy and intends to give it the most searching consideration. Various UK conservation bodies are producing a report suggesting how the Strategy might be implemented; and, in their capacity as the Government's advisors, the Nature Conservancy Council and the Countryside Commissions have been asked to suggest how best Government might respond.

There has been speculation as to the United Kingdom's attitude to the World Heritage Convention of 1972. The question of UK adherence to this Convention has been under consideration for some time, and I am now happy to announce the UK Government's decision to ratify the Convention. This will be done as soon as the wishes of UK dependent territories have been established. We will then consider appropriate areas for identification in terms of the Convention. The UK has of course long protected its natural environment under its domestic legislation; and the formal ratification of the World Heritage Convention will be further international evidence of the United Kingdom's continuing commitment to protection of appropriate aspects of the world's natural and cultural heritage.

A Brief History of the Origins of the Scottish Wildlands

Drennan Watson

Fine tracery of larch trees against a low-lying Highland mist

In considering the Scottish wildlands, I have confined myself largely to the Highlands and Islands of Scotland, though there are considerable stretches of semi-wild country in the area of the southern uplands commonly known as the Borders. The Highlands stretch north from the northern boundary of the rift valley that cuts across the waist of Scotland and west from the coastal plains that stretch round much of the eastern coast. The rock of the Highlands and Islands is very ancient, ranging from 400 million years at the most southerly boundary of the Grampians, to nearly 2,000 million years in the Lewisian gneiss of the island of Lewis in the North West. The topography of the present landforms derives indirectly from a low-lying plain. This plain was uplifted to give a high plateau, probably not much higher than the summits of the present mountains, and rivers eroding back into this plateau produced the main river systems that persist to this day. The glaciers of successive ice ages deepened and steepened these to produce the classical ice-moulded topography that now characterises the Scottish mountains.

The climate of these mountains is a mixture of oceanic and subarctic and is not an easy combination for humans. The only important trend

246

across the spread of the land is that rainfall declines steeply as you go east. The summit of Ben Nevis on the west coast receives an annual rainfall of about 4,000mm but Cairn Gorm, some 90km to the east, gets only 2,200mm. Climate declines more rapidly with altitude than in almost any other mountain range in the world. Wind steadily buffets the islands and mountains, sweeping over the bare and treeless landscapes.

With the exception of small restricted areas of base rich material, the underlying rock is poor in minerals. This, combined with the heavy rainfall and low soil temperature, has produced heavily podzolised soils of low fertility, with extensive areas of acid peaty bog. The vegetation is thus largely characterised by grassy heathlands. The natural vegetation is dominated by northern forms of the boreal forest, except in the most northerly parts where only birch is extensive. On the low ground, oak is the natural dominant species. On the higher ground on poorer soils, and in the northerly areas, its place is taken by the Scots pine. Mingled with these are various other species such as common birch, silver birch, rowan and aspen, along with a number of shrubs. The original animal inhabitants included red deer, elk, reindeer and beaver, along with wolf, brown bear and lynx.

It is uncertain when human beings first entered this scene, but the early colonisers were only the first of waves of peoples that in time included Celts of various kinds, Anglo Saxons and Vikings. By the year 1746 their activities had fundamentally altered the vegetation of most of Scotland, with extensive clearing of forests for agriculture. Prolonged grazing prevented regeneration of trees, as did burning to clear large areas of 'robbers' and wolves. With the habitat went many of its typical denizens. The lynx died out very early, while the bear lasted till about the 9th or 10th century. The beaver, once the basis of the country's valuable fur trade, probably lasted till the 15th century, and the wolf till the early 18th century. Nobody knows when the elk and reindeer disappeared.

1746 was the year of the battle of Culloden, a great watershed in Highland history and the beginning of much that was to affect the Scottish wildlands.

Culloden has always touched Scottish people more sadly than almost any other event in their history. This is not because it saw the defeat of Prince Charlie, but because it was the last battle when Scot fought Scot, and because of the fate of Highland society in the years thereafter. The Gaelic clansmen who fought at Culloden were the living representatives of the oldest society and culture in Europe, and one of the oldest in the world—the tribal society of the Scottish Highland clans.

Early Scotland was a land of several small kingdoms until the 8th century AD, when Kenneth McAlpine, ruler of one of these small kingdoms, managed to unite them under his rule by a judicious mixture of murder and marriage among the other ruling families, particularly among the dominant Picts. Thus was established the Gaelic kingdom of Scotland, with much the same boundaries as it has today.

However, in 1058 Malcolm Canmore (Malcolm Bighead), a king of largely English upbringing, succeeded to the Scottish throne, thanks largely to a policy of vigorous and selective murder of more senior claimants to the throne pursued by his immediate forebears. This introduced another major influence into Scotland, which overthrew the dominance of Gaelic civilisation and eventually produced the Scotland of the two cultures who were to battle at Culloden. Malcolm Canmore also introduced the system of feudal land tenure, which is still today the basis of Scots land law. At the same time, his queen and second wife, the blessed and determined St. Margaret, Romanised the old Celtic church.

In the 13th and 14th centuries the country came under attack from the imperial ambitions of England. The sheer brutality and ferocity of the punitive campaigns of the armies of Edward the First of England aided the evolution of a sense of national identity in Scotland which, under the leadership of resistance leaders such as Wallace, Moray and then the superb and brilliant Bruce, became the rock on which English ambitions foundered at the battle of Bannockburn in 1314.

When the seed of the Bruce eventually failed to produce a stable and enduring dynasty, the royal house of Stuart succeeded to the throne and attempted further to strengthen the authority of the crown, especially in their remoter Highland lands. However, bad luck, Stuart ineptitude and the difficulties of the mountainous terrain, all led to the failure of this policy. In the power vacuum that was left, the tribal system known as the Scottish clans evolved as a development of the ancient Celtic tribal tradition, and as an effective system of self-protection.

'Clan' is an anglicised form of the Gaelic word for children, and reflects the underlying belief in the clan as representing the descendants of one person. Hence the importance of the prefix 'Mac' meaning 'son of' in Scottish names. The function of the chief included almost all aspects of looking after the interests and welfare of his people—the children of the clan. His chief function, however, was to maintain the fighting strength of the clan and lead it in battle.

One disastrous result of this historical development was that it produced a growing gulf between Highland and Lowland Scottish societies, with a Lowland view of the Highlands as the haunt of barbarians and the source of raiding bands of cattle thieves and rebellious Highlanders. The union of the crowns of Scotland and England in 1603, and of their parliaments in 1707, did little to help matters. Neither did the supplantation of the Stuarts by the house of Orange in 1688 and later by the house of Hanover. Serious social problems were developing in the Highlands that the clan system could not handle. The Whig governments of the 18th century, with their almost bottomless corruption and stunning impotence, made matters worse. It was probably desperation born of this situation, rather than a romantic loyalty to the Stuarts, that fuelled a series of rebellions that burst out of the Highlands in these years, culminating in the rebellion of 1745 and the battle of Culloden in 1746.

The 1745 rebellion finally decided the Whig government that the clan system must be destroyed, and they proceeded systematically to dismantle it, principally by converting chiefs into feudal landowners and removing their inherited obligation towards members of their clans. This, combined with a population explosion and with changes in Highland land use, was to have fateful results.

In the century after 1745, the Highlands' population increased by about 50% to its highest ever level of around 400,000. This was due to several factors, including the introduction of the potato and innoculation against smallpox. Poverty, destitution and hunger increased, and with it the rate of outmigration, which was further encouraged by the government's substantial road-building activities that for the first time made the Highlands comparatively accessible.

Simultaneously, changes occurred in the agriculture of the area that were to have dire results. Traditionally, Highland agriculture had been a mixed pastoral one, based on common grazings holding cattle, sheep and goats. A system of transhumance, known as the shieling system, was widely practised, whereby stock were grazed on the low ground from autumn to spring, but summered on the high pastures, leaving the low ground free to be cropped for hay for winter keep. The cattle were particularly important to the cash economy of the area. Far more were reared than could be overwintered, and the surplus were annually driven to the southern markets over a system of tracks and routes known as the 'drove roads', and eventually the meat fed the people of the larger population centres in the south.

From about 1815 onwards, this market was gradually lost. A new style of agriculture was spreading over the Highlands, based on extensive sheep farming using introduced breeds of sheep. This system required large areas of open range and little labour. Many landowners began to regard the inhabitants of the land as a burden on the land and an impediment to 'progress' and profit. The feudal system of land tenure created a fateful link between land ownership and power, and allowed many landowners to clear their lands of this burden. Some did this with a ruthlessness that has become legendary, not only in Scotland but wherever in the world the cleared Highlanders went. Sometimes these landowners were incomers, bent on increasing profits from their newly acquired lands, but equally often they were descendants of the patriarchal chiefs, untramelled now by obligations towards their people. Often the people were moved to coastal areas and encouraged to take up work in fishing or the kelp industry, to further the profit, in most cases, of their landlords. Each family thus settled was given enough land to earn part of its living by agriculture, but not enough to earn all of it lest this deplete the labour available to the kelp industry. Thus was founded the crofting lifestyle that survives over much of the Highlands and Islands to this day.

Not all Highland landowners indulged in these inhumane clearances, and some were at least in part motivated by the belief that the desperate plight of their tenants required desperate measures. Poverty and famine also played a great part in causing the migration that cleared the Highlands of much of their population.

Thus the 'wilderness areas' of Scotland were becoming largely delineated along the lines we see them today. Much of the upper areas, with their shortage of ploughable land, vicissitudes of climate and infertility of soils, have never been permanently settled. Nonetheless, large areas that once supported sizeable populations are now deserted, leaving wild unpopulated areas such as Knoydart.

It is important to realise that the attitude of today's indigenous population towards the Highland lands is still dominated by the memory of the clearances. The wilderness areas of Scotland, with the exception of the Cairngorms plateau, are not as nature left them but have been substantially deforested and otherwise altered by human beings. In the minds of most Highlanders today these lands are not among the nation's treasures as wildlands. Rather they are lost lands, the lands of their forefathers. In some essential and fundamental way they are *their* lands, and need some day to be reclaimed and made productive again. In an area with few jobs and high unemployment, this seems a much more attractive prospect than making them into 'designated wilderness areas', since such people equate the word wilderness with wasted land, the graves of their forefathers and former communities. Politically, this is a major factor for any 'wilderness movement' in Scotland.

Even as 'the great sheep' was spreading through the Highlands and ousting the human population, another trend was following that would in turn oust it—the growth of the sporting estates. Also contributing to the decrease in sheep farming was a decline in prices for sheep products as cheaper imports flooded in to Britain from the Empire, as well as the deterioration of pastures under purely sheep grazing as more nutritious heaths and grasses were selectively grazed out and swards became irreversibly dominated by less nutritious grasses such as moor mat grass.

The industrial revolution had produced a new wealthy class, who turned to the Highlands for sport and leisure. The interest and patronage of such influential members of society as the Duke of Bedford and later the Royal family itself, encouraged this trend. Though

Red deer stag (*Cervus elaphus scoticus*)

A Highland Stalker

grouse and salmon were important quarries of the sporting fraternity, it was the red deer that was the aristocrat of the hunt. From the mid-19th century onward, deer forests—large areas of land given over exclusively to the hunting of red deer—became increasingly widespread. By about 1912, an incredible 20% of Scotland's land area was given over more or less entirely to the hunting of red deer by a small fraction of the populace.

Hunting lodges and extensive paths were built in wild areas, and there were further clearances of people from hunting areas. As a result, the total area of wild land—land without human artefacts and largely without human inhabitants—at this point probably reached a maximum in Scotland to date.

The era of the sporting estate saw further serious and ruthless depredations in Scottish wildlife. The elimination of all raptors and other carnivores, including even fish-eating birds such as mergansers, was considered part of efficient estate management. Thus the sea eagle, osprey, polecat, goshawk and various others became extinct in Scotland, while other species such as the golden eagle, peregrine, pine marten and wildcat were persecuted to the verge of extinction. In this, the gamekeepers and stalkers were assisted by the Victorian collectors of eggs, plants, birds, animals and generally anything that moved or grew. This era, up to the beginning of the First World War (which drastically thinned the ranks of gamekeepers and landowners alike), marked a nadir in the levels and variety of wildlife in the Scottish Highlands.

Since the end of the Second World War, many previously persecuted species have revived. This is due partly to the comparative lack of keepers over sizeable areas of the countryside, and partly to the influence of voluntary and statutory protection agencies and appropriate protective legislation. The pine marten and wildcat have spread, as have the peregrine, harriers, buzzards and golden eagle. The osprey has returned, and the sea eagle once again spreads its great wings over the land.

However, the influences of the sporting estates continue to be destructive in several ways. Poisoning and trapping of protected species is still widespread. Further, in the last twenty years, hundreds of kilometres of bulldozed tracks have been created to give hunting parties easy access and to allow the easier extraction of shot deer. These tracks have often penetrated into previously roadless areas, are usually badly engineered, and are constructed with disregard to effects on landscape and soil erosion. Only recently, after much of the damage had been done, was some fairly mild legislation enacted against this practice. In addition, the standard of management in many of the sporting estates is low. Burning to produce habitats suitable for grouse is often badly carried out, and fires frequently run out of control. Deer numbers in deer forests are often excessively high, preventing regeneration of shrub and tree layers, and divesting them of needed winter browse. Deaths due to winter starvation can be extensive, and deer carcases often litter areas of the hill in spring. The carrying capacity of the land for deer themselves is much reduced, and the habitats of many other forms of wildlife almost eliminated. The combination of overgrazing and burning is probably causing accelerated soil erosion and scree formation on many slopes, but this remains largely uninvestigated in Scotland.

Since the First World War, two other land uses have arisen that have affected the wilder areas of the Highlands—hydro-electric power and forestry. The development of hydro-electric power in the Highlands began as early as 1885, but it was chiefly after the Second World War that it proceeded apace. In the 15 years between 1948 and 1963, some two dozen schemes involving some fifty power stations were built. The trend finally ground to a halt in the 1960s against a wall of public opposition to schemes planned for areas in Glen Nevis and Lochs Fada and Fionn. However, it was the political pressure to use cheaper sources of power such as coal, rather than the cry to preserve wild or scenic areas, that was the principal factor in stopping a good idea carried too far. While some of these schemes served to increase the remoteness of areas cut off by rising waters in reservoirs, the associated dams, pipelines, access roads and powerlines caused very considerable intrusion into wild areas. Many lochs were greatly damaged in their value for scenery, wildlife and recreation by the rise and fall of their waters, exposing and recovering their margins.

Intensive forestry began in the Highlands after the First World War, following a German U-boat campaign against the British timber trade aimed at cutting off the supply of pit-props to the coal mines. As Britain's stocks of home-grown timber were then extremely low, this stratagem would have been a fatal blow to the coal mining industry, and thus to the iron smelting which supported the munitions industry, and almost succeeded in winning the war. Consequently, to develop a strategic supply of standing timber, the Forestry Commission was established after the war, and government encouraged planting by private landowners through tax benefits and planting grants. Intensive forestry has continued to expand ever since. Because of its techniques of dense planting (mostly of exotic species), deep ploughing, and high fencing to exclude deer, it totally destroys the wild qualities of land wherever it is practised. Once well established, the plantations cannot even be penetrated. Though they have aided the spread of some forms of wildlife such as roe deer and red squirrel, they generally harbour impoverished communities. In recent years there have been increased requirements to landscape these plantations in certain areas, but there has been inadequate restraint in the development of this land use.

The growth of organised lobbies to defend wild areas in parallel with these trends has been patchy and irregular, though it has a long and curious history. It was the influence of Sir Walter Scott, the great Scottish writer who invented the novel, that did the most to cause a *volteface* in the average Scot's perception of the Highlands. Previous views of these areas, noticing all too clearly the sad state of the inhabitants, had viewed the wild beauty of the mountains as a dreadful prospect, and the wild lands as just so much land that was totally wasted till properly tamed. Scott's novels, with their romantic tales of the Scottish Highlands, their warlike inhabitants and savage mountains, put forward a new view that was intensely aware of the beauty and appeal of the landscape. However, as this outlook either ignored the condition of the less fortunate inhabitants, or adopted some ill-informed romantic view as to their condition, it was in a sense as unrealistic as its predecessor. Nonetheless, Scott established that romantic attachment of Scots to wild Highland scenery and its peculiar association with national pride that was a reflection of his own deeply patriotic feelings.

By the mid-19th century, wilderness appreciation ran strong among a group of men of letters and affairs which included James Bryce, an associate of John Muir, another Scot. Bryce even tried to get a bill through Parliament giving freedom of access to moors and mountains in Scotland, though the attempt failed.

In 1890 he became the first president of the newly-formed Cairngorm Club, and in the same year the Scottish Mountaineering Club was formed. After the First World War, many climbing and mountaineering clubs were formed in Scotland, partly as a result of the increasing availability of public and private transport, including the push bike, which gave more access to the countryside. Widespread unemployment during the great depression also caused a movement into these activities in the Scottish hills that for the first time involved the working class. Mountaineering had previously been a 'gentleman's' leisure pastime until unemployment gave the working classes involuntary leisure. Since the Second World War there has been another and greater increase in persons going into the mountains, with the increased use of the private car being an important contributory factor.

The increase in appreciation of wild and mountainous areas was not, however, paralleled by their protection or even by political organisation of their users to protect them. Although individuals like Tom Weir and W.H. Murray have been active in various causes in the past, they have till recently remained isolated voices, without the backing of a large and organised constituency. Recently, however, there have been signs of this changing, with some significant steps being taken towards the protection of our finest mountain areas. Most importantly, from the early 1930s on, the National Trust for Scotland has been enabled, largely by money contributed by several wealthy mountaineers, to buy some of the finest areas as they have come on the market, including Ben Lawers, Glencoe and parts of Torridon. Despite considerable political activity in the 1940s, however, and various proposals about national parks, etc., nothing effective has ever been done. To this day, the protection given to the most important wild areas such as Knoydart (recently proposed as an army training ground by the Ministry of Defence), the area around Lochs Fada and Fionn, and above all the Cairngorms, is flimsy in practice, despite designations such as National Nature Reserves and National Scenic Areas that look good on paper. Increasingly, it is public opinion that is their most effective protection, and since there are still proposals for hydro-electric schemes in areas such as around Loch Lomond and Loch Maree, and since many of our finest national estates, like the land around Loch Lomond or in the Cairngorms, can still be bought and sold like baubles by anyone in the world wanting a private sporting playground going cheap, there are likely to be battles ahead.

This likelihood is raised by the increasing instability of land ownership in the Highlands. It is difficult to run Highland sporting estates profitably, for they were never set up as economic entities but rather as the playgrounds of rich men who could afford to support them. With the economic depression, fewer people have been able to afford to pay for sport of this kind, and even fewer to run the estates. Thus increasing areas of wild land have come on the market. In addition, a new kind of landowner, 'the institution' (pension funds etc.) has appeared, providing an even more remote landlord.

Some Aspects of the Scottish Countryside

Jean Balfour

Mute swan (*Cygnus olor*) with cygnets

Wilderness is an emotive word in Scotland. To many it suggests the inhibition of production from the land and the removal of people from the countryside. In Scotland, wresting a crop from the ground has been a toil against climate, bog and rock, and as a result the improving hand of human beings has been seen as bringing a cultivated productive landscape and a better way of life. As late as the 1790s James Robertson wrote: "All unproductive land which is abandoned as unimprovable may be called *waste* (or wilderness)."

When Thomas Pennant visited Bruar in Highland Perthshire during his Scottish tour in 1770 and wrote "It is but late that the Scots became sensible of the beauty of their own country", he was remarking on a new attitude which was developing under the influence of the writings of Sir Walter Scott and Robert Burns, and as a result of better living conditions. This change of attitude paved the way to the present-day concern about wild places and wildlife in Scotland.

Today 'wilderness' encompasses both people's attitudes and perceptions about certain places, and its meaning is certainly not as simple as the term 'waste' used by Robertson and others in the 18th century. To many, wilderness suggests a quality of remoteness, naturalness and beauty often associated with uninhabited and largely inaccessible land

Hillwalking is a popular Scottish pastime, even in winter

where wildlife is undisturbed, and where those visiting it require some degree of physical and mental resourcefulness.

In Europe, real wilderness exists in northern Scandinavia, Greenland and Iceland, where there are large areas of uninhabited natural landscapes often barely accessible. In Scotland, although some of the qualities associated with wilderness are to be found, the situation is different, for Scotland is inhabited, and it is this that distinguishes the wild places of Scotland from real wilderness. Small rural communities continue where there is better land and where forestry, fishing, recreation and, to a much lesser extent, industry provide modest employment. Paradoxically these communities are the guardians of our hills and wild places, since without them a rather different kind of wilderness might develop.

Today only about 20% of Scotland's land surface can be described as good agricultural land, lying mainly in the south and along the eastern seaboard. Much of its quality is due to the work of the 18th and 19th century improvers, who drained the land and carried off endless stones. Eleven per cent of the land is under managed forest, 70% of which has been planted since the Second World War. Native forest—Caledonian Pine and mixed deciduous woodland—exists only in small isolated remnants. Most of the rest of the land is described as rough grazing and hill, with about 10% of the whole country lying above the 460 metre contour. Much of the rough grazing area supports sheep and red deer and includes grouse moors. About 9% of Scotland is designated as

258

Sites of Special Scientific Interest, rising to nearer 14% north of the Highland Line, where it includes blanket bogs, arctic alpine vegetation, important birds of prey and remnant woodlands, and where the nature conservation interest generally is recognised internationally. Just under 13% of Scotland is designated as National Scenic Areas and a high proportion of these lie north of the Highland Line.

Proportionally, Scotland's population has four or five times as much space per capita as south of the Border. However, 80% live in the industrial belt, making Scots predominantly urban dwellers. It is in the uplands north of the industrial belt and the Highlands Line that high rainfall, low temperature and acid infertile rock make themselves really felt, and where there are comparatively large areas with little habitation.

However, most of Scotland's countryside, even the hills and uplands, have been influenced by human beings and are not therefore truly natural, except perhaps above the 700 metre contour. The countryside today is very different from what it was like in the 16th century, when there was certainly more woodland and scrubland, fewer deer, more cattle and no sheep. Much of today's beautiful naked hill landscape is the result of over-burning and over-grazing, which in places still continues today. The Highland landscape, largely shorn of its cover and some of its soil, is fragile and easily marked by human impact, particularly in the high sub-arctic hills where people and animals cannot live and only arctic flora inhabits sparsely.

The inherent problems of land quality in the Highlands and Islands which restrict its development for agriculture have led to extensive sheep farming, with densities as low as one ewe to four hectares in north-west Sutherland. Though sheep, along with red deer, can inhibit tree regeneration and contribute, along with burning, to the destruction of native woodland, their presence hardly intrudes on the remoteness of the hills. Acid soils and high rainfall can provide suitable conditions for the planting of trees, but exposure, bog and rock can inhibit tree growth, thus limiting the potential extent of new forest—forest which can create its own special qualities and wildlife habitats, while contributing to the local economy. The right balance between forests (including native remnants) and red deer, whose numbers have expanded greatly in the last 50 years, has yet to be achieved.

Because the Highlands and Islands are not a wilderness, individuals, groups and government organisations have sought to keep people in the hills and glens and to help create employment opportunities for them beyond the difficult and limited agriculture on which, along with fishing, they used to survive. This is not easy. So far forestry, modest tourism and recreation have the best track record.

Paradoxically, it is not production from the land that today threatens the qualities of remoteness and undisturbed wildlife, particularly vegetation, in the Scottish Highlands, but rather the development of recreation, if this is not properly planned and guided. The rise of the motor car and car ownership has given people a mobility unseen by previous generations and has provided the opportunity for many town dwellers to visit and enjoy the countryside. Much of the wilder remoter country unsuitable for any intensive use has been turned over to some form of recreation, and this has given rise to new pressures. For over a decade the Countryside Commission for Scotland and others have addressed their efforts to how to conserve the countryside under these circumstances, to help people understand it better and make them more aware of its sometimes fragile characteristics, and yet also to contribute to their enjoyment.

One of the threats to the countryside in the development of recreation is the conflict that may arise between different kinds of recreational activity. The concept of different kinds of countryside recreation, ranging from the gregarious to the solitary, from intensive use to occasional use, is not always fully recognised. For example, the potential conflict between downhill skiing with activities such as hill-walking or climbing was central to the use of Lurchers Gully and the public inquiry which investigated the issue. Another example is the construction of hill tracks for sporting (hunting) purposes, which increases vehicle accessibility to some of the remoter hills.

In a report on *A Park System for Scotland*, the Countryside Commission discussed the relationship between different kinds of countryside recreation and conservation, and said: "The overall responsibility for enjoyment of the countryside must take account of all types of activity. The generalisation that man is a gregarious animal does not reduce the importance of providing for enjoyment alone or in small groups....The conservation responsibilities must run hand in hand with the intensities of recreational use, and outdoor recreation objectives should be seen as providing as strong a support for countryside conservation as might arguments based on other values such as landscape character or wildlife conservation."

The key to maintaining the remote and undisturbed qualities of the hills lies primarily in the limiting of vehicle access, particularly of so-called non-traditional vehicles, while also taking account of the need for forest roads, access for stock feeding, and to some extent sporting interests.

Ways through the hills on foot are traditional in Scotland and were developed for cattle droving, raiding or journeying. Some of these paths remain today and parts have been incorporated into new long-distance footpaths such as the West Highland Way, designated by the Secretary of State for Scotland under the Countryside (Scotland) Act. These provide attractive walking routes through hill country, but do not and should not penetrate the wilder and remoter mountain areas.

Over the last 20 years skiing has become a major recreational development in the countryside, with the development of uplift facilities used in summer as well as winter. Much more thought needs to be given to both where and how such developments should be sited, with a recognition of both conservation interests and other kinds of recreation.

There is still room in the Highlands of Scotland for different kinds of recreation and for, hopefully, expanding economic activities. However, if we are to conserve the whole quality and experience of the hills, a careful balance of use, access and appropriate development must be found. It is no longer acceptable that these kinds of issues be the subject of uncoordinated and *ad hoc* decisions. There is a need for better planning, for a better framework within which to take decisions in a place like the Cairngorms, and for taking a long-term and not just a short-term view.

North of the Highland Line is not a wilderness, though it has some of the qualities associated with wilderness. It is a place where people live, and has very special and sometimes unique qualities. It is a place which needs very special care and encouragement.

Wilderness Values and Threats to Wilderness in the Cairngorms

Adam Watson

The Cairngorms National Nature Reserve, an arctic outpost in Britain

Wilderness is a concept of the human mind, not an objective description of an area. It emphasises our perception of solitude and beauty, and our understanding of nature, in environments which are essentially as nature left them. As environments world-wide become less natural because of the impact of modern industrial society, even partly altered environments become important to the many who appreciate the values of wilderness experience at first or second hand.

Some say there is no real wilderness in the Scottish Highlands. In fact, nowhere in the world is there now absolute wilderness, unaffected by industrial society. Radioactive pollution, acid rain and increases of carbon dioxide have spread all over the globe. There is now only relative wilderness. On this relative scale, the arctic-alpine zone on the Cairngorms would rate high, and some of it very high. Smaller areas on other Highland hilltops would also rank high, along with much of the coast, substantial tracts of ancient pine and birch forest, and some wetlands. The fairly natural upper moorland in the Cairngorms would rate fairly high.

The bulk of the extensive Highland moorlands is land degraded by deforestation, burning and over-browsing by sheep and deer. Nevertheless, this land—even some of the lower moorland—has a much more natural vegetation and animal life than do the coniferous plantations or agricultural grasslands which are the two commonest changes in British moorland, due to big subsidies of public money. The vegetation is semi-natural, and virtually natural on exposed high ridges and unburned moors near exposed coasts. Even the more altered parts of it below the potential tree-line and scrub-line have a semi-natural vegetation; many species occur naturally in the ancient forest as an understorey, and others abound in the more open conditions of the forest bogs.

At a distance the moorland looks like a subarctic tundra, and the higher moors have a wet, oceanic, subarctic climate. The lower moorland, even though greatly affected by humans, has developed into a semi-natural tundra-like environment which does not occur on a large scale in Europe outside Iceland and the Atlantic Scandinavian coast. Moorland below the potential tree-line in western Ireland and the Scottish Highlands thus formed important world sites for the International Biological Programme's Tundra Biome studies. Even the least natural moor can provide a strong experience of wilderness, particularly in deep, hard-packed winter snow when it resembles the undulating surface of an arctic ice-cap.

The Cairngorms form the largest block of relatively natural wild country in Britain, and the most arctic-like area in the EEC countries, with interesting arctic plants, animals and landforms. They are Britain's foremost area for nature conservation and wilderness, and one of the foremost for hill walking and other mountain recreation. The value of the Cairngorm National Nature Reserve as a wilderness area is enhanced by its relative accessibility to urban people.

I know the Cairngorms not only as a scientist who does research there but also, since the age of 13, as a hill walker and later a climber and cross-country skier. Almost as far back as I can remember, I have had a deep love and affection for the area, and have received much inspiration from it. There is nothing odd about a scientist speaking of love and inspiration: both are important for good science. But in themselves they are not enough to defend wilderness against modern threats; good, rigorous research is needed too, and helps all sides come to sensible decisions that provide the greatest benefit to most people in the long run.

The higher parts of the Cairngorms were too infertile and had too severe a climate for much human exploitation. Although formerly used for summer shielings and stock grazing, most of the high glens never had farms. Nevertheless, tree roots in the moorland peat bogs show that the lower moors were formerly a forest. Most deforestation had occurred by 1650: Ritchie and others have exaggerated the deforestation from commercial exploitation in the 1700s and 1800s. On the lower slopes, the relics of old pine and birch still comprise the largest area of near-virgin boreal forest in western Europe. Even in the extensive boreal forests of Scandinavia, centuries-old trees such as in Scotland are uncommon, except in a few small reserves.

The lower glens had small human settlements, but some were cleared in the 1800s. Most glens, however, emptied because tenant farmers left voluntarily, often in the last 40 years. Some glens are a sad sight with ruined houses, and in others most houses are holiday homes, with scarcely a local community left.

The moorland zone in and near the Cairngorms is extensive and varied, and contains the most remote ground in the east Highlands. It supports important populations of golden eagles and peregrine falcons, which showed less contamination from toxic chemicals than elsewhere in Britain during the years of marked global contamination of birds of prey in the 1960s.

Wilderness values in the Cairngorms have come under increasing damage and threat, particularly since 1960. Roads, lifts and other access facilities for downhill skiing have led to large-scale damage to wildlife, severe soil erosion, and flood damage in and near ski grounds. Crows attracted by food dropped by tourists have come from the valley to roam the high ground, where they rob nests of hill birds and greatly reduce the breeding success of ptarmigan. Ptarmigan have become virtually extinct on the ski grounds at Cairn Gorm, due to their flying into the ski-lift cables.

There has been a failure to balance tourist developments with what the hill can withstand. The easy access of chair lifts in summer has attracted thousands of people who would not otherwise have gone to the high plateau outside the ski grounds. This, the most outstanding arctic-like part of the Reserve, has also suffered locally severe vegetation damage and soil erosion. It will take decades to recover, and in some exposed places probably centuries. The Nature Conservancy Council, the government organisation charged with managing the Reserve, cannot control damage on the plateau as the cause of it—easy access from the ski grounds—is outside their control. This demonstrates the importance of a buffer zone with controls, as a protection for the core of a nature reserve or wilderness area.

The proposed road, chair lifts and other facilities in the Lurcher's Gully scheme in 1981 provoked the biggest conflict so far on a mountain issue in Scotland. Many people, having seen the construction litter, bulldozed pistes and soil erosion on the ski grounds, objected to this proliferating south-westwards towards the heart of the massif. The Lurcher's Gully Public Inquiry was unnecessary in the sense that, given proper anticipatory planning, such an area would have been out of bounds to development, which would have saved both sides money and time. However, Lurcher's proved a major turning point. For the

Recreation: Ski development on Cairn Gorm

Forestry: Tube seed planting in deep ploughed furrows

first time hill walkers, climbers and skiers, together with voluntary wildlife conservation bodies, joined those with a growing appreciation of the wilderness aspects of nature conservation, raising funds and preparing evidence for the Inquiry. They are now tackling other environmental issues in the Highlands.

At the Inquiry, confrontation was mentioned between local community and outside conservationists who oppose development. However, many conservationists say that what they seek for environmental protection in the Cairngorms is what is best for the long-term sustainability of local people. Most developers themselves have in fact come from outside the Highlands, and much of the population increase is due to outsiders to whom many of the jobs have gone; local people have tended to get menial work. Over-development of hotels and other tourist facilities at Aviemore has harmed smaller communities in Speyside. Compared with the Swiss Alps, Highland communities lack control of land and decision-making, and hence are not in charge of their own destiny.

A long-standing problem of nature conservation is that the relics of old forests are dying because severe browsing by too many red deer prevents tree seedlings from growing. Subalpine scrub above the potential timber-line has been almost wiped out by deer browsing and burning. Hill tracks bulldozed to ease access for deer shooters have been allowed far inside the Reserve, and caused severe soil erosion. Recent regulations to bring construction of such tracks under planning control were violated in 1983. High deer stocks also cause serious soil erosion. The worst-damaged hillsides have so many deer tracks and such heavy grazing that they are largely bare, with many gravel slides and gullies. Such land management is not sustainable in the long run as it severely damages soil, the resource upon which all life depends. The shooting of red deer for sport, a dominant land use over most of the Highlands, clearly conflicts with nature conservation interests in the Cairngorms.

The only solution is to cut deer stocks until monitoring of seedlings, ground vegetation and soil shows trends towards recovery. In the most heavily used glen bottoms, even big reductions of deer may not be enough to restore the more palatable hardwood trees and hardwood scrub; fencing and elimination of red and roe deer may be necessary. The eventual aim would be to increase greatly the ratio of low-ground forest to wintering deer.

Although Scottish Caledonian pine woods cover less than half per cent of Britain's woodland area, intensive modern afforestation with its fencing, ploughing and dense, uniform planting is a major threat. The Native Pinewoods Grants are resulting in afforestation next to the old woods, even though some owners would prefer natural regeneration. Many believe that grants on such ground should be run by the NCC rather than the Forestry Commission, with no grants for plantations next to old woods and with all the incentives going into natural regeneration.

The NCC owns only 12% of the Cairngorms National Nature Reserve. Management of the rest, under short-term agreements with landowners, has not prevented serious intrusions on wilderness and damage to nature conservation interests, such as ploughing and dense-planting of exotic conifers in or beside old forest, and poorly made bulldozed hill tracks. As areas owned by NCC are better managed for conservation interests than areas with Nature Reserve Agreements, an obvious step is for NCC to aim to own more of the Reserve.

Protection of the rest of the area needs to be improved in order to rise towards international standards. The recent Wildlife and Countryside Act offers NCC a new opportunity to strengthen protection measures for wildlife and wilderness in the Cairngorms. The NCC now has to notify landowners of damaging activities on Sites of Special Scientific Interest (which include National Nature Reserves). Thereafter land-owners must tell NCC if they wish to do a damaging activity, and NCC can compensate them for not doing it or buy the land by compulsory purchase.

Planning measures for protecting the Cairngorms area as a whole have clearly been insufficient. An overall management plan, with clear long-term aims and means for sound management of the area's outstanding features, has been lacking for years. However, Grampian Regional Council is now showing interest in such a management plan.

A powerful voluntary movement of hill users has arisen in the last few years as a major challenge to developers, traditional land users and statutory bodies. The hill users press for the same better protection as wildlife conservationists. They seek a reduction of access facilities in places suffering severe damage, a stop to forestry plantations and bulldozed tracks, and a cut in excessive deer numbers to allow tree regeneration and decrease the cruelty of having many deer starving to death in winter.

The National Nature Reserve and the most outstanding ground out-side it need special protection as a core area. Within it, NCC will achieve its aims of adequate nature conservation only if it gets the full backing of hill users and voluntary wildlife bodies. Outside the core there has to be a buffer where the local planning authorities operate tighter planning, in consultation with NCC and other bodies.

Events in 1983, with threats at Knoydart, Creag Meagaidh and Glen Affric, and with the Cairngorms as a chronic case, highlighted the lack of protection for Scotland's best mountain areas for wilderness. We need to emphasise these cases and call for something better.

Looking towards St. Kilda from Boreray, on top of a 1200 ft cliff which houses the largest gannetry in the world

The Seas Around Scotland

Hance Smith

A month old grey seal pup (*Halichoerus grypus*). The Scottish Islands contain over 60% of the world population of grey seals

(See the chapter on Marine Wilderness Areas and Multiple Sea Use Management *(p. 103) for an overall outline of sea uses, the development of marine conservation approaches, and the problems of designation of marine wilderness areas.)*

The seas around Scotland are situated on the periphery of industrial Europe, and also open into the widespread influences of the stormy North East Atlantic. They are richly endowed with both living and mineral resources, with a strong demand for these in both industrial Europe and North America. The principal pressure on the marine environment is resource extraction, in contrast to more central sea areas such as the southern North Sea and Channel, where the full range of sea uses provides intense pressure and conflicts among uses.

The patterns of shipping activity derive to a substantial extent from these resource uses, the international shipping routes (Fig. 1) carrying a relatively low density of traffic and being of great strategic importance. Shipping activity generated by the offshore oil industry (Fig. 2) and at the shore terminals is associated with extensive safety provisions, notably in the arrangements for traffic management at Sullom Voe, which extend throughout most waters around the north of mainland Scotland and include aerial surveillance measures for oil pollution control. The other main foci for commercial shipping are the Firth of Forth, Firth of Clyde and the port of Aberdeen, while Lerwick and Peterhead have large concentrations of fishing traffic.

The offshore oil industry has indirectly generated the most pressure for environmental conservation, including institution of monitoring schemes both by the industry itself and other bodies, especially in the Shetland area. There is also considerable impetus for planning measures in the coastal zone, where the impact of terminals, engineering yards and service bases is concentrated. The numerous public inquiries associated with these schemes are a rich source of environmental data, and conservation interests are strongly represented. Offshore activities have a strong impact on the coastal zone, and the relationship between land use planning on the one hand, and the need to plan the sea on the other, can be clearly seen. The apparently low priority often given to environmental factors may be a reflection of the corporate decision-making in which both government and oil companies have been anxious to obtain a maximum rate of exploitation of petroleum resources during the build-up phases of the industry.

The waters around Scotland are rich in fish stocks, and a focus for all the northern European fleets. Scotland is also the leading fishing region in the UK. Fishing is arguably most pervasive of all uses in its geographical range and potential influence on marine ecology. Included are the pelagic herring fisheries of the North Sea, Minches and Clyde, and the trawling and seine-netting activity both on the shelf and near shore, where there are complex patterns of hard and soft bottom which may be profoundly affected ecologically by fishing. Crustacean and molluscan resources are located close to the shore in similarly complex ecological situations, as are the considerable seaweed resources. Salmon fishing requires integrated land and sea management on a North Atlantic scale. Fish farming is now of substantial importance on the West Coast and requires strict environmental conditions, perhaps as rigorous as those required for effective wilderness conservation.

Waste disposal and associated pollution hazards are relatively low compared to the southern North Sea, with the exception of the oil spill hazard, for which extensive emergency procedures exist. Land-based pollution hazards on a large scale are localised to the densely populated coastlands of the Clyde and east coast, together with the oil terminals and a limited number of large coastal installations such as power stations.

The evaluation of the marine environment, though at first sight somewhat piecemeal, has been considerable, mainly as a result of existing and perceived pressures due to industrialisation and recreation in the coastal zone, together with the offshore hazards of the oil industry. Scotland is notable for the comprehensive survey of the beaches instigated by the Nature Conservancy Council and carried out by the Geography Department of the University of Aberdeen; for the protection of seabird and seal colonies as a result of the influence of special interest groups; and for the current survey by the NCC of offshore

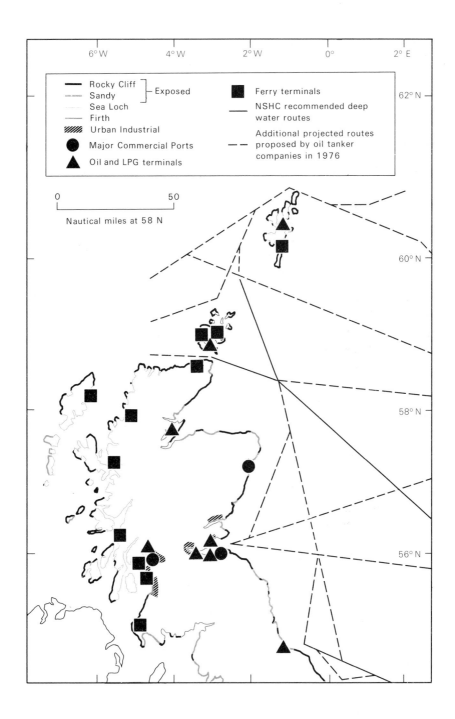

Figure 1   The coastline and navigation activities

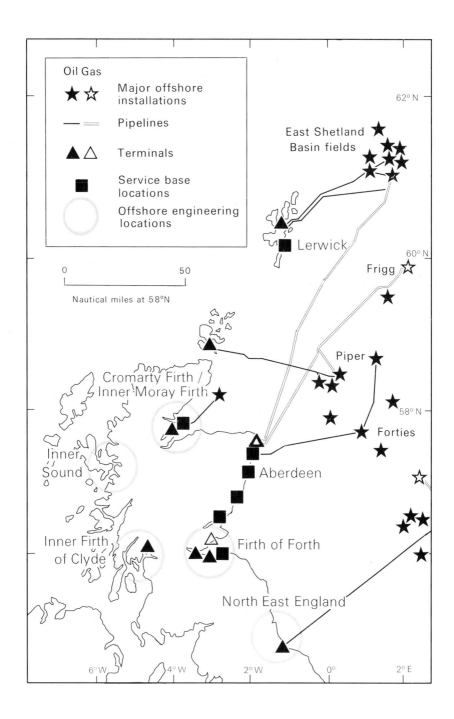

Figure 2   The offshore oil industry

seabirds at sea. Perhaps the most significant, though not exclusively maritime, is the long-term monitoring work being undertaken in the Shetland area, including the establishment of an ecological data base by the Institute of Terrestrial Ecology. A considerable amount of marine archaeological work has also been undertaken in Shetland and elsewhere.

The sea areas around Scotland require a coordinated policy for marine wildernesses within a multiple sea use context. Such a policy may readily be conceived in terms of geographical areas and localities on the one hand, and effective integration with other uses on the other.

Quite apart from oceanic scale problems associated with, for example, salmon management or diffusion of radionuclides from nuclear re-processing plants, a substantial area with a Scottish administrative and political dimension is involved (Fig. 3). Whatever the outcome of the dispute settlement on boundaries, the sea area that requires management is several times the size of Scotland's land area. Much of it—especially to the west—includes the deep water of the Faroe-Shetland Channel and Rockall Trough. Favoured for wave generators, much of the western area is relatively little used, with inshore waters of high amenity value for recreation, conservation and fish farming. To the east, by contrast, the intensity of uses is much greater.

Within this vast area, only the waters around Shetland have been to any extent systematically considered from a management standpoint. These considerations have ranged from the likely maritime boundaries of a devolved Shetland sea area, through the ITE ecological survey, to the Sullom Voe Oil Spill Plan and associated monitoring and surveillance, and the framework for a fishing plan already put forward in the course of Common Fisheries Policy negotiations. There has even been a call for the creation of a marine park, and the Shetland Islands Council have powers to license works and dredging within the territorial sea. In Orkney and the Western Isles there are fishing plan developments, and generally there is increasing recognition of regional management approaches to the Scottish fisheries. Other notable administrative moves include the Coastal Planning Guidelines and the rationalisation of port management on the major firths.

From the conservation viewpoint, most progress has been made in the coastal zone with the designation under existing UK legislation of Sites of Special Scientific Interest and National Nature Reserves, which has resulted in conservation of seabird and seal breeding colonies and of certain geological, geomorphological and ecological sites. Relatively restricted areas are involved and thus, in theory at least, a sufficient degree of control may be exercised over use. Such an approach may profitably be extended to human artefacts, especially the protection of historic wreck sites.

The protection of habitats on a large scale by marine parks is a

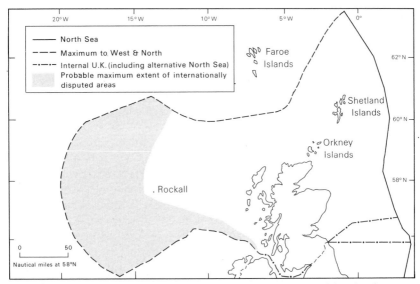

Figure 3   The political and legal limits of the waters around Scotland

development for the future. As the Exclusive Economic Zone becomes
subject to the creeping jurisdiction of state power, it is conceivable that
national park type legislation could be applied. At present this is
unlikely as treaty arrangements over internationally disputed areas
might be necessary. The position in Scotland might also be complicated
by the absence of comprehensive national park legislation for land
areas. In any event, the key management problem would be the integration of uses, possibly by the development of zoning policy similar in
principle to that adopted for parts of the Great Barrier Reef, with combinations of uses for geographical areas legally specified. In such an approach it would be necessary to coordinate the existing conservation interests who could probably provide most of the data and expertise required (including environmental data bases), fisheries management interests, and all those users (principally navigational, oil companies,
ports, recreation and defence) concerned with the establishment of fixed installations and routes.

Such a sea use planning approach has been widely advocated for all
uses of the North Sea, and there is a substantial amount of research
concerned with the data bases for such an approach. A preliminary
assessment of the complex legal implications has also been made. It is
likely that there is a long way to go politically before any such integrated approach becomes reality, but the pressure of events already
points towards practical, albeit piecemeal, coordination of interests to
safeguard the marine wilderness interest.

Human Nature

Robert Cowan

The crofting township of Howmore, South Uist

I would like to begin by saying somewhat nervously, if not in total fear and trepidation, that I am an unashamed, indeed professionally employed, developer. Many of you are predominantly on the side of conservation. My hope is that you may regard me as an endangered species, and so be gentle with me.

A developer is, as recent readers of the *Financial Times* will know, a person who wants to build a log cabin in the woods—while a conservationist already has a log cabin in the woods.

I have given this talk the title of 'Human Nature' because I wish to address the problem of increasing polarisation and conflict between those who profess a concern for people and those whose concern is nature. In doing this there are four propositions I should like to make: We are not a wilderness; development needs conservation; people must be conserved too; and conservation should be positive.

I have frequently heard Knoydart and other parts of the Highlands described as 'wilderness' or even 'the last great wilderness area in the UK'. This view displays a profound misunderstanding. Not since prehistoric times could the Highlands with any accuracy be described as wilderness—though it does contain huge areas of desolation caused by human activity. This desolation is the result of several factors, particularly the over-exploitation and over-use of land, combined with people's inhumanity to one another.

After years of bitter history, it is perhaps understandable that many Highlanders feel strongly when others describe areas that used to support large numbers of their ancestors as 'natural wilderness'. We do not regard more recent examples of human-created desolation as wilderness (eg the West Midlands), so why the Highlands? As journalist James Hunter of *The Scotsman* said recently, reminding us of Frank Fraser Darling: "To describe the Highlands as unspoiled is to abuse both language and history."

It is easy for us to agree in theory with the proposition that development needs conservation, but I could wish for more practical recognition of this. The World Conservation Strategy says that the positive goal of conservation should be maintaining 'sustainable resource' for development. I support this wholeheartedly, and would like to point out that the body I represent, the Highlands and Islands Development Board, is not exclusively concerned with industrial or even economic development. It also has a social remit and a statutory duty to 'have regard to the desirability of preserving the beauty of the scenery'.

The increasing national awareness of the attractions of open spaces and wildlife is resulting in the development of a more intelligent and demanding tourism industry, and nowhere is better able to cater for a wide variety of interests and activities than the Highlands. Our tourism industry has benefited greatly from our wildlife, and you can be sure that developers do not want to kill off the wildlife that lays such golden eggs!

Furthermore, today's newer and smaller industries no longer need to be located next to coal fields or large centres of industrial labour. I think electronic engineers and biotechnologists will increasingly choose to live and work in pleasant environments such as ours.

To address the point that people must be conserved too, today we are seeing—and I believe this is not wholly unrelated to the activities of the HIDB in the last 18 years—a reversal of a trend that has depopulated the Highlands and Islands for more than 100 years. Much of this can be related to our natural resources which include water suitable for building oil rigs or farming fish, agricultural land, trees, and fish in the sea around us.

In this sense, HIDB is very much a conservation body. We want to preserve and sustain the remaining human settlements in the remote parts of Scotland. The very rapid spread of conserved or sterilised land in recent years has, however, given many cause for concern.

Almost one third of the HIDB's area—which in turn is half the land area of Scotland—has been designated for conservation in some way, such as nature reserves, scenic areas or Sites of Special Scientific

In the conservation vs development debate, each side often views the other in an extremist manner

terest. Many people who live here are worried about when this process of sterilisation is going to stop.

However, this picture can be looked at from a different perspective. Half of the area classified in various ways by the Nature Conservancy Council is over 300 metres high, of little interest to developers other than skiers. Only about one third of it could be said to be suitable for development anyway, and much of even this area might be ruled out by other constraints—for example, inaccessibility or crofting tenure.

These figures illustrate how there can be two ways of looking at the situation, each supporting polarised views. In fact, so far there have been very few cases where conservation interests have prevented development.

In an endeavour to resolve this conflict situation, I must stress that much of the fault lies with conservationists. Not many people in the Highlands and Islands are in fact against conservation, but we are certainly against *some* conservationists.

The HIDB can and do work well together with responsible bodies such as the NCC and the Countryside Commission. But we must all resist the conservationists who are intent on deep-freezing the *status quo* and resisting all change at all cost. Even more must we resist the conservationists who want to keep the countryside for themselves and their elite bunch of friends who alone are sufficiently attuned to appreciate it. Conservation, if it is to be supported as it should, must be—and must be seen to be—for the benefit of people in general, and not just for mountaineers or botanists, for example.

What gets conservationists the bad name they undoubtedly have in the Highlands is that they too often say 'Thou shalt not' rather than 'Thou shalt'. There are many instances where positive developments can encourage conservation—for example, by replanting mixed forests of traditional species rather than regimented lines of Sitka Spruce. If money is to be paid to compensate for lack of development, then it should be specifically designated for local projects.

Most of all, conservationists should learn to speak with more local knowledge. Highlanders have a history of resisting government, either from Edinburgh or Westminster. Likewise, they do not want to be conserved from Bedfordshire.

My message, therefore, is a simple one: down with polarisation. Many conservationists see developers as 'baddies', while many of us in the Highlands see conservationists as perhaps a dangerous, creeping paralysis. Both views are unenlightened. Looked at from a different perspective, there is no reason why developers should not get together with conservationists, enjoy a fruitful marriage and live happily ever after.

Edge of the World: Fraser Darling's Islands

Morton Boyd

Shell-sand beaches, dunes and machair at Seilbrost, Harris which is a Site of Special Scientific Interest

"When I was a little boy the Garden of Hesperides, Hy Brazil and the Hebrides had a curious oneness in my mind. Two of these are mythical; the Hebrides are real but they reach into the legendary past and the limbo of my own mind and so however romantic they may have been in their beginnings in me, the Hebrides became a country which had to be trod."

So said Fraser Darling, when, in his old age, he recalled his earliest childhood recollections of the Western Isles of Scotland. His inward vision was of the awe-struck faces of the first Hebrideans—those Mesolithic people of dark Mediterranean stock—as they beheld the Hebrides stretching north-westward into the sunset. He saw the milestones of humankind through the ages from the Callanish Circle to the missile launchers of today. There were reflections of people in a golden age of plenty sustained by the seemingly endless resources of land and sea. Seasons of winter poverty were offset in summer plenty by an indigenous culture of provisioning of food and fuel harvested within sight of home.

279

The golden age of the Hebrides, that time of plenty in a clement climate when people and environment were a harmonious whole, is more of the imagination than of historical fact. The sensitive balance between the needs of the population and the resources of land and sea was probably gained and lost many times in different islands, but the course of history is punctuated by a very odd collection of events, all of which affected greatly the way of life and the environment. Fraser Darling saw these as the arrivals of Columba, the Vikings, the potato, the sheep, paraffin, the steam windlass on the fishing deck, wrapped bread, long-life milk and Wellington boots—all of which are the outward symbol of great social and ecological changes. The sage saw the grand interrelationship of the elements of air, land, sea and people in the great drifts of shell-sand. Shadowy figures of yesterday, men, women and children, break the undulating skyline of the sandhills with heavy loads of seaweed on their way 'twixt shore and the lifesupporting patches of potatoes and oats, grown often on *feanagan,* or cultivation ridging on shallow soils.

The tidal pool is a microcosm of the ocean, where the great generative power of the sea is in full display; sunlight and living creatures in the crystal setting of pure sea water. Seaweeds, molluscs, coelenterates, arthropods and sea squirts are all there in seeming chaos—yet the pool is fashioned for strength, stability and visual beauty. The shelving shores of the Hebrides provide an excellent substrate for a vast concourse of marine animals and plants which extract carbonate from the sea water. Their dead shells are fragmented by burrowing sponges, acmaeid limpits, chitons, echinoids, algae and fungi and are milled in the surf to produce a highly calcareous sand which occurs on the west coasts of the Outer Hebrides, Tiree, Coll and other smaller islands. This sand changes the ecology of the islands, giving an enrichment of agriculture and wildlife.

The combined effect of the weather, the sandy loam and the grazing of sheep, cattle and rabbits creates a unique maritime complex of grassland communities called the *machair.* Sandwiched between the sand dunes by the shore and the peat moorlands which form the spine of the islands, it is often cultivated in long strips, all unfenced. Between *machair* and moorland are the enclosed croftlands with their system of botanically rich fresh-water lochs which attract large numbers of water birds. The croftlands often possess old haymeadows, floristically very rich and excellent habitats for breeding meadow birds like the corn-crake which are now rare in other parts of Europe. Both dry and wet *machair* have a wide assortment of recovery stages from cultivation and possess the highest breeding assemblies of dunlin, redshank and ringed plover in Britain. As a whole the *machair* and croftland is both the basis of the agricultural economy of the Hebrides and a natural wildlife asset.

During 1983, an Integrated Development Programme for the Western Isles has been in progress through a 'less favoured' areas scheme of the EEC. Some £21 million were assigned for agricultural improvement over five years. The IDP has raised much controversy between agricultural and conservation interests which appeared to be in conflict, primarily over the improvement of stock production on *machair* grasslands. However, experience in the implementation of the programme has shown that fears that agricultural improvements would cause widespread harm to wildlife on the one hand, or that conservation restraints would be a blight on agriculture on the other, have not been borne out in practice so far. It is early days yet, but the machinery is on hand through a strengthened organisation on the ground and the provisions of both the IDP grants scheme and the Wildlife and Countryside Act to deal with the problems as they arise. In fact, there is a strong positive correlation between the numbers of breeding birds, plus the rich, floral hay meadows, and the number of native Gaelic speakers still crofting their land in their native tradition. If the crofting way of life with its traditions of small-holding agriculture is *conserved* in the socio-economic sense of the word, then there need be much less fear for the magnificent flora and fauna of the croftlands on *machair, hill and loch.* The IDP should be a comprehensive conservation experiment in which the way of life and cultural traditions of the Gael should be integrated successfully with that of the wildlife with which they have co-existed for several thousand years. Human beings and nature are, after all, two parts of one creation, and there is a fine opportunity in the IDP to demonstrate how this can be achieved in practice. As an example of conservation of both traditional lifestyles and wildlife, it is of wide international interest.

The islands of Scotland are on the extreme western edge of the vast landmass of Eurasia on the one hand, and on the eastern edge of the North Atlantic on the other. They are a microcosm caught between two enormous global systems of opposite character. Across the meridians eastwards to Central Asia and the Far East, plants and animals of the same genera—including that endangered species, *homo sapiens* —live on enormous ranges of habitat, producing species and races adapted to the needs of their particular home. Even the tiny archipelago of St Kilda, though bereft of its people, still has its own wren and mouse and ancient breed of sheep resembling the wild sheep of the High Pamir. Similarly, across the lines of latitude, the Hebrides are also in a crux position where Lusitanian and Mediterranean conditions fade into the boreal and sub-arctic, typified by the southern pink-butterwort at its northern limits and the northern red-necked phalarope at its southern limits. Geologically, this small country lies on the parting line of the Continental Drift of Europe and America, with the Archaean rocks of Scotland matching those in Labrador and Greenland.

Lunga, Treshnish Isles, Argyll, showing ruined house beside which Fraser Darling had his camp during his seal study in 1937

An old hay meadow at Elgol, Isle of Skye, showing the density and variety of flowering plants which are now absent in such quantity from areas of improved agriculture. Towering behind are the range of the Black Cuillins

The gannet (*Sula bassana*) breeds at seven stations in the Western Isles of Scotland, comprising most of the world's breeding population of this species. Their proximity to tanker routes and oil installations makes them very vulnerable

There is little wonder that Fraser Darling and many other naturalists before and after him found a deep fascination in the Scottish islands. During his island years, Fraser Darling brought a new dimension to natural history, making it a way of life. His studies of deer, seabirds and seals were self-contained essays in ecology and animal behaviour, but he also saw in the small, remote islands a clear expression of ecological interdependence among living creatures and of the basic processes of life and death. He had an unswerving belief that people and nature are parts of one whole system and that our moral and political conditions are as potent ecological factors as rainfall and erosion, and he gave expression to this in the *West Highland Survey* in 1955 and in his *Reith Lectures* in 1969.

The position of the Scottish islands in the great marine pasturage of the North Atlantic is of great importance in seabird conservation. St Kilda alone has 17 species; recent surveys have shown the following numbers of pairs: over 100,000 puffins, 59,000 gannets, 40,000 fulmars, 20,000 guillemots and 11,000 kittiwakes. The many seabird islands lie close to the tracks of tanker traffic to and from the oil ports on both sides of the Atlantic, in particular the new terminals at Sullom Voe in Shetland, Flotta in Orkney and the Firth of Forth. Great care has therefore to be taken in the management of this traffic to avert oil spillage of any sort. The foundering of a loaded tanker in the Scottish islands, particularly in summer, would mean a major seabird disaster, while continuous minor pollution from accidental spillages and clandestine tank washing might also cause devastation among seabirds in the long term. Happily, industry, government and conservation bodies are all jointly determined to see that such events do not occur.

The Hebrides, Orkney and Shetland remain a stormy frontier, yet the frontier is changing through modernisation of services and the pollution of air, land and sea. The remote outliers frequented by Fraser Darling and to which he found access so painfully difficult—North Rona, Sula Sgeir and St Kilda—can now be reached easily by helicopter. The notion of pure air and sea vanishes when the pollutants reaching Hebridean waters from the industrial mainland are measured. Traces of heavy metals and PCBs become concentrated in seabirds through their fish and planktonic food. These substances can affect the breeding success of the seabirds and also that of seabird predators such as the golden eagle, sea-eagle and peregrine. Seabirds and their predators are sensitive indicators of the cleanliness of the sea. Fraser Darling wrote:

"We shall try to perpetuate forest, moor, sand dunes, salt marsh, Hebridean islands and the denizens and vegetation of all these places but the national ethos has changed towards a greater respect for the natural world around us and a sense of trusteeship."

The roots of the Gaelic and Norse cultures go down with those of the plants, into the shell-sand and peat, and the tenacity with which the people—Hebrideans, Orcadians and Shetlanders—hold to their islands may be likened to the holdfasts of seaweeds and shellfish on their stormy shores. Within the Islanders' minds there is an awareness of the strength of nature—the immensity of the sky, the power of the sea and the benevolence of the land. Humans and wildlife in the Scottish Islands share a common destiny in the ritual of survival on what has been called 'the edge of the world'.

Afterword

Wilderness:
Trail to the Future

Ian Player

On the last evening of the 3rd World Wilderness Congress Colonel Sir
Laurens van der Post and I talked in the Universal Hall at the Findhorn
Foundation. To begin with I found it difficult to talk but I could sense
the understanding and sympathy of the audience.

We had all been through an intense week of talks that ranged from
Professor Meier's Jungian perspective of wilderness to a stunning lecture on the devastation of the Brazilian jungles by José Lutzenberger.
Finlay MacRae, our magnificent Scottish chairman, had played the
bagpipes and we had heard Gaelic poetry and singing from island
people. From the opening ceremony in Inverness to the final *indaba*
(gathering) there were very few delegates who were not moved by the
emotional atmosphere and the extraordinary kindness of the local Scots
and the multinational people of the Findhorn Foundation who were the
hosts to the Congress. The role of spirit in wilderness had full rein and
after a moving speech or the fading notes of the bagpipes many people
including myself had tears in their eyes.

It was a most difficult congress to organise. Vance Martin and I, with
the help of Sir Laurens van der Post, had struggled to ensure that it
took place. Raising money in the United Kingdom met with little
tangible response, though the concept received much praise. A whole
year passed before we had our first donation—£50. We were on the
point of giving up, but synchronistic events led to a dribble of money,
just enough to keep us going. Delegates were slow in registering and
some speakers took months to reply. It was only the knowledge that we
were working for a cause far greater than ourselves, and the support of
wonderful conservation friends in Britain, the United States, Australia
and South Africa, that kept us going. Resolution was finally rewarded,
and on the day the Congress began we had a capacity number of
delegates and we turned away many speakers, for we had too many.

These were some of the thoughts passing through my mind as
Laurens van der Post and I sat facing the crowd. As is customary in our
friendship and in keeping with the way we have given public lectures

285

together, I spoke first. In all the years I have known Sir Laurens I had always referred to him as Colonel. That evening I called him Laurens. Our friendship had deepened as a result of the problems and travails of this 3rd World Wilderness Congress. His wisdom, kindness, humility and great inner strength had been a source of help in all our labours. I was very proud to be sitting with him and to be called his friend.

Vance had asked us to speak on 'Wilderness: Trail to the Future'. I was reminded of the mpafa tree *(Ziziphus mucronata)* with its most characteristic thorn: one points forward and the other is hooked. It illustrates a fundamental principle of Zulu philosophy. We are always thrusting forward while also being hooked into the past.

So I began by telling how the idea of the world wilderness congress had been born in the Umfolozi game reserve in Zululand, during the long wilderness treks along the banks of the White and the Black Umfolozi rivers and into the hills with their lovely poetic Zulu names of Dengezi—Place of Broken Pots, Monfu—Pouting Rocks, and Mpila—Hill of Good Health, because it rises to a high point from the hot plains. My guide, companion and mentor was an old Zulu, Magqubu Ntombela. He was born and brought up here and served all the Zululand game conservators. We would camp near the rivers and cook impala meat on long green sticks next to the fire. With a dusting of coarse salt, a dash of black pepper and a handful of stiff maizemeal, it made a good meal. Tea or coffee was then boiled on the red embers of the fire, which reflected against the giant sycamore fig trees. We lay on the sand and he told me stories of the old Zulu heroes, his voice reverberating down river. Out beyond the fire the jackal were yipping and screaming as they followed a pack of hunting hyena. We heard the nightjar call, the grass owl hiss and the cries of bushbabies from the high tops of *acacia robusta* trees. It was in such a setting that the earliest of our human ancestors lived. The pattern of the land and the sounds of Africa were deeply imprinted on their evolving brains, so it can probably be said that the original memory of wilderness was in Africa.

I told Magqubu my plans for sharing this wild African Eden with people who would be prepared to walk here and experience it as we were doing. He understood what I wanted to do and we took out Natal Parks Board trails in the Umfolozi game reserve for many years. Later I founded the Wilderness Leadership School and we trekked with people from all over the world into the wilderness of Umfolozi. At the end of a trail we had our small *indabas* (gatherings) and from this came the idea of the big *indaba* for those who had experienced wilderness in other parts of the earth and who wanted to share their knowledge. This led to the 1st World Wilderness Congress in South Africa, the 2nd in Australia and now here we were in Scotland at the 3rd.

Sitting amongst the audience in this Findhorn Hall which had been built with much loving care were two close friends of mine, Hugh Dent and Paul Dutton. We had worked together in Zululand 28 years ago at a time when game rangers were not only extremely poorly paid but were shunned by society, for only a handful of people appreciated the game reserves. Both are men of great personal courage and for years they had faced the antipathy of local farmers and public officials who would not understand the importance of the conservation of natural resources.

Hugh and Paul were nourished, as I had been, by the wilderness of the game reserves they worked in—Umfolozi, Lake St Lucia, and Ndumu. The wilderness concept as defined in the American Act had gripped their imagination too and they were on fire about it. The audience listened as I told stories of Hugh Dent canoeing on moonlit nights, gliding past hippo herds that sheltered in small bays and alongside giant Nile crocodiles that were chasing shoals of mullet in the shallows. This was the closest that anyone could get to African wilderness. It made its impact on Hugh and he became another protagonist of wilderness.

Paul Dutton and I first met competing against each other on the 110 mile canoe race from Pietermaritzburg to Durban down the Umsindusi-Umgeni rivers. Paul had been stationed on Lake St Lucia in 1957 and canoed its vast expanses. He had an intense love for the Lake and its wildlife and an intimate knowledge of the hippo, crocodiles and water birds. We all served the Natal Parks Board and fought to have wilderness areas set aside within the game reserves.

T.E. Lawrence (Lawrence of Arabia) says in his book, *Seven Pillars of Wisdom*, that some 40,000 prophets left the city and went out into the wilderness, had their visions then returned to the city to try to spread their message to their doubting associates. We were like those prophets, but in our world the wilderness had shrunk to tiny pitiful remnants, mere witness areas of the once huge wild landscape of southern Africa. We watched the deterioration of the wild lands as more roads were built, villages grew and a mass of tourists visited the parks. It was only where people were made to walk, or ride a horse, or canoe that the landscape did not feel the human population explosion.

In the 1970s Paul Dutton went to Moçambique and stayed there when the communist Frelimo government took over from the Portuguese. After ten years of loyal service Paul was arrested. It was a displacement action of Frelimo in retaliation for a raid by South African forces into Moçambique. Paul had committed no crime and no charges were laid; he was simply the victim of politics.

I will always remember him telling me how wildlife had come to his rescue. In his prison cell in the feared high security Machava prison there was a tiny slit in the wall and he could see the sky. He was able to identify 80 different species of birds. There were spiders in the cell and

he spent hours watching the way they spun their webs and caught passing insects.

He was in solitary confinement. The lack of contact with people was
a terrible strain. He used to think up ways to keep his gaolers in con-
versation. This was only possible when he was sweeping his cell or
receiving his plate of maize meal. He had a small tube of toothpaste
which he mixed with his pipe tobacco and used it to paint animals and
birds on the walls. Each day his gaolers would stop to look at what he
had done and point to an animal they knew from their particular tribal
area in Moçambique. This gave him the chance to talk to them and
they became very interested in the stories of his adventures in wild
country with rhino, elephant and lion.

I had been away working on the tamaraw project in the Philippine
Islands and returned to hear that Paul was incarcerated in this dreadful
prison. No one had publicised it for fear of antagonising the Frelimo
authorities. I knew this was the wrong decision and contacted Laurens
who immediately took action. Laurens had been a prisoner in Java
under the Japanese and he knew what solitary confinement meant. He
contacted the British Ambassador in Pretoria, Sir John Leahy, and I
was introduced to him and explained the position and Paul's inno-
cence. Sir John promised help. We cabled Ray Arnett in Washington
and other friends in New York and Switzerland.

Paul was eventually released and chose to stay in Moçambique to
complete his contract. He later attended a reception at the Palace of
President Samora Machel. The President was impressed with him and
wanted him to stay in Moçambique. When Paul left, he had forgiven
his captors and praised Samora Machel for his interest in conservation.
Paul's life had been saved by wildlife and his belief in wilderness. He
came to the 3rd World Wilderness Congress not only to be present at
the proceedings but also to meet Laurens and to thank him personally.

The wilderness has made it possible to have these friendships and I
knew there were people in the audience who had made new friends and
renewed old friendships. This is one of the functions of the world
wilderness congress and this particular one in the Highlands of
Scotland, with the wild heather and snow-clad hills, had woven a
special magic, and on this last night I doubted if anyone would ever
forget the experience.

What of the trail to the future? Wilderness has become one of the
most precious resources on our planet. Only a few countries give it
legal protection. It is the task of everyone who knows the power of
wilderness to fight for its retention and to persuade all governments of
its importance to humanity.

The world wilderness congresses in their own way have become
trails into the wilderness of the mind based upon the profound experience of scientists, politicians, artists, writers and poets. Those

people attending know that the congresses are evidence of the quickening pulse of our concern for the world in which we live. They know too that it is not only the scientific factual warnings of unparalleled disasters facing us that will save our species. It requires the ancient knowledge of tribal people, the emotion of art, poetry and literature, religion and the practical guidance of those who have been through the fire of politics. The environment needs a holistic approach in the widest sense of the word.

The principal strength of wilderness is that it is impartial to short-term benefit, or to imbalanced or egocentric thinking. The wisdom in wilderness is long-term and evolutionary. Therefore increasingly in the minds of people, especially those who are concerned with a balanced future for themselves and their children, wilderness has become a symbol of environmental quality. I have personally led a thousand people of many races, nations and creeds on the trails in the Umfolozi game reserve and Lake St Lucia with the Wilderness Leadership School. These wilderness participants have a deep personal experience which affects the way in which they make decisions and view their future. There are many who echo the same phrase: "This experience changed my life."

Many challenges stand between ourselves and the true understanding of what it means to live in harmony with our environment. Perhaps the greatest of these challenges is to overcome the persistent sense of ineffectiveness and the visions of doom in the human psyche. Here we need to urge the psychologists to look deeper into the human mind and to find answers to the paradox of people as wilful and destructive beings and people as loving and concerned beings. The reconciliation of these opposites is our most urgent quest. Carl Gustav Jung knew and understood this, and continually voiced it. It is my personal conviction that wilderness in all its definitions is a key to resolving this paradox. Above all we must never overlook the spiritual impact of wilderness.

The trail to the future lies in the hands of all of us who have experienced wilderness. It must be our task to make the wilderness a moveable feast and bring it into the cities through the mind of human beings.

Perhaps there is a moral in Paul Dutton's experience. We are all in a kind of prison and daily need to take note of what lies through the slit in the prison wall. All about us is the natural world and even in the most densely populated cities there is the sight of a bird or an insect, something to remind us of other life.

Thoreau's famous statement, which has been repeated countless times, contains an inescapable truth. He said, "In wilderness lies the preservation of mankind."

The bush....
the night
moves through the bush
the bird
calls through the bush
the hyena
laughs through the bush
the man
thinks through the bush
the lion
coughs through the bush
sound scatters—
seeps through the bush;
intoxicates the weary mind
weeps through the soul
  of days gone by
    of days to come.

The soft cocoon
the sharp reality
    light softly calls in the east,
and the day bursts through
the bush
always the bush.

God secure me from security,
  now and forever,
    Amen.

Jonathan Bailey

Summaries of Talks
Not Included in This Book
and
Additional Material on the
3rd World Wilderness Congress
at Inverness and Findhorn,
Scotland.

Under the Pole Star.
Hans Anderson

The lands under the Pole Star in the most northerly part of the European land mass are filled with variety—from towering mountain ranges to mighty rivers, from the luscious green of larch woods in summer to the cracked ground where the permafrost rules, from forest tundra to stunted scrubland, and from virgin spruce forests filled with ancient 500 year old pines to ocean shores scattered with trees and driftwood torn loose by violent spring floods and the breaking up of the winter ice. These areas are home to a wide variety of bird and animal life, increasingly threatened by the inroads of industrial civilisation.

The land is filled with ancient trails that can be covered only on foot, on skis or by reindeer sled. But this is not a wilderness devoid of humans, for signs can be found of a long-dead people and their dwellings, and of more recent inhabitants. Nomads continue to tread the ancient trails leading from summer to winter. The people known as the Lapps live in four nations—Norway, Sweden, Finland and the Soviet Union. The Lapps protect and preserve the ancient traditions, showing respect for the spirits and the sacred places. They are dependent on the reindeer for their survival, and their word for these animals means life.

Even today, the gentle rhythm of the old world still continues in these remote places, but the continuation of this idyllic lifestyle is not necessarily guaranteed. The search for oil and gas is in full swing and much of the tumbling living water is now constrained by dams and tamed to serve human needs. The mountains and soil are raped of their riches.

There was a time when these resources seemed endless and from that misconception we planned and overdeveloped the factories and industrial complexes that demanded and devoured more and more. Even the remotest wilderness forests are now under threat. However, large areas of undisturbed land still remain, and it is imperative that we all make a concerted effort to influence politicians and those in positions of power to work out and implement a policy of protection for our waters, mountains and forests, for the sake of the animals, birds and fish, and for the coming generations of humankind.

The New Zealand Experience.
Eric Bennett

New Zealand evolved in isolation over millions of years, with no herbivorous or predatory mammals. Its forests, especially lowland ones, are unique and of crucial international importance in the study of stable and self-perpetuating ecosystems. When the first Polynesians arrived, about 80% of the land was covered in forest and 70% still was when the first European settlers arrived in 1840. Today native forest covers only 22% of the land. Some 11 million ha have been cleared and other types of wilderness have also been modified. This and the introduction of herbivorous and carnivorous animals has led to the extinction of many of the life forms that once characterised NZ. Nearly a quarter of the world's endangered species are confined to this country.

NZ's present system of nature reserves does not fully represent the range of areas which should be protected. The Biological Resources Centre has now set up an ecologically-based framework of 286 natural areas against which the adequacy of the existing system can be assessed.

The NZ national parks system originated in 1887 when Maori chiefs gifted sacred land as a national park. NZ now has ten national parks, with two others proposed. The existing parks were selected under criteria emphasising wild scenery, so a strategy to achieve a better representation of biota and ecosystems is urgent. There is also a State Forests System and a Reserves System.

Wilderness has been a preoccupation of the Federated Mountain Clubs of New Zealand. In 1977 FMC, concerned about the confusing standards developing under the different management systems, publicly promoted the concept of a Wilderness Commission of private individuals who would set policy and coordinate management. In 1980 the Dept of Lands and Survey, the Forest Service and the National Parks Authority published their Joint Wilderness Policy.

However, little progress has been made in the formal establishment of wilderness areas outside national parks. In 1981 a Wilderness Advisory group was set up as a result of FMC's first New Zealand Wilderness Conference, to advise government on potential wilderness areas. Their first task was formulating a draft wilderness policy *(which has since been formally adopted by the NZ government)*. This policy proposed a minimum of 20,000 ha for wilderness areas, with suitably large or difficult-to-traverse buffer zones, and laid down specifications concerning developments and activities in these zones.

Ten large wilderness areas have been proposed by FMC. They are the last chance to provide a wilderness opportunity for future generations and would provide an enviable national wilderness system. Some areas are under threat, hence there is urgency to establish reserve status. In March 1983, the Minister of Forests gave approval in principle to the Raukumara wilderness area and noted a 'definite demand' for wilderness areas which the government would attempt to cater for in future.

NZ's early European settlers saw the forest wilderness as something to be tamed. Now New Zealanders are beginning to see wilderness as a wonderful asset. The NZ nature heritage is quite distinct as a result of its isolated evolution. In the face of today's idolatrous commitment to material growth, we should take pride in deciding consciously to forgo development and to leave some places forever unspoiled as a symbol of the value of nature and of life in its own right.

Look Up—The Sky's the Limit.
Eleanor Franey

The sky has set the stage for an intellectual adventure in a learning programme begun in 1982 for third-graders at the Thompson School in Arlington, Massachusetts. The ever-changing beauty of the sky has captivated the children's imagination, prompted curiosity and stimulated the pursuit of knowledge, as well as providing me, the teacher, with a fresh outlook, approach and enthusiasm for teaching.

It begins with looking up and becoming aware. The sky is always there; you don't have to go anywhere to get to it, and it's free. It is something we can all experience and relate to at any time as long as we *see* it. After the students turn to the sky, it's simple. They begin wondering about and questioning everything in their environment. They practise writing skills by composing and sending letters to all sorts of people with requests, suggestions and thanks. For example, letters were sent to weather-people at TV and radio stations suggesting they mention the beauty of the sky in their reporting. The students read sky poetry continually. This has developed vocabulary and reading skills, and also gives confidence to slower readers. They keep sky journals, in which they explore astronomy, weather, the seasons, night and day, the solar system, legends, folktales, mapping skills, plant growth and so forth.

The library has become a very popular place. The students develop critical thinking skills, spelling and vocabulary, as well as sharing creative stories and research and developing oral communication skills and confidence. Art activities provide a strong thread of visual stimulation and exploration. Significantly, these children become zealously turned on to all environmental concerns, but only after they become enthralled by the wondrous beauty of the sky.

The Alaskan Wilderness.
Glenn T. Gray

Alaska's 1.5 million sq km represent some of North America's most spectacular wilderness. Towering mountain ranges contrast radically with vast areas of flat tundra and taiga (northern boreal forest). Alaska is the largest of the United States, with the smallest population—only 400,000 people. It is a land of extremes. Temperatures range from

294

30°C to -26°C. The coastal rain forest receives up to 635 cm of precipitation each year, while the arctic tundra is desert-like in comparison. Glaciers up to 2201 sq km large flow from even larger icefields, slowly gouging out mountainsides. Active volcanoes erupt periodically and earthquakes are not uncommon. In the interior taiga, wildfires regularly alter the landscape.

Alaska's relatively unspoiled fish and wildlife habitat supports a wide variety of species. Musk oxen, caribou, moose, wolves, wolverines and three kinds of bear roam the land. The waters provide a home for endangered species of whales as well as sea lions, walruses and a wide variety of fish. Alaskans are almost as diverse, ranging from those living a subsistence lifestyle in the bush to the more conventional urban dwellers. The native people encompass three distinct groups: Eskimos, Aleuts and American Indians.

Over 56 million ha of Alaska are included in various state and federal protective designations, with more than 22 million ha of these managed as wilderness and preserved from development. Their preservation has involved a long and strenuous struggle.

During the 1970's, the future of Alaska's federally managed land was being shaped by many opposing forces. Conservationists united in an effort to protect Alaska's wild lands from possible ecological degradation due to oil development. Aboriginal land claims delayed completion of the trans-Alaska pipe-line. Making things more complex, the state was in the process of selecting some of the 42 million ha as authorised by the Alaska Statehood Act. In 1971, the Alaska Native Claims Settlement Act (ANCSA) awarded the indigenous people one billion dollars and 18 million ha of land. This legislation ignited a controversy that ultimately divided Alaska physically and emotionally. Section 17(d)(2) of ANCSA gave the Secretary of the Interior authority to withdraw up to 32 million ha for study as possible inclusion in the national forest, park, wildlife refuge and wild and scenic river systems. The land was protected until December 1978, presumably allowing enough time for Congress formally to designate the land. However, the process evolved into a long and heated debate involving developers and preservationists from all over the country. Finally a compromise was reached and on December 2, 1980, President Carter signed the Alaska National Interest Lands Conservation Act into law.

More than one third of Alaska has been included in some kind of protective designation. But there is no guarantee that these lands will continue to be preserved in the future. Conflicts between wilderness use and land development can be expected to escalate. The degree of consideration given to conservation will depend on the attitude of people in Alaska in coming years. Environmental and political education for youths may be one answer. Understanding land use problems and politics will enable future Alaskans to participate actively in environmental planning and legislative processes, influencing management decisions on both private and public lands.

Environmental Law:
Recent Developments in South Africa.
P.D. Glavovic

In most systems, law is traditionally regarded as the servant of society and not its master. Laws are passed or evolve relative to society's needs, but they tend to lag behind those needs. At this time there is little doubt of the need for specific legislative adoption of a legal conservation ethic. This should not be by way of a general policy statement, but enacted as a matter of law. There is no reason why precise and unequivocal provisions should not be enacted, for example, for the interpretation of statutes and subordinate legislation, and for judicial review of administrative actions, on the basis of a declared conservation ethic.

In South Africa, common law affords inadequate environmental and wildlife protection. The time is clearly ripe for re-introduction, in some form, of the *actio popularis* (public interest) of Roman Law, to complement the current bias of individual rights.

In relation to developments in other countries, a clear statement of national policy has taken a long time to emerge in South Africa. There are a multitude of laws touching upon environmental matters, contained in numerous acts of parliament and ministerial regulations, provincial ordinances and municipal by-laws. Whilst it would be neither practical nor desirable to attempt to consolidate all environmental laws into one all-embracing statute, some degree of rationalisation is clearly desirable.

In 1980, the then Department of Water Affairs, Forestry and Environmental Conservation published a White Paper on a National Policy Regarding Environmental Conservation. In consequence, a Select Committee of the House of Assembly was appointed to enquire into and report on the subject of the Environment Conservation Bill, with power to take evidence. In February 1982, the Commission adopted the recommendations of the White Paper and drafted the Bill which became law in July 1982.

The main purpose of the Act, as stated in its long title, is 'To make provision for the coordination of all actions directed at or liable to have an influence on the environment.' This general statement of intention does not have the force of law. South Africa could benefit from the experience of other countries, and the Act should be amended so as unequivocally to establish a conservation ethic as a substantive rule of interpretation for our courts in respect of all laws affecting the environment.

The way in which the Act seeks to achieve its declared purpose is by the establishment of a Council for the Environment, which is purely advisory. While it serves the very useful function of an environmental watchdog, it has no teeth. It does not have any power of enforcement.

The Act gives the Minister wide-ranging powers to make law by regulations affecting matters of particular concern to conservationists, and there are recurring references to the advisory capacities of the Council and management committees. This form of legislation concentrates too much power in the hands of bureaucrats, while the usual checks and balances of parliamentary debate and publicity prior to promulgation are lacking. The South African common law is inadequate and, in its present form, so is the Environment Conservation Act. Further legislation is necessary.

Wilderness Politics, Public Participation, and Values.
Daniel H. Henning

The survival, quantity and quality of wilderness everywhere will be basically determined by political and governmental processes. Yet these processes tend to avoid value exposure and emphasis. Governmental approaches toward wilderness and environmental affairs tend to hinge around economic development, techno-scientific, factual and statistical considerations, while underlying and basic values are often not brought to the forefront but disguised under an 'objective' and 'professional' image. This avoids basic conflicts and threats to alliances and compromises, but has negative consequences for wilderness. Under this orientation, public participation loses a great deal of opportunity to influence decision-making.

Wilderness values are unique, complex and intangible, generally non-economic and long-term, while opposing non-wilderness values are more concrete and quantifiable, emphasising economic and short-term considerations. Non-wilderness value positions are consequently more oriented toward government approaches in public participation. Ironically, both non-wilderness and wilderness interests may follow these approaches in their public participation efforts in order to fit into the established governmental system. This results in the exclusion of important and needed values underlying the various interests and positions. By not articulating and involving wilderness values more, the public often misses opportunities for affecting far-reaching wilderness decisions. Wilderness values need to be more explicitly as well as implicitly stated, and implemented politically.

More study and emphasis needs to be given to wilderness values *per se*, which are often complex and difficult to describe and identify. We also need to develop more innovative ways of educating the public on wilderness values in terms of their lives and welfare and of ensuring that their value inputs are effectively incorporated into public participation and political processes. Articulate and powerful public support, through a value emphasis, can do a great deal to determine the survival, quantity and quality of the remaining wilderness on planet Earth.

People, Nature and Conservation.
Douglas Hey

A new approach is needed to the entire nature conservation issue. Among the problems which must be debated and resolved are those of human behaviour and human numbers. Despite extensive and intensive conservation education programmes in many countries, poaching, vandalism and the desecration of nature proceeds apace. People are still exploiters rather than stewards of the 'garden'. In addition, human populations, particularly in the developing countries, are growing at an alarming rate, and if this trend continues many thousands of species and most wilderness areas will disappear. Increasing numbers, together with demands for improved standards of living, put increased pressure on the natural resources. It is essential to compromise and reconcile conservation and development.

We need also to address the question of whether we in the modern world still need nature or whether we can live a full and healthy life in an environment of our own creation. There is also the fascinating issue of whether nature conservation is for the sake of humankind, or whether fauna and flora as part of Creation have a right to exist *per se*.

Wilderness and Dams:
Destruction by Insignificant Increments.
Geoffrey E. Petts

Reservoirs have attracted considerable attention from conservationists because human-created lakes can inundate vast areas of terrestrial habitat, interrupt important faunal migrations, and destroy the socio-economic basis of indigenous cultures. Dam construction usually involves the provision or improvement of route-ways into remote areas which often encourage agricultural, industrial and recreational developments subsequent to project completion. Yet the impoundment itself can markedly alter the entire river downstream. These changes may take place over a period of tens of years after dam closure. In the short term the effects may be manifested by relatively minor changes to individual components of the ecosystem but the cumulative long-term effects of these changes may totally alter the characteristics of a river, and are not necessarily only confined to the channel itself.

One striking downstream manifestation of river impoundment is the loss of pulse-stimulated riparian and floodplain habitats. Under natural conditions rivers experience a wide range of discharges during the year, and low-lying land adjacent to the river, often produced by the migration of the river itself, will be regularly inundated. The high primary productivity of these floodplain ecosystems is controlled by the dynamic interaction of the annual flooding and associated sedimentation. The world's rivers once provided vast floodplain ecosystems: the Zambezi, for example, regularly flooded up to 16 km on either side of the channel. Today, major floodplain rivers are rare and many of the pulse-stimulated habitats have been lost because of river impoundment. The fringing floodplains of the Zambezi, Danube, Don and Missouri, for example, have virtually disappeared and the 53,000 sq km floodplain of the Mekong is but one example of a regularly inundated habitat that is currently being altered by dam construction.

It is unfortunate that the conflict which exists between the objectives of river impoundment and the needs of the floodplain ecosystem is so intense. More than 300 large dams are being completed each year, and by the year 2000 it has been estimated that more than 60% of the world's total streamflow will be regulated. Perhaps we have now reached a point when the preservation of a few river systems should be considered seriously, at least until we can gain a fuller understanding of the long-term environmental changes resulting from river impoundment.

The Big Mountain Legal Defence/Offence Committee.
Laura Kadenehe

Under the guidance of our Creator and upholding the spiritual responsibilities and oral traditions which we recognise as our law, all that we offer this Congress is within the context of our understanding of the urgency to uphold our entire way of life. It is always an honour to participate with a great circle, where hearts and minds unite with power and wisdom to find solutions that will allow us to uphold our spiritual life for a continued future.

Indian people have been faithful to their responsibility to the Earth and all life originating from her, and to the generations of our past and our future, our ancestors and our unborn. In this spirit, our nations unite continuously to discuss the plight of our Indian people and the struggle for survival that is upon us today.

Big Mountain Legal Defence/Offence Committee was established at the request of the traditional Hopi elders of Big Mountain to provide the people with an independent legal network. The elders wanted lawyers who would recognise their claim to exercise jurisdiction as a sovereign nation and their struggle to rebuild their nation, Big Mountain Dine Independent Nation. Standing up to defend their nation and enforce their jurisdiction, to protest against relocation or to defend their Mother Earth from rape and desecration, often meant encounters and arrest. The elders wanted lawyers who would be sincerely committed to their resistance struggle, literally a struggle for survival against genocidal attack and their forced displacement from their ancestral homeland.

The fact that this legal committee needs to exist highlights the difficulties encountered by Indian people attempting to organise themselves in the southwest. The people themselves survive in very poor living conditions, isolated from world view by dirt roads and no communications systems whatsoever. It is convenient for the Government, who do not recognise the people's abhorrent situation, that they remain hidden. And it must be recognised that these conditions of under-development are what the people chose, thinking this would allow them to continue with their way of life uninterrupted. As it became apparent that this was not the case, the elders have stepped forward, and one of the difficulties they encountered is profound culture shock. Thus special organising efforts have to be made.

BMLDOC is establishing itself as the central clearing house which national support group networks can plug into. All legal efforts are conducted through the Big Mountain Legal Office. Our office documents legal information, processes litigation, and represents individuals from the Joint Use Area with various legal problems. Our outreach involves speaking on legal, cultural and historical issues, and explaining the need to examine bills on the issue of relocation. We continue to explore ways to stop relocation of the people, and document and expose statistics on the mining conducted on Indian lands by outside concerns. Our minimal resources have meant we have been unable to launch a large-scale campaign of support, but this office is an important symbol and accomplishment to those of us who have been organising out here for so long without one.

Over the last few years, we have realised that the US Government is intensifying its efforts at relocation. We have continued to stand firm, hoping that groups and individuals would slowly jump on the bandwagon to help us stop relocation, fencing and stock reduction. Four years later, however, relocation continues and we are only two years away from the 1986 deadline, waiting to see what measures the Government will resort to in removing those unwilling to cooperate. Our elders continue to go on to the Spirit World before our eyes, pressured with all the effects of relocation, arrests, trials and imprisonment, while they watch their homeland being destroyed.

Progress and Offshoots of the World Campaign for the Biosphere.
Nicholas Polunin

The term 'biosphere' has been variously used by different authorities, but here I use it to denote the envelope involving and surrounding the Earth in which any form of life exists naturally. We human beings, together with some eight million species of plants, animals and microbiota, owe our origins to the biosphere. We are an integral part of it, and are utterly dependent on it. Yet we are increasingly and most gravely threatening it. However, we also have the capacity to save it.

The World Campaign for the Biosphere was declared by concerned environmentalists on Environment Day, 1982, initiating a movement to help the 'person in the street' to be more aware of our absolute dependence on the biosphere. The Summer 1982 issue of *Environmental Conservation* published the Declaration of the World Campaign for the Biosphere. Recently the World Council for the Biosphere was established. Its main function will be to monitor global conditions from a holistic point of view, and to alert governments, leaders and the public of any widespread tendency or foreseeable change that could be harmful to the biosphere or any major part of it. Concurrently, the International Society for Environmental Education is being established, advising but not directing the many regional, national and local associations for environmental education that have sprung up in recent years. Mention should also be made of the new International Association for Research on Impounded Rivers, dealing with one of the ways people have done most to alter the face of our planet.

The Imperative of Nuclear Disarmament.
Mostafa K. Tolba, Arthur H. Westing, Nicholas Polunin

Nuclear weapons have the deadly capacity to destroy the life-giving systems on which we all depend. Plants, animals, and their habitats both terrestrial and aquatic can be utterly devastated by nuclear detonations, of which the existing capability is sufficient practically to destroy our Earth several times over. The peoples of the world face the stark choice of survival or virtual annihilation.

As the world has never experienced a large-scale nuclear war, predictions of possible environmental effects must remain widely conjectural. However, studies of the effects of the Hiroshima and Nagasaki attacks, of numerous test explosions and of other circumstances including natural catastrophes, help to suggest the type of impact and extent of effects of such an event. These effects comprise four main categories which may be treated as follows.

1. **Blast energy.** This comprises half or more of the energy of a nuclear bomb, and its dissipation is responsible for much of the physical damage caused on detonation. A single one-megaton airburst would knock down virtually all trees over about 14,000 ha and force thousands of tonnes of water vapour from the lower to the upper atmosphere; groundburst, it would blast out a huge crater extending over perhaps 12 ha and with a maximum depth of 90m, and thrust some 50,000 tonnes of rock and soil materials into the upper atmosphere as fine dust; burst underwater, it would lift tens of thousands of tonnes of water droplets into the atmosphere.

2. **Heat energy.** Another one-third or more of the energy of a nuclear bomb is dissipated in the form of an intense thermal wave, igniting wildfires over a vast area whose extent depends on the terrain, weather conditions and vegetative cover.

3. **Radiation energy.** The remaining 10% or so of the energy of a nuclear bomb is dissipated in the form of nuclear radiation, of which a portion is released in the initial burst and the remainder, much more slowly and widely, as radioactive fallout.

4. **Synergistic effects.** Among the more disastrous of these would be those that could be set in motion by the large-scale injection of fine particles of dust and droplets of water into the stratosphere, by the addition of vast quantities of smoke to (or generation of smog in) the troposphere, and by introduction of large amounts of oxides of nitrogen into the ozone layer.

There is nothing to do about nuclear war except avoid it (which means also avoiding accidental or other nuclear flare-up). This will require destroying all current capability of waging such war and henceforth monitoring the world against any manufacture of nuclear weapons. It additionally demands a close world-wide monitoring of the civilian nuclear-power industry in order to detect and forestall possible clandestine production of weapon-grade plutonium and thence the manufacturing of nuclear weapons. These avoidances are everybody's imperatives and the more we insist on them, the sooner and more effectively will politicians prevail on governments to conform to them and save people and nature from the threat of annihilation.

Wilderness under Attack—The Politics of Wilderness Conservation in the United States, 1981-83.
William Turnage

I feel it is most important that James Watt has been forced to resign as Secretary of the Interior of the United States. In my opinion there has never been an anti-environmental organisation like Ronald Reagan's current administration, which has come to office absolutely determined to dismantle most of the environmental protection legislation enacted over the past century.

It is impossible to overstate the difference between previous administrations, both Republican and Democrat, and this one. Officials in the resource area in the current administration come largely from the industries which their agencies are supposed to regulate. Another fundamental flaw in these appointments is that they are people who do not believe in government and the traditional roles and missions of the agencies which they are running. Historically, people who do not believe in government do not make good governors.

However, we have an incredibly strong and talented conservation movement in the United States. The four major national conservation organisations dealing with wilderness issues are the National Wildlife Federation, the National Audubon Society, the Sierra Club and the Wilderness Society. These organisations employ highly professional staff with, for example, the Wilderness Society having more registered lobbyists than any other organisation in the nation's capital. Each group focuses a lot of attention on legislation, but also works at a grass-roots level through their membership or local chapters.

The United States has what is probably the largest pure wilderness system in the world, composed of 80 million beautiful acres. In the next six years final decisions will be made about another 63 million acres of wild, roadless land. It could be the last big apportionment of land in our history, and it is a crucial one. The nature of the administration and people in office are critical—there won't be another chance.

Will-of-the-Land:
Wilderness Among Early Indo-Europeans.
Jay H. Vest

The ancient Celts, a sub-group of the Indo-European race, worshipped nature: for them it was alive with the same creative force humans share. Their conception of *Will Power* or *will-force* was extended wholly to nature—even solid earth. this notion of 'will' is akin in origin to the term 'wild'. Nash tells us that 'wilderness' means 'wild-dēor-ness'—the place of wild beasts, the root probably being 'will', meaning self-willed or uncontrollable, from which came the adjective 'wild'. 'Wild-dēor' denotes creatures not under the control of humans. 'Ness' in Middle English was apparently retained only in place names. Nash maintains that 'ness' suggests a quality producing a certain mood in an individual who assigns it to a specific place. However, considering the Middle English application of 'ness' to place names, it may well have been combined with 'wild' in an entirely different sense from that Nash suggests, meaning 'willed-land'. If the 'der' of wilderness represents 'of the', then in 'wilderness' there is 'will-of-the-land' and in 'wild-dēor' there is 'will of the animal'. The primal people of northern Europe were not bent on dominating all environments and the 'will-of-the-land' concept demonstrates a recognition of the land for itself.

Indo-European nature worship evidences a tradition of sacred places—wilderness in the deepest sense, imbued with *will-force* and spirit. Although most contemporary scholarship implies that only modern cultures can appreciate such wilderness, there is a reverence for 'wild' nature that predates the homocentric mediaeval/renaissance world view. With Roman Christianity an imperialism emerged where the wild took on connotations of a desolate waste filled with demons, and the primal Indo-Europeans, in failing to acknowledge the God of the Bible, were defined as barbarous. Nature and nature worship were consequently perceived as evil. 'Heathen' means 'dweller on the heath', and 'pagan' originally meant 'a rural or rustic person'. As Christianity became the religion of the towns, the rural people who retained the ancient deities became known as 'pagan heathens'. They worshipped on the heath or in the grove—that is, in the wilderness.

Among ancient Indo-European cultures are many examples of wild sanctuaries. The Celts held sacred certain groves known as *nemetons*—related to the Breton *nemu*, 'the heavens'—reflecting the Celtic belief that the real and the surreal were two facets of a whole. The sacred grove continued in its wild—willed or uncontrollable—condition, and thus the will-of-the-place, its spirit, manifested itself. Such groves were the site of worship, particularly on earth festival days. When these festivals were discontinued, usually because of imperial compulsion, the primal culture disintegrated.

In these sacred groves the Druids, the spiritual leaders of the Celts, developed their lore, wisdom and ecological ethics, glimmerings of which can be gleaned from Arthurian legend. The archetypal Druid, Merlin, explains to Arthur what it means to be king: "You will be the land and the land will be you; if you fail, the land will perish, as you thrive, the land will blossom." Kinship with the land and its continued health are central themes of the Celtic world view.

One Man's Wilderness
Heinz Steinmann

'Cape York Rainforest'—painting by Heinz Steinmann

3rd World Wilderness Congress

The Congress was opened to the sound of Scottish bagpipes

The World Wilderness Congress is a project of the International Wilderness Leadership Foundation, and is a platform designed to promote the international exchange of conservation experience. Centred around wilderness as a symbol of environmental purity, the Congress allows scientists, developers, artists, traditional peoples, politicians, hikers and hunters to meet and share perspectives in order to:

- further worldwide understanding of the need for and meaning of wilderness areas
- enable the general public to understand that industrial, agricultural and commercial growth must go hand in hand with the preservation of wild and natural areas
- formulate plans of action to assure that specific natural areas be established and properly managed as wilderness areas, to be held in trust for future generations.

The 1st Congress convened in Johannesburg, SA, in 1977, the 2nd Congress in Queensland, Australia in 1980, and the 3rd Congress in Scotland in 1983. The published proceedings of the 1st Congress, *Voices of Wilderness*, are available from the Wilderness Leadership School, PO Box 15036, Bellair, Natal 4006, RSA. The proceedings of the 2nd Congress, *Wilderness*, are obtainable from the Findhorn Press, The Park, Forres IV36 0TZ, Scotland. This book, *Wilderness: The Way Ahead*, is available from both the Findhorn Press (address above) and from Lorian Press, PO Box 147, Middleton, WI 53562, USA.

Ceilidh in the Universal Hall, Findhorn Foundation

The 4th World Wilderness Congress will convene in Colorado in 1987. The Secretariat can be contacted at the **Department of Forestry and Natural Resources, Colorado State University, Fort Collins, Colorado, USA.**

Resolutions from the 3rd Congress, as well as the full text of the papers presented, are also available from the Congress Secretariat at the above address.

Col. Sir Laurens van der Post

Panel discussion: Ian Player, Sally Ranney. Hans Anderson, Laura Kadenehe, Ramakrishnan Palat, Laurens van der Post, Adam Watson

The opening weekend was held at the Eden Court Theatre, Inverness

Hon. Barry Cohen, Minister of State,
Home Affairs and Environment, Australia

Carolyn Tawangyawma and Laura Kadenehe of the Hopi nation with children from Treverton School, South Africa

Karen Blair

The stained glass window in the front foyer of the Universal Hall of the Findhorn Foundation was completed just before the Congress, and was an attractive addition to the display of artwork

The art exhibition at the Congress included work by more than 40 artists and craftspeople of regional and international distinction, and featured painting, sculpture, photography, engraving, printing and weaving

Contributors to the 3rd World Wilderness Congress

Hans Anderson. Writer, Sweden

G. Ray Arnett. Assistant Secretary of the Interior, USA

Bill Bainbridge. Regional Director, Department of Environment Affairs, Republic of South Africa

Dr. Jean Balfour. Former Chairman, Countryside Commission for Scotland, UK

Very Rev. Prof. Robin Barbour. University of Aberdeen; Former Moderator of the General Assembly, Church of Scotland, UK

Felipe Benavides, O.B.E. President, PRODENA, Peru

Eric Bennett. Conservationist, New Zealand

Karen J. Blair. The Duke of Edinburgh Award Scheme, UK

The Hon. John R. Block. Secretary of Agriculture, USA

Dr. Morton Boyd. Director, Nature Conservancy Council, Scotland, UK

Michael Brown. Human Resources Consultant, USA

Ian Campbell. Gardener, musician, UK

Sheldon Campbell. President, Zoological Society of San Diego, USA

Hon. Barry Cohen. Minister of State, Home Affairs and Environment, Australia

Robert Cowan. Chairman, Highlands & Islands Development Board, UK

Gerald B. Dix. Lever Professor, Department of Civic Design, University of Liverpool, UK

Anthony Fairclough. Director for the Environment, European Commission, Belgium

Eleanor Franey. Spacious Skies Learning Program, USA

Bernard Gilchrist. Chief Executive, Scottish Wildlife Trust, UK

Peter D. Glavovic. Howard College School of Law, University of Natal, Republic of South Africa

Alan Grainger. Author, editor; Commonwealth Forestry Institute, UK

Glenn Gray. Formerly of US Forest Service, USA

Dr. John Hendee. Department of Agriculture, Forest Service, USA

Prof. Daniel H. Henning. Eastern Montana College, USA

Dr. Douglas Hey. SA Nature Foundation, Republic of South Africa

Laura Kadenehe. Big Mountain Legal Defense/Offense Committee, USA

313

Sir George Trevelyan. Founder Director, Wrekin Trust, UK

William A. Turnage. Chief Executive, The Wilderness Society, USA

Jay H. Vest. University of Montana, USA

Dr. Adam Watson. Institute of Terrestrial Ecology, UK

R. Drennan Watson. N.E. Mountain Trust, UK

Prof. Arthur H. Westing. Senior Research Fellow, Stockholm International Peace Research Institute, Sweden

The Hon. George Younger. Secretary of State for Scotland, UK

Franco Zunino. Italian Wilderness Society, Italy

Chairing Sessions

Roger Collis, Lorian Association, USA

Bernard Gilchrist, Scottish Wildlife Trust, UK

Sir John Lister-Kaye, Bt. Aigas Field Centre, UK

Finlay MacRae, Forestry Commission, UK

Verne McLaren, World Wildlife Fund, Australia

George Petrides, The Wildlife Society, USA

Robert Pickering, Minister of Parks and Renewable Resources, Saskatchewan, Canada

Ian Player, Wilderness Leadership School, RSA

Vincent Serventy, World Wildlife Fund, Australia

Secretariat of the 3rd World Wilderness Congress

Leona Aroha, Registrations

Tracey Barton, Secretary

Frances Edwards, Tours

Michael Lindfield, Liaison

Virginia Lloyd-Davies, Press Officer

Dobrinka N. Popov, Art Exhibition Coordinator

Leonard Sleath, Honorary Treasurer

Vance G. Martin, Executive Officer

Advisory Committee to the
3rd World Wilderness Congress

Finlay MacRae, UK (Congress Chairman)

G. Ray Arnett, USA

Sir David Checketts, UK

Colonel Sir Laurens van der Post, UK

Ian Player, RSA

Edmund de Rothschild, UK

Lieutenant Colonel Tom Welch, UK

Dr. Felipe Benavides, Peru

Wally O'Grady, Australia

Edward Posey, UK

Sir John Lister-Kaye, Bt, UK

Vance G. Martin, UK (Congress Executive)

Sponsors

Participating Sponsors:

Highlands & Islands Development Board

Gulf Oil Corporation

Commission of the European Communities

Office International (TM Sparks and Son Ltd)
R.T.Z. Services Ltd
Barclays Bank, plc
General Electric Company (USA)
Collins Publishers
Godfrey Davis/Europcar
Christian Salvesen
Rothman's International, plc
British Gas Corporation
R.& R. Urquhart
J.M. Younie & Sons Limited
Findhorn Bay Caravan Park
John Harvey and Son Ltd
National Film Board of Canada
Scottish Television

Tiger Trust
Dartington Hall
Elsa Wild Animal Appeal
Michaelmas Trust
N.M.R. Charities Committee
Rothschild Trust Co Ltd
Ronson Charitable Foundation
Oppenheimer Charitable Trust
Threshold Foundation (USA)
One Earth Foundation Inc
Wilderness Foundation (UK)
Game Conservation International
Wilderness Leadership School

Findhorn Foundation
Centre for Human Ecology (Edinburgh)
Moray District Council
Highland Regional Council
Inverness District Council

Verne and Jean McLaren
Alan Massam
Mr and Mrs T.O. Martin
Lord Astor of Hever
Major General Victor Campbell
R.H. Barraclough
Anna Allen
Sheldon Campbell
Lord Strathnaver
The Hon James and Mrs Stuart
The Earl and Countess of Moray
The Earl and Countess Cawdor
Sir William Gordon Cumming
Major Nigel Graham and the RSPB
Ann and David Jevons
Elinore Detiger
Ray V. Collier (NCC)
Michael and Gail Shaw
Simon and Sarah Fraser
John Busby
A.D. Barton
Angus and Abbie Marland
Moray Mackintosh
Ann Player
Kate Martin

Many other kind people, too numerous to mention, have also given freely of their time on behalf of wilderness and Wilderness '83.

World Wilderness Congress International Committee

G. Ray Arnett, USA, Department of Interior, Assistant Secretary for Fish, Wildlife and Parks

Dr. Felipe Benavides, OBE, Peru, President PRODENA; former Trustee, World Wildlife Fund

Lloyd Brookes, Canada, Consultant; Parks, Wilderness and Resource Management

Dr. Gerardo Budowski, Costa Rica, Head of Forest Sciences Dept, Graduate School and Research Station of Turrialba

Dr. W.E.G. Butler, Australia, Medical Doctor, Farmer

Edmund de Rothschild, UK, Banker; Philanthropist

Dr. John Hendee, USA, Science Advisor, Assistant Station Director, US Forest Service

Sir John Lister-Kaye, Bt, UK, Director Aigas Field Centre

Vance G. Martin, UK, President, International Wilderness Leadership Foundation

Verne McLaren, Australia, Trustee, World Wildlife Fund (Australia)

Wally S. O'Grady, Australia, Conservationist, Farmer, Chairman of 2nd World Wilderness Congress

Professor George Petrides, USA, Michigan State University

Ian Player, RSA, (Honorary Chief Executive Officer) Founder of Wilderness Leadership School, Chairman of 1st World Wilderness Congress

Vincent Serventy, Australia, Trustee, World Wildlife Fund (Australia)

Stan Studer, USA, Attorney, Rancher

Harry L. Tennison, USA, President, Game Conservation International

Captain Percy Trezise, Australia, Author, Anthropologist

Stewart Udall, USA, Former Secretary of the Interior

Col. Sir Laurens van der Post, UK, Author, Explorer

R.W. Whitely, RSA, Businessman, Provincial Councillor

Professor Scott C. Whitney, USA, Professor of Law, College of William and Mary

The Findhorn Foundation

The Findhorn Foundation, which hosted the 3rd World Wilderness Congress, is an international spiritual and educational community in the north of Scotland. It was founded in 1962 by Peter and Eileen Caddy and Dorothy Maclean on a caravan park a mile from the fishing village of Findhorn, from which it takes its name. The community now consists of some 200 permanent members, and thousands of guests visit each year to take part both in the educational programmes and in the working life of the community.

The Foundation has no formal doctrine or creed. It is based on the idea that humanity is involved in an evolutionary expansion of consciousness which will, in turn, create new patterns of civilisation and promote a planetary culture infused with spiritual values.

In addition to its regular educational programmes, the Foundation also hosts arts festivals and international conferences several times a year. The 3rd World Wilderness Congress was the first outside conference to be hosted by the Foundation. The completion of the Universal Hall now allows the community to expand its work by offering full conference facilities to groups and organisations who seek to give their own expression to the development of a positive future.

For more information, write to the Findhorn Foundation, The Park, Findhorn IV36 OTZ, Scotland.

The Findhorn Village

The centuries-old village of Findhorn is situated at the mouth of the Findhorn River and on the edge of the Findhorn Bay, in a beautiful and tranquil setting which added much to the *ambience* of the 3rd World Wilderness Congress. As a token of appreciation for the hospitality shown to the Congress by the residents of the Findhorn village, the International Wilderness Leadership Foundation has given the village a grant to enable an educational cairn to be erected which explains the significance of the sand-dune system on the Moray coast.